HILDE GAUTHIER-PILTERS has observed camels in the Sahara for extended periods during the past twenty-five years. She has published many books and articles on her research in France and Germany.

ANNE INNIS DAGG is the author of eight books, including works on the giraffe, on locomotion in animals, and on the interaction of wildlife and human beings. She is currently teaching at the University of Waterloo, Canada.

The Camel

The Camel

Its Evolution, Ecology, Behavior,
and Relationship to Man

**Hilde Gauthier-Pilters and
Anne Innis Dagg**

Photographs by Hilde Gauthier-Pilters

The University of Chicago Press
Chicago and London

HILDE GAUTHIER-PILTERS has observed camels in
the Sahara for extended periods during the past
25 years. She has published many books and articles on her research in France and Germany.

ANNE INNIS DAGG is the author of eight books,
including works on the giraffe, on locomotion in
animals, and on the interaction of wildlife and
human beings. She is currently teaching at
the University of Waterloo, Canada.

The University of Chicago Press, Chicago 60637
The University of Chicago Press, Ltd., London

Library of Congress Cataloging in Publication Data

Gauthier-Pilters, Hilde.
   The camel, its evolution, ecology, behavior, and
relationship to man.

   Bibliography: p.
   Includes index.
   I. Camels.   I. Dagg, Anne Innis, joint author.
II. Title.
QL737.U54G38   599.73'6   80-23822
ISBN 0-226-28453-0

To Jo and Ian

Contents

Preface

Many books have been written about the camel (*Camelus dromedarius*), some by veterinarians (Cross 1917; Leese 1927; Droandi 1936; Curasson 1947), some by military men or members of camel corps (Leonard 1894; Cauvet 1925–26; Vitale 1928; Finbert 1938), some by historians (Marsh 1856; McKnight 1969; Bulliet 1975), and one by a camel man (Barker 1972). No one, however, has written about the camel as an integral member of the desert environment. Because the camel is a domesticated animal, we know a great deal about its diseases (studied so that healthy animals can be maintained) and its anatomy (measured and analyzed from body parts collected from abattoirs), but little about its behavior in the desert or its drinking and feeding habits. Zoologists have studied the physiology of camels in the laboratory, where food is supplied by man, but almost no one has observed them in the dunes or wadis to record, for example, how much of a plant they actually consume. Our first aim in writing this book, then, is to describe the camel in its natural habitat in the northwestern and western Sahara.

Our second aim is to point out the importance of camel men in the ecology of the desert, for without them, there would be no camels to utilize the desert's resources. Camel men are of necessity nomads, and we have paid special attention to the Reguibat, the last great nomads of the Sahara. Unless they receive assistance from their governments, these nomads may be forced, because of the recent great drought, to settle permanently in slum towns of the Sahara, leaving the desert unused and uninhabited by man.

Our third aim is to present a comprehensive bibliography of scientific references dealing primarily with the camel. Although these have been drawn largely from *Biological Abstracts*, many other sources are listed.

This book is based largely on the field studies of Dr. Gauthier-Pilters, whose research papers have all been published in French or German (see the bibliography). She wrote chapters 2, 3, 4, 6, 9, 10, and 11. Dagg wrote chapters 1, 5, 7, and 8 and prepared the bibliography.

Dr. Gauthier-Pilters would like to thank all the people who encouraged and helped her in her work, including her husband, Mr. Jo Gauthier, former manager of the Centre de Recherches Sahariennes at Beni-Abbès, who often drove her to distant nomad camps and facilitated her work in many other ways; Prof. N. Menchikoff, former director and creator of this research station; Prof. Th. Monod, former director of the Institut Fondamental d'Afrique Noire and member of the Institut Français; Mr. J. Adam, former chief botanist at the Institut Fondamental d'Afrique Noire; Mr. J. P. Lefranc, geologist; Prof. J. Dubief, meteorologist; the library of the Centre de Hautes Etudes Administratives sur l'Afrique et l'Asie Modernes in Paris; the Agence pour la Sécurité de la Navigation Aérienne en Afrique et Madagascar in Nouakchott; the members of a French petroleum research company working in her area in 1961 for their hospitality; and especially Mr. L. Treuffet, who commanded troops at Djebilet. She is particularly indebted to Ms. R. Hartung, biologist, who accompanied her on three field trips totaling 7 months, and to Arab guides Bouzidi Boudjema from Beni-Abbès and Reguibi Mbarek Ould Ali, whose helpfulness far surpassed our expectations.

Dr. Dagg is grateful to the many people who made her work possible, especially Dr. I. R. Dagg, Ms. R. Rowe, Ms. J. Spowart, Mr. D. Leach, and Ms. D. Anderson, and to the National Research Council of Canada for supplying her with photographic materials.

Both authors are pleased to acknowledge financial aid from the many institutions mentioned in appendix A; the assistance of the government of Mauritania; the help of friends and acquaintances from Algeria and Mauritania, particularly from MIFERMA; discussions with Knut Schmidt-Nielsen; the support of their families in France, Germany, and Canada; and the great assistance of their Arab guide in Mauritania, Sidi Mokhtar Ould Bontemps.

Introduction

We studied camels in the western Sahara (1) on 8–14-day trips from a base camp, (2) on long expeditions with the free-grazing camel herds of nomads or their herdsmen, (3) at wells where we were stationed for periods of 1 day to 1 month, and (4) during expeditions we organized to study working camels that we hired especially for this purpose. (See appendix A.)

Our 8–14-day field trips were based either at the research station at Beni-Abbès or at the oasis of Atar, where equipment, provisions, and guides were available. We always had to travel long distances to reach the nomads, who sought pastures for their herds far from the overgrazed and firewood-depleted areas surrounding the oases and villages. Sometimes we went by car, but usually we had to inform a distant nomad by means of the "Arab telephone" (oral communication from man to man) to send pack camels for us. During the usual wait of several days, we bought foodstuffs and, with the help of a hired guide, prepared water bags, saddles, and camping gear.

Once we reached the nomads' or herdsmen's camps after a 1- or 2-day journey, we pitched camp ourselves, using a tent as protection against the cold nights of winter and as a shield from the midday sun of summer (pl. 1). This camp was supervised by our guide, who interpreted our conversations with the nomads, helped with some of the research activities, renewed our supply of water when necessary, and prepared meals (pl. 2). During the day we observed camel herds in the pastures over a radius of 10–20 kilometers from our camp, noting how much of each type of plant the camels ate and collecting plant samples. The camels fed for 8–10 hours each day, covering 20 kilometers or more in the process. In the late spring and summer, when temperatures usually exceeded 40° C, our efforts were hindered by burning winds, occasional sandstorms, and lack of food, water, and shade.

Our long expeditions to study the free-grazing camel herds of the nomads were similar to our trips from a base camp except that we moved when the nomads moved. Our camp cots and supplies had to be packed on camels each morning, were partially unloaded for the lunch break, and were completely unpacked each evening.

We organized a number of trips to wells to measure the water consumption of camels. Because of the time involved, the camel owners visiting a well often refused at first to allow their animals to be watered separately so that we could measure the amount each drank (pl. 3). Only after long discussions between them and our guide would they agree to cooperate. (For such reasons the help of a guide of high social standing [in Mauritania] or well known to the nomads [Algeria] was essential.) Often the measurements were taken over an entire day in sun temperatures of up to 60° C.

In order to monitor camels' food and water intake and urine and feces output under working conditions, we hired camels for 1–4-week journeys in the desert. To ensure that the camels were under maximum stress, these journeys were all taken in the summer, when the daily temperature usually exceeded 40° C and the night temperature often stayed above 30° C. We generally traveled 10–40 kilometers per day, going from one well to the next, carrying water and resting at midday.

For our fieldwork in the desert, we had to adapt completely to the life of the nomads. Because we shared their interests and knew a variety of camel-related words in their language, we were accepted as friends (pl. 4). Such a relationship is essential if one is to understand completely the ecological interdependence of camels, nomads, and the desert.

Part 1

Evolution, Ecology, and Behavior

1 Evolution and Present Status

The family Camelidae is divided into an Old World group (camels) and a New World group (lamoids, comprising the wild vicuña and guanaco and the domesticated llama and alpaca of South America). The only two living species of camels are the dromedary (or one-humped, or Arabian) camel (*Camelus dromedarius*) and the Bactrian (or two-humped) camel (*Camelus bactrianus*). (In this book the word *camel*, when used alone, refers to the dromedary.) The embryos of both species at first have two hump primordia, but in the one-humped camel these apparently fuse during subsequent fetal development (Lombardini 1879). The adult Bactrian camel's humps tend to flop to one side in a flaccid state, especially in old individuals, when the humps (especially the posterior) lose their fat, whereas the skin of the dromedary's hump is more elastic, so that as the animal loses fat during periods of stress the hump simply shrinks in size. Compared with the one-humped camel, the Bactrian camel has longer and darker-colored hair, shorter legs, and a more massive body, which are cold-adapted features. In general, Bactrian camels are found in mountainous, rocky regions while dromedaries are restricted to dry, arid climates and a mainly flat terrain.

Living members of the Camelidae belonging to the infraorder Tylopoda and the order Artiodactyla share a number of characteristics: a reduced number of upper incisors, with only the lateral ones retained; long upper and lower diastemata between the small canines and the reduced premolars; postorbital bars in the skull; tympanic bullae filled with spongy bone; a long neck; long legs with the ulna and fibula much reduced; no trace of lateral toes; a digitigrade stance, with the divergent toes ending in nails spread nearly flat on the ground except for the underlying heavy pads; and a stomach with three compartments (Romer 1966). The infraorder Tylopoda is more primitive and not closely related to the infraorder Pecora, whose members possess cloven hooves, a stomach with four compartments, and even fewer teeth. There are also important embryologic differences between them (Baptidanova et al. 1975). Both groups of animals eat vegetation, which they later ruminate.

Evolution   The first camelids can be traced back through the Tertiary of North America to primitive Upper Eocene ancestors no larger than hares, with four toes per foot and an undifferentiated dentition. A later descendant, the North American Oligocene *Poëbrotherium* of about 35 million years ago, was much more camellike, but somewhat smaller than a sheep. It also had a complete dentition (44 teeth), with canines and incisors of similar shape, and no diastemata. The crown of the molars, however, was fairly high, as if they were already adapted to browsing on sandy and tough vegetation. The orbit was not yet closed, although the bony processes behind the eyes were long. The legs were short, the lateral toes (II and V) had already disappeared, and the two separate remaining metapodials presumably ended in hooves.

Along the main evolutionary line of the camelids in the Miocene and Pliocene, body size increased, the teeth and skull became more specialized, the metapodials fused into a cannon bone, and the typical flat, spreading camelid foot came into being. In *Procamelus* (with 40 teeth) and *Pliauchenia* (with 38 teeth) the orbit was completely enclosed by bone, the two inner upper incisors were absent, and diastemata were present. During the latter half of the Tertiary the camelids were numerous in North America, with many side branches, such as the gazelle-camel *Stenomylus*, a small, slight animal, and the giraffe-camel *Oxydactylus*, with a very long neck and legs, both from the Miocene.

Toward the end of the Tertiary, camelids first emigrated via the Beringia land mass to the Old World. Emigrations continued sporadically through the Pliocene, when the genus *Camelus*, to which our present-day camels belong, left North America. *Camelops*, a camelid well over 2 meters high at the shoulder, existed in what is now southwest North America until well into the Pleistocene. It may eventually have been wiped out by early man, because there is evidence that *Camelops* and early man coexisted (Irwin-Williams 1967; Frison et al. 1978).

At the end of the Tertiary, while *Camelus* and other camelids were emigrating to the Old World, relatives of the llama (*Lama*) were moving south through Central America into the mountainous regions of South America. Camelids there were used by man about 5500 B.C., with domestic forms evolving by 2500–1750 B.C. (Wheeler Pires-Ferreira, Pires-Ferreira, and Kaulicke 1976) or earlier (Pollard and Drew 1975). *Camelus* and *Lama* have been discrete genera for several million years, but their karyotypes are strikingly similar (Taylor et al. 1968). Their basic structure too is similar: the camel's hump and the llama's heavy hair are superficial features apparently acquired in recent times in response to each genus's modern habitat. There is no evidence that these genera can interbreed, even by artificial insemination (Treus and Lobanov 1976).

The camelids were plains animals, adapted to life in open areas. When *Camelus* reached the Old World, it spread rapidly west along the dry belt of Eurasia, with some animals moving south into India, where remains of *C. sivalensis* and *C. antiquus* have been found in the northern hills (Zeuner 1963). Bones of the former have been uncovered in this area in close association with human artifacts from the Lower Pleistocene (Verma 1975). In western Asia the camelids separated into two groups. The Bactrian-like species stayed in the east or migrated farther west, *C. knoblochi* reaching southern Russia, where it was hunted by man, and *C. alutensis* migrating to Romania (Zeuner 1963); beyond these areas the climate was less dry, and thus unsuitable for camels. At least one species moved south, because bones of *C. thomasi*, a close relative of the Bactrian camel, have frequently been found from about 40,000 B.P. levels at Mousterian sites in the Nubian Desert (Gautier 1966; Wendorf et al. 1976). The ancestors of the one-humped camel, or dromedary (from the Greek *dromas*, "running"), meanwhile had spread south into Arabia, the Middle East, and, by the Middle Pleistocene, North Africa. Fossils of *C. dromedarius* from Morocco have been described by Charnot (1953), and camel bones have been found in Algeria in association with Paleolithic artifacts (Mikesell 1955). However, by historic times the wild one-humped camel was extinct. The domestication of the camel and the uses to which it has been put by man are discussed in part 2. At present, among camels living in Africa, at least 20 distinct breeds can be identified (table 1).

Present Distribution

Although the dromedary is found in almost all the arid and semiarid regions of the Old World, its main home is in North Africa. In the western and central part of that area it ranges south to about 13° north latitude. To the east it is found in the northern Sudan, in northern Kenya almost to the equator, in eastern Ethiopia, and (in great numbers) in Somalia. South of these limits, the more humid climate, diseases, and sedentary human populations limit its distribution.

In Asia the dromedary occurs throughout the Arabian peninsula, in Syria, Lebanon, Israel, Jordan, Turkey, Iran, Iraq, Afghanistan, Pakistan, in northwestern India, in China (western Sinkiang), and in the southwestern Soviet Union, mainly Turkmenistan. Because of the exportation of dromedaries in the past, they are also found in Australia and the Canary Islands.

In Turkey, Afghanistan (where dromedaries are especially common in the south), and Turkmenistan, dromedaries and Bactrian camels coexist and may interbreed. The northern limit of the cold-resistant Bactrian camel is about 52° north latitude. It is present in northeastern Afghanistan, the steppes of the southern Soviet Union, where it replaces the dromedary from Turkmenistan eastward, Siberia east of Lake Baikal, Mongolia, and northern China. In Tienchan and Pamir it exists at altitudes as high as 4,000 meters, where the yak begins to displace it as a pack animal.

Present Population

The Food and Agricultural Organization of the United Nations (FAO) has published extensive census data on camels (tables 2 and 3), but the accuracy of these and other quoted figures is uncertain. The number of dromedaries in many desert countries is known only approximately, because camel owners, who in North Africa, the Near East, and Afghanistan are largely nomads or seminomads, tend to avoid official censuses. In addition, the numbers vary considerably from place to place depending on the availability of food. Bulliet (1975) quotes a world population figure for camels of 1.5 million in 1876, 6 million in 1925 (quoting Cauvet [1925–26], and more than twice that many today; but in reality the total number was surely

Table 1 Camel Types in Africa

Type	Region	Use	Body Features	Coat, Color	Comments
Sudani	Egypt	...	...	...	...
Maghrabi	Egypt, Iba, Algeria, Tunisia, Morocco	Pack	Slow, sturdy	Long hair, brown	Not a fixed type
Fellahi	Egypt	Pack	Large, heavy, large hump	White or sand colored	...
Mowalled (crossbred between the 2 above)	Egypt	Farm and desert work	...	...	The most common in Egypt
Rashaidi	Sudan	Pack	Light, relatively short legged	Reddish	Not as useful as the Kababish
Arab (Kababish)	Darfur, Kordofan	Pack	Heavy, large hump	Short, sandy gray	...
Anafi	NE Sudan	Riding	Light, leggy, small hump	Pale	...
Bishari	NE Sudan	Riding	Stronger than Anafi	Light	One of the best riding camels, excellent feeding
Ogaden	NW Somalia	Pack	Large	Pale, nearly white	...
Dolbahanta	E Somalia	Pack	Slow, large hump	...	Largest of Somali camels
Guban	Maritime plains of N Somalia	Pack	Very hardy	Sparse, reddish	Smallest of Somali camels
Mudugh	N Somalia	Pack	Medium, small hump	Tawny	Fit for work on stony ground, poor milker
Benadir (Gel Ad)	S Somalia	Pack	Large (500–550 kg)	White	...
Tibesti	Tibesti, S Fezzan	Riding	Small, hardy, for stony and sandy soil	Long hair, gray, often dark	Smallest riding camel of Africa
Manga	N + W Lake Chad	Pack	Heavy, unfit for desert	...	...
Air	Air	Riding	Tall, slender, small hump	Light	Fast
Berabish	NW Timbuktu	Pack	Medium size, strong, heavy	Long hair, brown	...
Adrar	Adrar des Iforas	Riding	Moderate hump	Short, gray	...
Sahel (Mehari)	Sahel	Riding	Large, slender, small hump	Fawn	...
Gandiol	Senegal	Pack	Large, heavy	...	...

Source: Epstein (1971).

Table 2 Camel Population of African Countries

	No. of Camels (× 1,000)													Density (camels/sq km), 1976
	1947–52	1960–65	1966–67	1967–68	1968–69	1969–70	1970	1971	1972	1973	1974	1975	1976	
Somalia	2,220	2,700	2,800	2,900	3,000	3,000	3,000	3,000	3,000	3,000	1,500	1,900	2,000	3.14
Sudan	1,550	2,001	2,420	2,662	2,918	3,000	3,000	3,100	3,200	2,500	2,620	2,736	2,827	1.13
Ethiopia	855	940	964	969	981	987	987	990	995	995	970	950	960	0.81
Mauritania	160	466	620	675	685	690	690	700	720	700	716	732	748	0.68
Kenya	152	252	290	300	312	315	315	320	322	520	530	530	564	...
Chad	266	338	350	355	355	370	370	370	370	330	300	305	310	0.25
Niger	224	352	370	380	390	400	345	345	350	285	235	250	260	0.22
Tunisia	186	158	238	260	270	280	280	280	290	180	180	180	195	1.56
Morocco	195	221	222	214	222	230	230	230	233	200	200	200	200	0.45
Algeria	147	165	175	173	178	175	175	175	179	165	165	155	157	0.07
Mali	79	172	224	231	218	218	218	215	215	150	158	168	178	0.14
Libya	324	266	256	232	206	163	163	120	100	120	120	120	120	0.69
Egypt	118	123	126	127	136	132	127	125	125	113	109	111	113	0.12
Former Spanish Sahara	65	29	37	43	56	58	58	61	63	70	77	80	83	0.31
Djibouti	15	18	20	20	21	22	22	23	23	23	24	24	25	...
Senegal	7	27	33	31	31	30	30	30	30	20	23	24	25	...
Nigeria	12	15	17	18	18	19	19	20	20	18	18	18	17	...
Upper Volta	1	3	5	6	6	6	5	5	5	5	5	5	5	...
Total	6,576	8,246	9,167	9,596	10,003	10,095	10,034	10,109	10,240	9,394	7,950	8,488	8,787	...

Source: FAO Production Yearbooks.

Table 3 Camel Population of Non-African Countries

	No. of Camels (× 1,000)													Density (camels/sq km), 1976
	1947–52	1960–65	1966–67	1967–68	1968–69	1969–70	1970	1971	1972	1973	1974	1975	1976	
India	638	903	1,050	1,080	1,100	1,120	1,120	1,100	1,100	1,130	1,130	1,154	1,178	…
Pakistan	466	682	820	840	870	900	900	930	850	800	833	866	899	…
Mongolia	741	729	664	644	655	660	660	670	670	670	650	650	650	…
Saudi Arabia	265	460	500	520	540	550	550	560	570	580	590	602	614	0.04
Iraq	181	202	210	215	220	220	266	280	300	313	315	322	330	0.74
Afghanistan	350	317	300	299	299	301	301	300	300	300	300	300	290	0.44
Yemen A. R.	48	54	56	56	57	58	58	59	60	110	100	120	120	0.82
Iran	450	234	190	185	180	180	120	115	110	80	70	60	60	0.04
Yemen Dem.	75	46	43	42	42	41	41	40	40	40	40	40	40	…
Turkey	107	54	43	43	42	39	39	31	29	25	21	19	18	0.02
China†	12	14	15	16	16	16	16	17	17	17	1,080	1,070	1,070	…
Jordan	10	17	17	11	13	13	13	10	9	18	16	18	18	0.19
Israel	4	10	10	11	10	10	10	10	10	10	10	10	11	0.53
Oman	…	…	…	…	…	…	…	…	…	10	7	6	6	…
Qatar	…	…	…	…	…	…	…	…	…	8	9	9	9	0.41
Syria	75	11	10	7	7	7	7	7	7	6	8	6	6	0.03
Kuwait	5	6	6	6	6	6	6	6	6	6	6	6	6	0.39
Lebanon	2	1	1	…	…	…	…	…	…	1	1	1	1	0.10
Bahrain	…	…	…	…	…	…	…	…	…	1	1	1	1	1.67
Cyprus	1	…	…	…	…	…	…	…	…	…	…	…	…	…
Australia	2	2	2	2	2	2	2	2	2	2	2	2	2	…
European USSR	306	247	251	256	263	244	244	238	230	249	245	253	253	…
Total	3,738	3,989	4,188	4,232	4,322	4,367	4,353	4,375	4,310	4,376	5,434	5,515	5,582	…

*The FAO groups both species of camels together. The camels are dromedaries except in Mongolia and China, where most are Bactrians, and in Afghanistan, Turkey, USSR, and Iran, where some are Bactrians.

†The FAO data given for China are obviously incorrect to some extent. Cockrill (1975) estimates that China has about 17,000 camels. A report from Reuter's (Jan. 1980) gives a current total of 600,000 in China.

Source: FAO Production Yearbooks.

never as low as 1.5 million and probably has not increased so dramatically in recent times. In three countries where camels have been important working animals, their numbers have declined significantly since 1947–52—by 88,000, or 82 percent, in Turkey; by 390,000, or 87 percent, in Iran; and by 67,000, or 89 percent, in Syria—perhaps partly as a consequence of the more or less forced settlement of nomads.

Figures from different sources may vary widely. The FAO value for Australia is 2,000 for 1947–75, although during that period the number of domesticated camels declined steadily; including feral camels, the values should have been 20,000 or higher for much of that period (McKnight 1969). Similarly, in the Sahel during the drought of 1972–73, the camel population declined 13 percent according to FAO figures but 95 percent according to another report (Temple and Thomas 1973).

A careful study of the tables indicates that the recent values for camels are fairly consistent from year to year (with the exception of those for China) and therefore probably fairly accurate, but the figures for 1947–52 are often not at all what one would expect from later trends and perhaps therefore are suspect. While the number of camels in most countries has remained fairly stable over the past decade, the number in the countries of Mauritania, Kenya, former Spanish Sahara, Djibouti, Saudi Arabia, Iraq, and Yemen Arab Republic has increased steadily and the number in Iran and Turkey has declined fairly steadily. Camel numbers in 13 African countries dropped between 1972 and 1974, the worst years of the great North African drought of the early 1970s, but camel migration to areas of better food availability presumably was responsible for a corresponding rise in three countries—Libya, Spanish Sahara, and Kenya (pls. 5–7). In Spanish Sahara the food was provided as extra rations by the government (see fig. 1).

It is impossible to estimate the density of camels in all the countries listed in tables 2 and 3, because some or perhaps most of each country may have no camels at all. In those that are uniformly arid, however, camels are widespread, and their density has been calculated as shown. The country with by far the highest density is Somalia, with 3.14 camels per square kilometer. Although also largely a camel country, Mauritania has only 0.68 camels per square kilometer, presumably because the vegetation is much sparser.

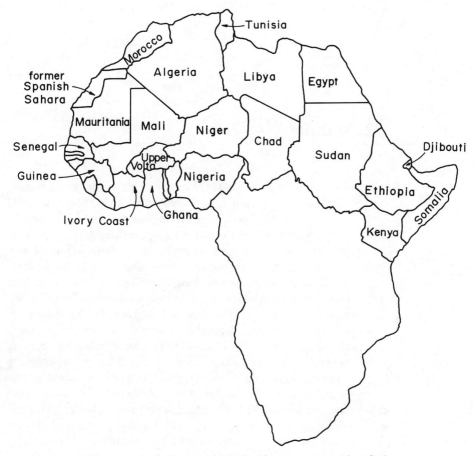

Fig. 1   Map of Africa, with North African countries identified

2 Habitat

Climate *General features.* One-third of the earth's land surface consists of arid terrain where evaporation exceeds rainfall, which, besides being minimal, is distributed irregularly in time and space. One-third of these dry lands occur in the Sahara, the largest, hottest, and driest desert of the world and the main habitat of the dromedary. Arid lands are defined as those receiving 50–150 millimeters of rain a year, while hyperarid lands receive less than 50 millimeters of rain a year (Planhol and Rognon 1970). The latter deserts are found along the west coast of South America, the west coast of South Africa, in central Arabia, and in central North Africa. The former border the central hyperarid deserts of Africa and Arabia, and include the central parts of the less continental deserts of Australia and the southwestern United States and the Kalahari. Arid regions can support many camels, but hyperarid regions can meet the needs of camels only temporarily (table 4).

Table 4   Aridity of North African Countries

	Total % of Country Hyperarid and Arid (<150 mm rain/yr)	% of Country Hyperarid (<50 mm rain/yr)	% of Country Arid (50–150 mm rain/yr)
Egypt	100.0	90.0	10.0
Former Spanish Sahara	100.0	0	100.0
Libya	95.2	64.8	30.4
Algeria	90.8	51.7	39.1
Mauritania	90.0	40.0	50.0
Niger	84.0	8.0	76.0
Tunisia	60.0	0	60.0
Sudan	56.0	21.0	35.0
Chad	52.0	4.0	48.0
Mali	50.5	23.5	27.0
Morocco	30.0	0	30.0

Source: Meigs (1952).

To provide a reliable and comprehensive weather description of a region requires a minimum of 20–30 years of continuous observations. Meteorological data are difficult to obtain from the Sahara (figs. 2 and 3), where some 120 meteorological stations, distributed irregularly—some in unsuitable places and some not always functioning—must serve 8.6 million square kilometers, an area almost the size of Europe. Indeed, in the central Sahara, 1,000 kilometers may separate one station from the next. The main characteristics of the Saharan climate as given here are based on the work of Dubief (1959, 1963), one of the preeminent climatologists of the Sahara.

The Sahara cannot be treated as a homogeneous climatic entity. Rather, it constitutes a complex climatic system, with characteristics varying according to region. There are two main climatic zones, the north and the south, with the rainfall increasing toward the south. The bodies of water on either side of the desert have different effects on its climate; in the west the cold Canary Current mitigates the desert climate of the Mauritanian coast, while in the east the hot Red Sea enhances the desert climate, making this area one of the most arid coastal regions in the

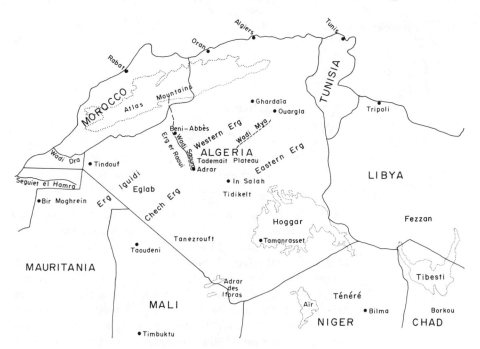

Fig. 2   Map of the northwestern Sahara

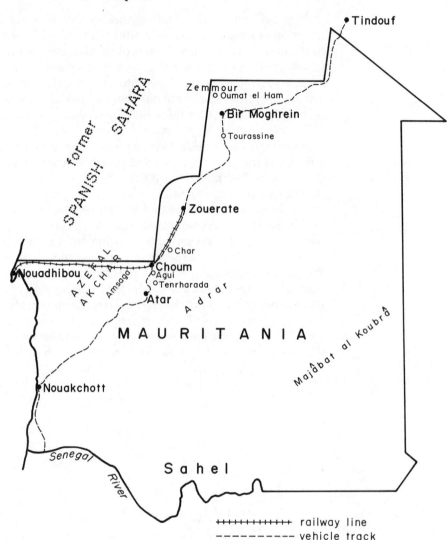

Fig. 3   Map of Mauritania

world. In the northwest the Atlas Mountains act as a barrier to the maritime influence of the Mediterranean Sea and North Atlantic Ocean. During the hot season the climatological effect of these bodies of water penetrates no farther than 500 kilometers inland from the northern coast and, at the latitude of Nouakchott, only 200 kilometers from the Mauritanian coast. In the northeast, however, the effects of the Mediterranean are felt in summer well into the interior of the continent, as far as southern Cyrenaica and the eastern border of the Hoggar. Temperatures are therefore generally higher in the western Sahara than in the northeast, with greater daily and annual fluctuations. On the other hand, the equatorial Atlantic Ocean has an important though temporary influence on the southern Sahara through the Sudan monsoons of summer. The influence of the Indian Ocean is blocked by the Ethiopian mountain massif.

Radiation and temperature. Because there are few clouds over the Sahara, the insolation is very high, indeed, almost equal to the highest possible insolation per year— 4,100 hours (~11.2 × 365). In most parts of the desert there are fewer than 10 cloudy days a year and between 9 and 11 hours of sunshine a day, depending on the season. The areas receiving the most sun are Egypt and the central portion of the western Sahara.

The heat in the desert is very great in summer, not only because of the direct rays of the sun but also because of diffuse reflection from the soil (which can equal 44 percent of the sun's radiation on sand, almost as much as on old snow) and because of radiation from the soil, which may heat up to a temperature of 70° C. This radiation makes summer nights in rocky areas much hotter than those in sandy areas, where the temperature of the soil changes more rapidly, both daily and annually.

The temperature of the soil, which in summer is frequently 60° C at its surface, drops to 55° C a few centimeters above the surface, and to 40° C 1 meter above the surface. Sand heated to 60° C is very painful to human feet, even in sandals, and kills most small animals that cannot find shade or dig underground. The annual temperature range at the ground's surface is sometimes as high as 60–70° C. Daily temperature variations cease about 50 centimeters below the surface (Pierre 1958), while annual variations probably cease about 6 meters down (Dubief 1959). In summer, sand that was 57.5° C at the surface was 33.4° C at a depth of 50 centimeters, while in winter it was 3.4° C at the surface and 16.1° C at 50 centimeters (Pierre 1958). Because of the fairly constant temperature and high humidity underground, sand dunes offer favorable living conditions to many small animals. Camels, which cannot hide from the heat as burrowing animals do, have evolved various behavior patterns to help them cope with the desert climate (see chap. 5).

Maximum and minimum air temperatures are of much

greater ecological significance than mean values, which
are often misleading. Figure 4 plots the annual mean
maximum and minimum temperatures for two stations in
Mauritania in the area in which much of our work was
done: Bir Moghrein in the north and Atar in the center.
Figure 4 gives only a general idea of temperature differences. Figure 5, depicting the maximum and minimum
temperatures for the two hottest months in 1973, points up
the variations from place to place. Heat stress for men and
camels is less important in Bir Moghrein, 250 kilometers
east of the Atlantic coast, than in Atar, about 350 kilometers inland, for three main reasons: (1) The extreme heat
(greater than 40° C) lasts about 4 months in central
Mauritania but only 2 months in the north. (2) The summer heat is often interrupted by a cool week in the north
but at most by several consecutive cool days in central
Mauritania, although both regions have about the same

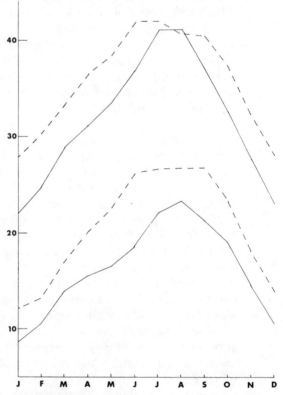

Fig. 4   Yearly maximum and minimum average temperatures for two towns in
Mauritania. *Dashes* = Atar, 1936–50; *solid* = Bir Moghrein, 1942–50
(Dubief 1959).

number of extremely hot days (greater than 45° C) in July
and August. At Bir Moghrein the temperature may drop to
33° C when cool winds, called *tagout* by the nomads, blow
from the north. Also, the summer sky in the north is often
cloudy in the early morning, clearing only as the temperature rises. (3) Night temperatures, also of great ecological
importance, are much higher in Atar than at Bir Moghrein.
In Atar the nights are already hot (greater than 25° C) as
early as June, and they remain so throughout the summer.
In the north about one-third of the nights have temperature lows of less than 20° C.

These differences explain why the camel needs more
water during the summer in Atar and farther east than at
Bir Moghrein.

In winter Saharan temperatures may drop to 0° C, and
occasionally to −10° C in the mountains or on high

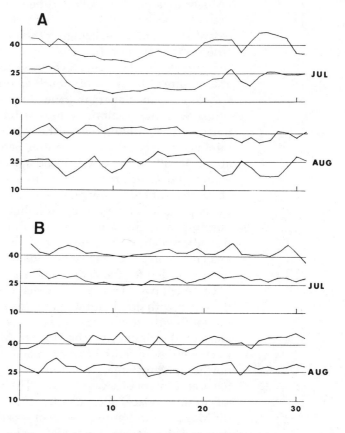

Fig. 5   Maximum and minimum temperatures during July and August 1973 for
two towns in Mauritania. A = Bir Moghrein; B = Atar.

plateaus. It is truly remarkable to see the dunes of the Western Erg on those rare occasions when they are covered with hoarfrost.

The heat of the desert ensures a high rate of water evaporation. Using a Piche evaporimeter, Dubief (in Schiffers 1971) obtained average evaporation values of over 3 meters per year for the whole Sahara, with the center of the western Sahara losing 6 meters and the southeastern Sahara 7 meters. The evaporation, of course, increases not only with temperature but also with drier air and stronger winds. Evaporation is so great that one's lips remain chapped and one's skin dry despite continual perspiration.

Rain. Since rain is rare in the desert and varies greatly in when it falls, where it falls, and how much of it falls, many years of data must be collected before conclusions can be drawn. The irregularity of rainfall makes nomadism essential, the nomads bringing their camel herds to areas where previous rain has ensured enough vegetation for the animals. Information on where good pastures are available is spread by word of mouth among nomads.

Rainfall in the Sahara in general increases from north to south, with mean annual values of 100 millimeters in the north and 150 millimeters in the south. The areas of least rainfall are located in the central Sahara (Taoudeni has about 5 millimeters a year) and farther east. The mean values, however, may reveal little of real significance about the rainfall in any one year; for example, they mask the importance of periods of drought (periods without any "useful" rain, i.e., at least 5 millimeters in a 24-hour period), which in some regions of the eastern Sahara may exceed 6 years. The longest periods without any rain have been recorded for the central and eastern Sahara.

There are two main rain systems, the Mediterranean in the north with dominant winter rains and the Sudanese in the south with summer rains, systems that may overlap in areas of Mauritania and the Hoggar. Most of the rain falls in September in central Mauritania, and somewhat later in northern Mauritania. In addition, there are Sudanese-Saharan centers of low pressure. The irregularity of rainfall in time, space, and quantity is illustrated for Atar and Bir Moghrein in figure 6. A fall of less than 5 millimeters a year scarcely affects the vegetation, while more rain is utilized by plants in varying degrees depending on the begun, they range from mild to severe, depending on the amount of sand carried by the wind, the area over which they extend, and the wind velocity. Sandstorms may last several days, depending in part on the direction of the wind; those blowing from the west generally last longer than those from the east. Only winds greater than force 3 on the Beaufort scale can carry grains of sand. This is presumably why the sands of the Western Erg, where the daily northeast winds are moderate, have not filled in the Wadi Saoura, which borders the dunes on the west. Sandstorms are infrequent in the central Sahara and are absent in the mountain massifs.

Relief   There are five main types of habitat in the Sahara, each with its own physiognomy, soil type, microclimate, and vegetation.

Hamada. A plateau covered with rocks and stones of various sizes from which sand and finer particles have been blown away, hamadas, which are especially common in the north, cover more than 70 percent of the surface of the Sahara. The plateaus are generally formed of horizontal beds of sedimentary rock of various ages (Cretaceous and Tertiary), sometimes topped with limestone slabs, which may terminate in abrupt cliffs. They are difficult to cross with camels because the vegetation present is confined mostly to wadis, low erosion ditches, and depressions of various sizes. One type of depression, the *daya*, has a subterranean drainage system that collects rainwater and allows soil to form; thus, relatively dense vegetation is present. The large number of dayas in the northern Sahara and in the steppes north of the desert but south of the Atlas Mountains is caused by the lack of drainage of rainwater to the ocean. Often more than 1 kilometer square, dayas also occur on the border of dune massifs, where floodwater from a plateau is blocked by dunes. Sometimes rainwater remains in such dayas for weeks, thus offering ample water for animal herds (pl. 9). In northern Mauritania, where wells containing sweet water are scarce, the people obtain drinking water from flooded dayas wherever possible. However, herds grazing on the hamadas must generally travel long distances to get from one daya to another.

Another type of depression, the *sebkha*, is usually larger than the daya. Sebkhas were formed as depressions dur-

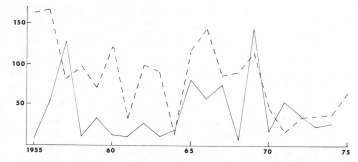

Fig. 6   Yearly rainfall (in millimeters) at two towns in Mauritania, 1955–75. *Dashes* = Atar; *solid* = Bir Moghrein.

season and time of day it falls, the intensity of the rain, the temperature, the nature of the substrate, and the latitude. Thus, rain that falls for several hours during the cool season, or during several successive days, ensures future good pastures, while summer rainfall, which is usually of short duration, of greater intensity, and more localized, often has little or no effect on the vegetation. There is great variety in monthly totals of rain in any one place from year to year (fig. 7).

Even where there is little rain, it may be enough to affect the vegetation if there are depressions in the ground with little permeable soil, or deep sand which retains the water and keeps it from evaporating. Walter (1970) noted that in

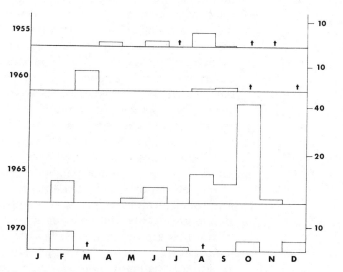

Fig. 7   Monthly amounts of rain at Bir Moghrein for four different years (t = trace of rain = < 0.1 millimeter).

regions near Kairo-Heluan receiving 25 millimeters of rain annually all depressions contained some vegetation; if we assume that approximately 40 percent of the rainwater flows into depressions or erosion ditches and that these depressions represent 2 percent of the total surface, then vegetation would receive the same amount of water through runoff as would vegetation growing on flat terrain receiving 500 millimeters of rain annually. Areas of the Sahara that are occasionally flooded represent 30 percent of the total surface.

Local rains may cause occasional minor floods, but the heavy rains in the Atlas Mountains may cause floods extending hundreds of kilometers. During a 57-year period the Wadi Saoura, which passes through Beni-Abbès and is usually completely dry, caused floods 200 kilometers in length 33 times, 300 kilometers 13 times, 400 kilometers 6 times, 500 kilometers 5 times, and, once, 800 kilometers. On one occasion, from October 1905 to May 1906, water flowed without interruption from the source of the Guir in the Atlas (which together with the Zousfana forms the Saoura) to a place 450 kilometers farther south. The Atlas Mountains contribute much more water to the riverbeds of the Sahara than does the Hoggar.

Floods occur suddenly and without warning when large quantities of rain have fallen many kilometers from the area being flooded. An exceptionally heavy rainfall of 50 millimeters in 2 days in 1960 caused flooding when the Wadi Mya rose several meters. Water flow can reach a volume of 3,000 cubic meters per second and progress at the speed of a person walking quickly, so it is not surprising that people and animals have been drowned in the desert and in villages and palm tree plantations seriously damaged. Even heavier rainfalls have been reported: in 1950, 37 millimeters (the annual average) fell within 40 minutes in Tamanrasset, and within an hour the noontime temperature had fallen from 32° C to 18° C.

Although most floods are of short duration, the underground flow of water may persist for months or even years at variable depths in an apparently dry riverbed, allowing fairly shallow wells to fill and relatively rich shrub vegetation to grow. This water may be salty if it has flowed over or through ground rich in salts. The Wadi Saoura flows almost every year and always has subterranean water near its surface; the many oases along its course have gained it the name "street of palms" (pl. 8). There are no major

wadis in the eastern Sahara or in the generally fla Sahara. In the northwest the Wadi Dra and Seguiet el Hamra flow only occasionally.

Dew. Dew is rare in the Sahara, even in the moun encountered it only in August in the wadis of mour in northern Mauritania, where the ter reached 40° C each day but dropped to abou night. One morning we collected about one-thir of dew on a nylon sleeping bag. On the wester the Sahara there are about 10–15 foggy days ea

Wind. There are very windy regions in the Saha the Rio de Oro coast and the Tidikelt, and som Borkou, where wind erosion has sculptured into fantastic shapes; but there are also wind where car tracks have remained visible for yea tensity of the wind often changes with the time with the season: it is less windy at night and at autumn and beginning of winter than it is at ot Most winds are of moderate strength and ar than they are in Europe because there is little to impede them; on the coast of Mauritania blows from the north the year around. In the Mauritania the prevailing winds usually are northeast, except in summer, when under the i the Sudan monsoons they blow in the south from the southwest. Steady, mild winds from tion produce accumulations of sand around bus tion that offer shelter to small animals.

Hot winds are particularly deleterious in a cause they accelerate dehydration. The winds h ent characteristics depending on where they *irifi* (from *araf*, "roast") in the western Sahara is dry wind from the east or northeast, frequent and autumn and often accompanied by sandstoi make the temperature rise to 50° C. Fortunatel does not last longer than 12 hours. Hot, dry w *chergui* in Morocco, *ghibli* in Libya, and *sirocco* and Tunisia sometimes blow from the desert t Europe. In Egypt the *khamsin* (meaning "fift; sometimes blows for 50 days, may cause si Egypt also has cold and dusty khamsins in wii

Sandstorms in the Sahara are more a result o soil than of wind velocity and variability. Once

ing the Tertiary and filled during the Quaternary cycle of arid and humid phases. Unlike dayas, sebkhas have no subterranean drainage and contain a great deal of salty sediment. Many wadis end in sebkhas, which are found adjacent to mountains and plateaus and may cover large areas, as in southern Tunisia. Sebkhas with a high concentration of salt are devoid of vegetation.

Reg. Vast, rather flat plains covered with fine gravel, sand, lime, or clay, regs—unlike hamadas, which are erosion areas—are accumulation areas (pl. 10). In the central and eastern Sahara a reg is called a *serir* (meaning "small"). Regs and serirs usually are fluvial in origin, and thus are found adjacent to the big hamadas of the western Sahara, the Libyan desert, and the central Saharan massifs, where large runoffs of water have spread fine sediment and gravel over large areas. Some regs and serirs, however, were created from the breakdown of rock *in situ*. The reg is the poorest environment for life in the Sahara (pl. 11). Only after "useful" rainfalls do annual plants spring up on the sandy regs and attract the nomads and their herds from distant places.

Wadi. Usually dry riverbeds (called *washes* or *arroyos* in America, *ennedi* in Tibesti, and *kori* in the Hoggar) that are cut more or less deeply into the terrain, and wadis form part of a typical landscape in the desert, their relatively rich vegetation contrasting sharply with their more barren surroundings. Most wadis do not have an identifiable source and never reach the ocean, terminating instead in depressions or disappearing into the soil, sometimes to continue flowing underground. The big wadi systems, which may be over 1,000 kilometers long, originate in the northern and central mountains of the Sahara. Lesser systems descend from the plateaus, for example, the Wadi Mya from the Tademait. In the rather flat western Sahara, where there are no large wadis, the occasional small riverbed and *thalweg* ("erosion ditch") offer favorable grazing (pl. 12).

Mountains. The Sahara has a crystalline-igneous rock base, which crops out in many places to form mountains of different heights. The lowest crystalline massif is the 800-meter Eglab in the western Sahara. Farther east are the 800–1,000-meter Adrar des Iforas and the more humid massifs of Aïr in Niger, which reach 1,900 meters. The best known mountainous area is the Hoggar; with a peak of 2,600 meters, the Hoggar is traversed by one of the principal trans-Saharan roads and is peopled by the Tuareg. Wind and water, together with the ever-burning sun and extremes of temperature, have produced an immense variety of rock forms in the Sahara. Many rivers from the mountain massifs have cut deeply into the surrounding sandstone plateaus (called *tassili* in the central Sahara) and hollowed out in the course of ages deep canyons, such as that in the Tassili n'Ajjer (maximum depth, 2,254 meters), a region famous for its prehistoric carvings.

Farther east, the volcanic massif of Tibesti in Chad has the highest mountain in the Sahara—the 3,415-meter Emi Koussi. To the southeast the Ennedi, a sandstone plateau, rises to heights greater than 1,500 meters. The eastern Sahara as far as the Nile is empty and flat, with only a few crystalline-igneous massifs and sandstone plateaus. East of the Nile this Precambrian base rises to 2,000 meters, then falls abruptly down to the Red Sea. In all, mountains 2,000 meters and higher constitute about 5 percent of the Sahara.

In Mauritania the main mountainous area comprises the sandstone plateaus of the Adrar, which have a maximum height of about 800 meters and extend 700 kilometers from southwest to northeast. In the smaller of several craters here, nomads formerly sought refuge in times of danger. Although the central Tagant massif is only 300 meters high and the southern massifs of Affolé and Assaba only 200 meters, these plateaus look like mountains because they rise so abruptly from the plains. They represent a serious obstacle to the nomads and their camel herds on their annual migrations from north to south and back. In 1964 Gauthier-Pilters joined a Reguibat family, who moved with their 300 camels from northern Mauritania to Tagant, 600 kilometers farther south. It took them 3 hours to herd the animals to the top of the 200-meter pass up a steep path where steps were cut in the rock.

A distinctive form of relief is the *inselberg*, an isolated mountain of granite or sandstone found in the northwestern Sahara and between the Atakor and Tassili plateaus in the central Sahara (pl. 13). Inselbergs have a conical form with steep sides and a gently sloping base covered more or less with erosion material. Unlike the inselbergs, the *gour* (singular, *gara*) are flat-topped mountains that have been "cut off" from plateaus by the slow erosion of river systems.

Sand regions. Sand regions in the Sahara exhibit a great variety of forms, including the chaotic dune massifs of the Eastern Erg (110,000 square kilometers) and the Western Erg (80,000 square kilometers); the very dry Erg Chech (180,000 square kilometers) with its flatter dune chains separated by large channels; the immense undulating Majâbat al-Koubrâ, 250,000 square kilometers without a single tree and with hardly any water, the favorite study area of the great Saharan scientist Th. Monod; and the almost flat sand areas of the Ténéré (280,000 square kilometers). There are also smaller groups of dunes and single chains more than several hundred kilometers long, such as the Abu Mohariq in Egypt, which extends over 600 kilometers from northwest to southeast.

In all, 26 extensive dune regions cover one-fifth of the Saharan surface. In the Eastern Erg and Western Erg interlapping dunes reach heights of 300 meters and are difficult to cross, but travel is fairly easy in the Erg Iguidi and other dune areas, where parallel dune ranges of lesser height (50–80 meters) are separated from each other by broad corridors almost free of sand. In the southern Sahara, where it is increasingly humid, the dunes have been largely leveled and the corridors filled with sand, forming undulating, monotonous expanses such as those covering vast areas of southern Mauritania.

The sand of the ergs is of fluvial origin, deposited during the Quaternary in large depressions by the big wadi systems. The fine dust particles were blown away by the wind, leaving the heavier sand grains behind. Many wadis disappear at the edge of ergs or run closely beside them, as does the Wadi Saoura. The extent of the dune massifs has not changed since they were formed, although the wind may alter their shape. Unlike European sand regions, particularly those on the coasts, desert sand regions offer a favorable habitat for plants and small animals. Sand is porous, so that rainwater penetrates quickly before it can evaporate. The plants that grow in deep sand have an extensive and deep-reaching root system that allows them to utilize the water deep in the sand. Such plants constitute a permanent food source for animals during the dry season, and the dunes, especially the big northern massifs (Western Erg, Eastern Erg, Erg er Raoui), are therefore important areas of pasture, with a varied, almost evergreen shrub vegetation. Some ergs, however, are almost barren.

One form of dune is the *barchan,* an isolated moving dune found on flat terrain where there is little other sand. Barchans exist where the wind always blows from the same direction, which gives them a crescent shape with symmetrical ends. The convex side of the dune is exposed to the wind, while the concave side falls steeply from a sharp ridge. Barchans are typical of the coastal region of Mauritania, where, near Nouadhibou, they move 10 meters a year (Capot-Rey 1953). In Egypt they form chains 100 kilometers or more in length.

Vegetation   Food for direct human consumption, such as dates, peanuts, wheat, and vegetables, can be grown on only 10 percent of the Sahara. About 30 percent of the Sahara is hyperarid, supporting at most only 20 species of plants (Tanezrouft, the Libyan desert, and part of the Ténéré are the three major hyperarid regions). The patchy scattering of vegetation on the remaining 60 percent is a function of the irregular rainfall. Most of the Sahara cannot be used for crops, therefore, but only for ranging livestock. The chief livestock species is the camel, the only domestic animal that in summer can forage far from any source of drinking water and that, because of its method of feeding, does not harm the soil or vegetation (see chap. 3).

The flora of the Sahara comprises about 1,200 species (Ozenda 1958). No extensive biome aside from the arctic is known to have so few species. The flora contains Mediterranean elements as well as Saharo-Sindian elements (dominant in the northern and central parts) and Sudano-Deccanian elements (dominant in the south). There is a gradual decrease in abundance and species of plants from south to north, corresponding to the increasing aridity. In Mauritania, which is mostly flat, there are 360 species (Sauvage, in Schiffers 1971), while in hyperarid parts, such as the Majâbat al-Koubrâ (meaning "big empty space without water"), Monod (1958) found only seven species in a 150,000-square-kilometer area. By contrast, Quézel (in Schiffers 1971) found 568 species in a 200,000-square-kilometer area in the Tibesti Mountains. Many plants living in the desert have evolved into new, endemic species, but rarely into endemic genera. Almost

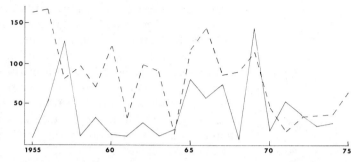

Fig. 6 Yearly rainfall (in millimeters) at two towns in Mauritania, 1955–75. *Dashes* = Atar; *solid* = Bir Moghrein.

season and time of day it falls, the intensity of the rain, the temperature, the nature of the substrate, and the latitude. Thus, rain that falls for several hours during the cool season, or during several successive days, ensures future good pastures, while summer rainfall, which is usually of short duration, of greater intensity, and more localized, often has little or no effect on the vegetation. There is great variety in monthly totals of rain in any one place from year to year (fig. 7).

Even where there is little rain, it may be enough to affect the vegetation if there are depressions in the ground with little permeable soil, or deep sand which retains the water and keeps it from evaporating. Walter (1970) noted that in

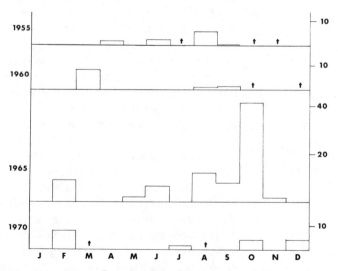

Fig. 7 Monthly amounts of rain at Bir Moghrein for four different years (t = trace of rain = < 0.1 millimeter).

regions near Kairo-Heluan receiving 25 millimeters of rain annually all depressions contained some vegetation; if we assume that approximately 40 percent of the rainwater flows into depressions or erosion ditches and that these depressions represent 2 percent of the total surface, then vegetation would receive the same amount of water through runoff as would vegetation growing on flat terrain receiving 500 millimeters of rain annually. Areas of the Sahara that are occasionally flooded represent 30 percent of the total surface.

Local rains may cause occasional minor floods, but the heavy rains in the Atlas Mountains may cause floods extending hundreds of kilometers. During a 57-year period the Wadi Saoura, which passes through Beni-Abbès and is usually completely dry, caused floods 200 kilometers in length 33 times, 300 kilometers 13 times, 400 kilometers 6 times, 500 kilometers 5 times, and, once, 800 kilometers. On one occasion, from October 1905 to May 1906, water flowed without interruption from the source of the Guir in the Atlas (which together with the Zousfana forms the Saoura) to a place 450 kilometers farther south. The Atlas Mountains contribute much more water to the riverbeds of the Sahara than does the Hoggar.

Floods occur suddenly and without warning when large quantities of rain have fallen many kilometers from the area being flooded. An exceptionally heavy rainfall of 50 millimeters in 2 days in 1960 caused flooding when the Wadi Mya rose several meters. Water flow can reach a volume of 3,000 cubic meters per second and progress at the speed of a person walking quickly, so it is not surprising that people and animals have been drowned in the desert and in villages and palm tree plantations seriously damaged. Even heavier rainfalls have been reported: in 1950, 37 millimeters (the annual average) fell within 40 minutes in Tamanrasset, and within an hour the noontime temperature had fallen from 32° C to 18° C.

Although most floods are of short duration, the underground flow of water may persist for months or even years at variable depths in an apparently dry riverbed, allowing fairly shallow wells to fill and relatively rich shrub vegetation to grow. This water may be salty if it has flowed over or through ground rich in salts. The Wadi Saoura flows almost every year and always has subterranean water near its surface; the many oases along its course have gained it the name "street of palms" (pl. 8). There are no major wadis in the eastern Sahara or in the generally flat western Sahara. In the northwest the Wadi Dra and the Wadi Seguiet el Hamra flow only occasionally.

Dew. Dew is rare in the Sahara, even in the mountains. We encountered it only in August in the wadis of the Zemmour in northern Mauritania, where the temperature reached 40° C each day but dropped to about 18° C at night. One morning we collected about one-third of a liter of dew on a nylon sleeping bag. On the western coast of the Sahara there are about 10–15 foggy days each year.

Wind. There are very windy regions in the Sahara, such as the Rio de Oro coast and the Tidikelt, and some, like the Borkou, where wind erosion has sculptured sandstone into fantastic shapes; but there are also windless areas where car tracks have remained visible for years. The intensity of the wind often changes with the time of day and with the season: it is less windy at night and at the end of autumn and beginning of winter than it is at other times. Most winds are of moderate strength and are steadier than they are in Europe because there is little vegetation to impede them; on the coast of Mauritania the wind blows from the north the year around. In the interior of Mauritania the prevailing winds usually are from the northeast, except in summer, when under the influence of the Sudan monsoons they blow in the south and center from the southwest. Steady, mild winds from one direction produce accumulations of sand around bushy vegetation that offer shelter to small animals.

Hot winds are particularly deleterious in a desert because they accelerate dehydration. The winds have different characteristics depending on where they occur. The *irifi* (from *araf*, "roast") in the western Sahara is a burning, dry wind from the east or northeast, frequent in summer and autumn and often accompanied by sandstorms; it may make the temperature rise to 50° C. Fortunately it usually does not last longer than 12 hours. Hot, dry winds called *chergui* in Morocco, *ghibli* in Libya, and *sirocco* in Algeria and Tunisia sometimes blow from the desert to southern Europe. In Egypt the *khamsin* (meaning "fifty"), which sometimes blows for 50 days, may cause sandstorms. Egypt also has cold and dusty khamsins in winter.

Sandstorms in the Sahara are more a result of bare, dry soil than of wind velocity and variability. Once they have begun, they range from mild to severe, depending on the amount of sand carried by the wind, the area over which they extend, and the wind velocity. Sandstorms may last several days, depending in part on the direction of the wind; those blowing from the west generally last longer than those from the east. Only winds greater than force 3 on the Beaufort scale can carry grains of sand. This is presumably why the sands of the Western Erg, where the daily northeast winds are moderate, have not filled in the Wadi Saoura, which borders the dunes on the west. Sandstorms are infrequent in the central Sahara and are absent in the mountain massifs.

Relief There are five main types of habitat in the Sahara, each with its own physiognomy, soil type, microclimate, and vegetation.

Hamada. A plateau covered with rocks and stones of various sizes from which sand and finer particles have been blown away, hamadas, which are especially common in the north, cover more than 70 percent of the surface of the Sahara. The plateaus are generally formed of horizontal beds of sedimentary rock of various ages (Cretaceous and Tertiary), sometimes topped with limestone slabs, which may terminate in abrupt cliffs. They are difficult to cross with camels because the vegetation present is confined mostly to wadis, low erosion ditches, and depressions of various sizes. One type of depression, the *daya*, has a subterranean drainage system that collects rainwater and allows soil to form; thus, relatively dense vegetation is present. The large number of dayas in the northern Sahara and in the steppes north of the desert but south of the Atlas Mountains is caused by the lack of drainage of rainwater to the ocean. Often more than 1 kilometer square, dayas also occur on the border of dune massifs, where floodwater from a plateau is blocked by dunes. Sometimes rainwater remains in such dayas for weeks, thus offering ample water for animal herds (pl. 9). In northern Mauritania, where wells containing sweet water are scarce, the people obtain drinking water from flooded dayas wherever possible. However, herds grazing on the hamadas must generally travel long distances to get from one daya to another.

Another type of depression, the *sebkha*, is usually larger than the daya. Sebkhas were formed as depressions during the Tertiary and filled during the Quaternary cycle of arid and humid phases. Unlike dayas, sebkhas have no subterranean drainage and contain a great deal of salty sediment. Many wadis end in sebkhas, which are found adjacent to mountains and plateaus and may cover large areas, as in southern Tunisia. Sebkhas with a high concentration of salt are devoid of vegetation.

Reg. Vast, rather flat plains covered with fine gravel, sand, lime, or clay, regs—unlike hamadas, which are erosion areas—are accumulation areas (pl. 10). In the central and eastern Sahara a reg is called a *serir* (meaning "small"). Regs and serirs usually are fluvial in origin, and thus are found adjacent to the big hamadas of the western Sahara, the Libyan desert, and the central Saharan massifs, where large runoffs of water have spread fine sediment and gravel over large areas. Some regs and serirs, however, were created from the breakdown of rock *in situ*. The reg is the poorest environment for life in the Sahara (pl. 11). Only after "useful" rainfalls do annual plants spring up on the sandy regs and attract the nomads and their herds from distant places.

Wadi. Usually dry riverbeds (called *washes* or *arroyos* in America, *ennedi* in Tibesti, and *kori* in the Hoggar) that are cut more or less deeply into the terrain, and wadis form part of a typical landscape in the desert, their relatively rich vegetation contrasting sharply with their more barren surroundings. Most wadis do not have an identifiable source and never reach the ocean, terminating instead in depressions or disappearing into the soil, sometimes to continue flowing underground. The big wadi systems, which may be over 1,000 kilometers long, originate in the northern and central mountains of the Sahara. Lesser systems descend from the plateaus, for example, the Wadi Mya from the Tademait. In the rather flat western Sahara, where there are no large wadis, the occasional small riverbed and *thalweg* ("erosion ditch") offer favorable grazing (pl. 12).

Mountains. The Sahara has a crystalline-igneous rock base, which crops out in many places to form mountains of different heights. The lowest crystalline massif is the 800-meter Eglab in the western Sahara. Farther east are the 800–1,000-meter Adrar des Iforas and the more humid massifs of Aïr in Niger, which reach 1,900 meters. The best known mountainous area is the Hoggar; with a peak of 2,600 meters, the Hoggar is traversed by one of the principal trans-Saharan roads and is peopled by the Tuareg. Wind and water, together with the ever-burning sun and extremes of temperature, have produced an immense variety of rock forms in the Sahara. Many rivers from the mountain massifs have cut deeply into the surrounding sandstone plateaus (called *tassili* in the central Sahara) and hollowed out in the course of ages deep canyons, such as that in the Tassili n'Ajjer (maximum depth, 2,254 meters), a region famous for its prehistoric carvings.

Farther east, the volcanic massif of Tibesti in Chad has the highest mountain in the Sahara—the 3,415-meter Emi Koussi. To the southeast the Ennedi, a sandstone plateau, rises to heights greater than 1,500 meters. The eastern Sahara as far as the Nile is empty and flat, with only a few crystalline-igneous massifs and sandstone plateaus. East of the Nile this Precambrian base rises to 2,000 meters, then falls abruptly down to the Red Sea. In all, mountains 2,000 meters and higher constitute about 5 percent of the Sahara.

In Mauritania the main mountainous area comprises the sandstone plateaus of the Adrar, which have a maximum height of about 800 meters and extend 700 kilometers from southwest to northeast. In the smaller of several craters here, nomads formerly sought refuge in times of danger. Although the central Tagant massif is only 300 meters high and the southern massifs of Affolé and Assaba only 200 meters, these plateaus look like mountains because they rise so abruptly from the plains. They represent a serious obstacle to the nomads and their camel herds on their annual migrations from north to south and back. In 1964 Gauthier-Pilters joined a Reguibat family, who moved with their 300 camels from northern Mauritania to Tagant, 600 kilometers farther south. It took them 3 hours to herd the animals to the top of the 200-meter pass up a steep path where steps were cut in the rock.

A distinctive form of relief is the *inselberg*, an isolated mountain of granite or sandstone found in the northwestern Sahara and between the Atakor and Tassili plateaus in the central Sahara (pl. 13). Inselbergs have a conical form with steep sides and a gently sloping base covered more or less with erosion material. Unlike the inselbergs, the *gour* (singular, *gara*) are flat-topped mountains that have been "cut off" from plateaus by the slow erosion of river systems.

Sand regions. Sand regions in the Sahara exhibit a great variety of forms, including the chaotic dune massifs of the Eastern Erg (110,000 square kilometers) and the Western Erg (80,000 square kilometers); the very dry Erg Chech (180,000 square kilometers) with its flatter dune chains separated by large channels; the immense undulating Majâbat al-Koubrâ, 250,000 square kilometers without a single tree and with hardly any water, the favorite study area of the great Saharan scientist Th. Monod; and the almost flat sand areas of the Ténéré (280,000 square kilometers). There are also smaller groups of dunes and single chains more than several hundred kilometers long, such as the Abu Mohariq in Egypt, which extends over 600 kilometers from northwest to southeast.

In all, 26 extensive dune regions cover one-fifth of the Saharan surface. In the Eastern Erg and Western Erg interlapping dunes reach heights of 300 meters and are difficult to cross, but travel is fairly easy in the Erg Iguidi and other dune areas, where parallel dune ranges of lesser height (50–80 meters) are separated from each other by broad corridors almost free of sand. In the southern Sahara, where it is increasingly humid, the dunes have been largely leveled and the corridors filled with sand, forming undulating, monotonous expanses such as those covering vast areas of southern Mauritania.

The sand of the ergs is of fluvial origin, deposited during the Quaternary in large depressions by the big wadi systems. The fine dust particles were blown away by the wind, leaving the heavier sand grains behind. Many wadis disappear at the edge of ergs or run closely beside them, as does the Wadi Saoura. The extent of the dune massifs has not changed since they were formed, although the wind may alter their shape. Unlike European sand regions, particularly those on the coasts, desert sand regions offer a favorable habitat for plants and small animals. Sand is porous, so that rainwater penetrates quickly before it can evaporate. The plants that grow in deep sand have an extensive and deep-reaching root system that allows them to utilize the water deep in the sand. Such plants constitute a permanent food source for animals during the dry season, and the dunes, especially the big northern massifs (Western Erg, Eastern Erg, Erg Chech), are therefore important areas of pasture, with a varied, almost evergreen shrub vegetation. Some ergs, however, are almost barren.

One form of dune is the *barchan,* an isolated moving dune found on flat terrain where there is little other sand. Barchans exist where the wind always blows from the same direction, which gives them a crescent shape with symmetrical ends. The convex side of the dune is exposed to the wind, while the concave side falls steeply from a sharp ridge. Barchans are typical of the coastal region of Mauritania, where, near Nouadhibou, they move 10 meters a year (Capot-Rey 1953). In Egypt they form chains 100 kilometers or more in length.

Vegetation Food for direct human consumption, such as dates, peanuts, wheat, and vegetables, can be grown on only 10 percent of the Sahara. About 30 percent of the Sahara is hyperarid, supporting at most only 20 species of plants (Tanezrouft, the Libyan desert, and part of the Ténéré are the three major hyperarid regions). The patchy scattering of vegetation on the remaining 60 percent is a function of the irregular rainfall. Most of the Sahara cannot be used for crops, therefore, but only for ranging livestock. The chief livestock species is the camel, the only domestic animal that in summer can forage far from any source of drinking water and that, because of its method of feeding, does not harm the soil or vegetation (see chap. 3).

The flora of the Sahara comprises about 1,200 species (Ozenda 1958). No extensive biome aside from the arctic is known to have so few species. The flora contains Mediterranean elements as well as Saharo-Sindian elements (dominant in the northern and central parts) and Sudano-Deccanian elements (dominant in the south). There is a gradual decrease in abundance and species of plants from south to north, corresponding to the increasing aridity. In Mauritania, which is mostly flat, there are 360 species (Sauvage, in Schiffers 1971), while in hyperarid parts, such as the Majâbat al-Koubrâ (meaning "big empty space without water"), Monod (1958) found only seven species in a 150,000-square-kilometer area. By contrast, Quézel (in Schiffers 1971) found 568 species in a 200,000-square-kilometer area in the Tibesti Mountains. Many plants living in the desert have evolved into new, endemic species, but rarely into endemic genera. Almost

25 percent of all plants growing in the northern, western, and central Sahara are endemic (Ozenda 1958).

Desert plants fall into two biologic types—the perennials and the ephemerals (annuals). The perennials are adapted to water scarcity and to heat by special morphological and physiological features. These include thickening of the plant covering; reduction of the leaf, sometimes to the size of a tiny shell around the twig (*Tamarix*) or of a rice corn (certain halophytes); curling of leaves, especially in grasses (*Aristida*); or the total disappearance of leaves (*Leptadenia, Retama, Capparis*) or side twigs (*Anabasis articulata*)—all features that have evolved to reduce transpiration. Often leaves have evolved into thorns, which, together with hairs on the leaves and twigs, cut down air movement and thereby reduce transpiration. Only a few species are succulents, with water reserves in their tissues, and none of these grows in the very dry central and eastern Sahara.

Desert perennials are characterized by their extended root systems, whose volume may be 5 to 20 times that of the other plant parts, depending on local water conditions (Planhol and Rognon 1970). The roots not only penetrate into deep soil, which is cooler and contains more moisture than soil nearer the surface, but have an extensive horizontal network to take advantage of even the slightest rainfall. Each plant needs a large area of soil for its survival, and the drier the climate is, the farther apart the plants grow.

The ephemerals show no adaptation to water shortage. They are, however, adapted to dry climates by their generally small size and their short life cycles; some species are ready to fruit 10 days after germination in response to a single rainfall. Such a plant may flower even if it is only a few centimeters high, whereas similar plants in rich moist soil might grow to 1 meter in height. Ephemerals have small roots, large tender leaves, and, therefore, high water needs. Their seeds can remain dormant for many years if it does not rain, so their overall survival is unaffected by drought. The ephemerals, called *acheb* in Arabic, occur all over the desert, even in the most arid parts, such as the Tanezrouft and Ténéré, where annual rainfalls of 10–20 millimeters are sufficient for their development. Groundwater is unnecessary for their growth, and they are found often in depressions, especially those in regs. In the uplands of the Hoggar a great variety of annual plants grows after the autumn rains, providing extended fodder resources for the 4–5 months they remain green and good dry fodder for another 4 months (Johnson 1969). The main representatives are the Cruciferae and the Compositae. These sporadic pastures draw the nomads from afar, even though the plants generally last only a month or 6 weeks. Acheb are absent from the large Saharan ergs because the sand there is constantly shifting.

The desert flora is subject to great variation in space and time. Although few species can survive the heat and aridity, one may encounter millions of individual plants of one of these species. We have seen completely barren regs transformed, after heavy rainfalls, into immense carpets of annual flowers. Once we walked for a week in dunes covered loosely with grasses of one species, *Aristida pungens*, with only a few plants of two or three other species.

The typical unequal distribution of vegetation is caused by edaphophysiographic factors such as penetration of water into the soil, retention of water, and speed of runoff, which reflect the extreme differences in water supply of the various areas. In arid regions with less than 100 millimeters of rainfall annually, the water, and hence the vegetation, becomes concentrated in depressions. Clay soils are the driest, and soils caught between rocks or in rock fissures the most moist.

The food of the camel consists mainly of grasses and the leaves and twigs of shrubs and trees, the latter represented by only a few species. Because of its dry summers and cold winters, the north has fewer trees than the south (Stocker 1971). Infinite varieties of plant associations can occur in the desert, where a single biotope may contain species that are found in several other biotopes as well. A certain plant may be dominant in one place, rare in an adjacent area, and completely absent from other regions nearby. Other plants are sometimes isolated, sometimes gregarious. In this study we take into consideration only the principal biotopes we have investigated. A camel may visit several such biotopes in an hour of grazing, or it may remain in the same biotope (for instance, a wadi) for several days. A camel may stay for weeks or months in a dune region grazing on almost monospecific pastures, or it may walk long distances to find food in dayas scattered over a hamada. We discuss below a few of the most important fodder plants that grow in the desert environments we studied.

Hamada and rocky plain. A typical plant of the northern rocky plateau is *Anabasis aretioides,* an endemic Chenopodiaceae found only in the south Oranais to a distance of 120 kilometers south of Tindouf (pl. 14). This compact cushionlike plant may be scattered over vast areas that are devoid of other vegetation. It is well grazed by the camel, even in summer, despite its very low water content and serried twigs filled with sand, which is said to wear down the teeth of camels severely. Most plants of the hamadas, however, are localized in low depressions where the wind has blown deposits of sand. There are a few trees like the evergreen *Maerua crassifolia,* often associated with another tropical species, *Acacia ehrenbergiana.* The former has very deep roots; Monod (1958) found roots in a well at a depth of 50 meters belonging to a *Maerua* growing 4 meters away. In Chad these trees reach heights of 7–8 meters, their dense foliage offering welcome shade.

Reg. The vegetation of regs, which tend to be devoid of topographical features, is restricted to almost imperceptible depressions. Plant associations vary depending on whether the substrate is predominantly sand, clay, gravel, or stone. The dense and monophyletic growth of a plant in an area indicates that one substrate prevails there. The least productive regs are the stony ones. Their vegetation typically includes *Pergularia tomentosa* (generally ignored by the camel), diffuse growths of *Haloxylon scoparium,* and *Salvia aegyptiaca.* The very common sandy regs support a richer vegetation, which may consist of a relatively dense cover of *Aristida plumosa* and *A. obtusa,* plus some other species in lesser density. On regs of clay and sand a typical association of plants is *Cornulaca monacantha,* a salty plant relished by the camel, and *Randonia africana.* After rainfall, annual plants (acheb) develop on the sandy regs. Species present on the regs grow in other biotopes with the same type of substrate.

Wadi. Wadis, because they collect water from the higher surrounding areas, often have a dense and varied vegetation of grasses, thornbushes, and trees. Indeed, they are the only biotope, aside from the oases, where trees are fairly numerous (pl. 15). The most common tree in the northern Sahara is *Acacia raddiana,* which is present in sandy wadis all over the Sahara and the Sahel (the southern border of the Sahara), providing excellent forage for camels (pl. 16). It is particularly common in the Zemmour, where it is green and in flower in summer. *Acacia raddiana* is often associated with the grass *Panicum turgidum* and one or more fodder shrubs. The vegetation of the wadis is especially rich in the central Sahara, where Maire (in Ozenda 1958) logged 80 species in a single inventory. This is twice as many as we counted in a wadi in the northwestern Sahara following a heavy rainfall. In Mauritania *A. raddiana* is associated with various tropical trees, such as the drought-resistant *Balanites aegyptiaca, Maerua crassifolia,* and the evergreen *Capparis decidua,* as well as with *P. turgidum, Cymbopogon schoenanthus, Calligonum comosum,* and the evergreen *Leptadenia pyrotechnica,* a large shrub found in an area spanning the southern Sahara eastward to Arabia. *Nitraria retusa* grows where the soil is moist. This 3-meter-high evergreen halophyte of Saharo-Sindian distribution is especially common on the dunes along the Mauritanian coast.

Other plants associated with *A. raddiana* in the northern Sahara are absent in the south. In the west, where the desert climate is ameliorated by the influence of the ocean, some tropical species, such as *B. aegyptiaca, M. crassifolia,* and *Calotropis procera,* are found as far north as southern Morocco, but do not grow as tall there as in the south. In the flood-prone wadis a typical genus is *Tamarix,* which has about 10 species in the Sahara. The most common, *T. gallica* and *T. articulata,* grow several meters high, sometimes in large clumps. Their wood is often used for fires and for making tent pegs. The roots of these species may reach a depth of 10–20 meters and extend horizontally for 50 meters (Stocker 1971). Where flooded soil is salty, various members of the Chenopodiaceae grow, such as *Atriplex halimus, Salsola foetida,* and various species of *Zygophyllum.*

Daya. Another favorable biotope, dayas support rather dense and varied vegetation resembling that of the wadis. In the north dayas typically contain mostly shrubs, such as *Zilla macroptera, Launaea arborescens, Ziziphus lotus, Randonia africana, Anvillea radiata,* and *Bubonium graveolens,* with trees very rare. *Anvillea* and *Bubonium* are particularly resistant to drought; in extended areas along the Algerian-Mauritanian border that had gone rainless for 18 months, these were the only two plants in innumerable dayas surrounded by completely barren regs. When there is some rain, there may be a wealth of ephemerals; because the relatively deep soil of the dayas retains moisture, the vegetation cover can reach 80 percent (Sauvage, in Joly et al. 1954).

Dune. Because the porosity of sand reduces the evaporation of rainwater, dune valleys are often moist enough to support herbaceous vegetation. Another source of moisture, completely independent of local rainfall, is the more or less deep underground water reserves. Largely extra-Saharan in origin and to a great extent fossil reserves, they provide the deep wells with water. The sand of the big dune massifs in the northern Sahara like the Western Erg and the Erg er Raoui is permanently moist below a depth of 2 meters. It is believed that this moisture is from the last heavy rains, which fell several thousand years ago. Near Beni-Abbès the sand in the erg 2 meters below the surface had a water content equal to 1.2 percent by weight (Demon et al. 1957). Because of the moisture in the dunes, the perennials there, which possess deep and extensive roots, remain green all summer.

Since the dune biotope is very homogeneous in the northern ergs, which cover almost 1 million square kilometers, the vegetation is very homogeneous too, consisting of only 17 species in our study area. However, the composition and density of the vegetation may vary considerably from place to place. Together with *Cornulaca monacantha*, a drought-resistant halophyte that also grows in deep sand outside dune areas, the shrubs *Genista saharae, Calligonum azel,* and *Randonia africana* are the most common plants and the favorite food of the camel in the northern ergs. Two other common shrubs, *Ephedra alata* and *Retama raetam,* are seldom eaten by camels. Among the important forage grasses, *Aristida pungens* is widespread in deep sand throughout the Sahara, *Danthonia fragilis* is common in the Western Erg only, and *Cyperus conglomeratus* is present in all the Saharan ergs, but only in localized regions. *Moltkia ciliata,* a small shrub with stiff and hairy leaves, is highly palatable to camels and the most common of all the small herbaceous dune plants. The

wind sometimes deposits sand around plants; in the
Iguidi old specimens of *C. monacantha*, which were very
spread out but only 0.5 meter tall, had collected sand into
hills several meters high.

In the drier ergs of the western Sahara, such as the Erg
Iguidi (50,000 square kilometers) and the Mauritanian
ergs, the vegetation is much more monotonous, consisting
mainly, and in very large areas exclusively, of grasses,
with *A. pungens* by far the most dominant. This species,
called *drin* by the Arabs and *sbot* by the Maures, is well
adapted to moving sand, with roots stretching down several meters and horizontally up to 20 meters, so that it can
grow even on the crests of arid dunes. It took Monod 8 days
to walk through a monospecific pasture of *A. pungens* in
the Majâbat al-Koubrâ. Such erg pastures furnish a smaller
amount of dry plant matter for camels than the southern
Algerian ergs, but still enough for good maintenance.

In the Sahel the vegetation becomes varied and more
dense, including trees (mainly *Acacia*), thornbushes, and
high grasses. Here the typical Saharan plants *A. pungens*
and *C. monacantha* are replaced by the cram-cram grass
Cenchrus biflorus, a typical Sahel plant and a basic food of
the camel most of the year. The southern Sahara includes
some of the most botanically impoverished regions, including the Djouf, Tanezrouft, Ténéré, Djourab, the Libyan desert, and the Nubian desert. In the almost barren
ergs of these areas, the only plants found are scattered
A. pungens and *C. monacantha*.

3 Feeding

In the Sahara, the camel both grazes and browses (words used interchangeably in this book) on the local vegetation, and only rarely receives supplementary food from its owner. Generally no heavy work is demanded of camels nowadays beyond carrying water and moving the baggage of nomad camps, but they are still valued for their meat, wool, and milk, which they produce from the scarce desert vegetation.

Unlike slow-moving cattle and intensively grazing goats, which crop plants down to the roots and even climb into trees to forage, camels are economical feeders that never overgraze the vegetation. They keep on moving while feeding; on a good hamada pasture, for example, they may cover 5 kilometers in 2.5 hours while grazing. No matter how rich or how poor the quality of the vegetation, camels take only a few bites from any one plant before moving to another. It may be that they like a varied diet, which causes them to move along in search of new plants or of remembered pastures, but they can subsist for months in a monospecific pasture. Most camels graze in herds where the individuals are spread far apart, which is another advantage to the vegetation. Indeed, under drought conditions the herds sometimes split up into groups of one or two, which preserves the vegetation even more. Lynch (1977) noted that sheep under extremely adverse foraging conditions also separate into very small groups.

Camels do not degrade the desert vegetation; in fact they may actually conserve it. It has been shown that in an area where camels have grazed on grass, the vegetation has fared better than in a similar area that has been protected from camels (Gauthier-Pilters 1969). The growth of desert plants in Australia and in the United States has also been shown to be stimulated by grazing (Pearson 1965; Trumble and Woodroffe 1954). Trees, however, from which camels obtain a significant amount of nourishment, may grow better if they are periodically protected from browsing. Barker (1972) noted that camels prefer browsing at some trees more than others and that if they fed at one tree year after year they could kill it.

Mechanism of Feeding   The upper jaw of the camel has one pair of incisors, one pair of canines, three pairs of premolars, and three pairs of molars, while the lower jaw has three pairs of incisors, one pair of canines, two pairs of premolars, and three pairs of molars, or a total of 34 teeth. The diastemata are well marked. Some camels in the Sudan and southern Sahara have an additional pair of teeth, third lower premolars, bringing their full complement to 36 (Cauvet 1929). The permanent teeth are fully erupted when the camel is 7 years of age. The canines of males, which are used as weapons for fighting among themselves, are larger than they are in females. Both the incisors and the canines in the lower jaw continue to grow throughout the camel's lifetime, so a diet of some hard plant parts, or even sometimes dried meat and bones, is essential to keep them worn down. If fresh branches supplied to camels in zoos do not abrade their teeth sufficiently, they must be ground down by a keeper (Dittrich 1976).

In feeding, camels often first grasp the vegetation between their long, hairy prehensile lips, the upper two halves of which are separated and move independently (indeed, the Arab term for harelip in people is *foum el djemel*, "camel lip"). The lower lip becomes stretched and often floppy in old camels. After the vegetation has been brought into the mouth, it is grasped between the extended lower denticulated incisors and the upper gum lying over the premaxilla. This upper palate is less highly evolved than in the other ruminants because the lateral incisors are still retained in the camel. The camel may either draw off leaves from a branch or clip off an entire twig, individual fruit, or flowers. Barker (1972) noted that camels browsing at mulga trees pulled down branches with their jaws (not their teeth) until they broke and then cleaned off the leaves with a downward pull. By stretching its neck straight up, a camel can browse to a height of 3.5 meters (pl. 17). In the desert only giraffes and climbing goats can reach vegetation higher than this.

Chewing and Cudding Each mouthful of food is chewed slowly and completely, especially if it contains long thorns (pl. 18). If the thorns are numerous, the camel has to chew with its mouth open because it cannot close it around the food. Because the lower jaw is narrower than the upper, the camel must chew at any one time either on the left or on the right side of the mouth so that opposing teeth will come into contact. Like most ungulates, it chews vegetation a number of times on one side before switching to the other, but when cudding it chews each bolus on alternate sides in successive movements. Each bolus is generally chewed 40–50 times, but sometimes as little as 20 or as much as 70 times, with each chew taking about 1 second. These figures are similar to those for the giraffe, which eats similar food. Like the giraffe also, the camel cuds while lying, standing, or walking, regurgitating each bolus a few seconds after the one before it has been swallowed. In summer, camels tend to ruminate at midday and during the night, feeding much of the rest of the time.

Food Intake The weight of a bite of each species of food plant varies from 1 to 20 grams, with several bites making up a mouthful, which is chewed and swallowed. Camels take the smallest bites from very thorny plants, plants with leafless twigs, flowers or stalks of dry grasses, and small annual plants. The flowers of *Aristida pungens*, for example, are eaten one by one. Camels take bigger bites from fleshy halophytes, large sturdy annuals, plants with well-developed leaves, and plants with long succulent twigs, such as *Calligonum azel*. Bites from these plants weigh between 10 and 20 grams. The bite size, which tends to be larger in a hungry animal, varies with the season. For example, a bite from *Genista saharae* weighs 15 grams during flowering but only 3 grams after flowering. Similarly, a bite from a salty plant may weigh 10 grams when it is green but only 3 grams when it is dry. The number of bites taken each hour varies between 200 and 700, with fewer where the vegetation is relatively rich.

Since the size of a bite that a camel takes from a plant is fairly constant for each plant species during a given season (i.e., when green, dry, in flower, in pod, etc.), it was possible for us to estimate the quantity of food a camel ate by weighing a portion of vegetation similar in size to what a camel would break off at a bite, and multiply the weight by the number of bites. This was the only method that allowed us to take into account both the scattered feeding of the camel and the uneven distribution of the vegetation.

We monitored 150 normally grazing adult camels during a total of 500 hours as described above, sometimes observing one individual for 8 hours at a time. The camels all belonged to guarded herds and fed only during the day. Whenever we made such counts, we also collected samples of the plants the camels were eating. We weighed, dried thoroughly, and reweighed these samples to determine their water content. Data for a variety of regions and seasons are presented in table 5.

In most pastures the camels ate 10–20 kilograms of green food each day depending on the plants available; this intake corresponded to 5–10 kilograms of dry matter. In the most succulent pastures of salty or annual plants consisting of up to 80 percent water, the camels ate 30–40 kilograms of fresh vegetation (or 8–12 kilograms of dry matter) per day. Our estimates were generally lower than the 30–50 kilogram daily fresh food intake thought necessary to sustain a camel; this latter range would be appropriate for working animals, such as those in a camel corps.

How much a camel eats depends on the kind of plant it is feeding on. Individuals can manage quite well for several months on a daily ration of 5 kilograms dry weight of *A. pungens,* a highly nutritious grass—and reliable source of food, covering 3–10 percent of the area of the vast dune regions of the western Sahara—which can be eaten dry as well as green. Camels must eat six times as much acheb (ephemerals) as of *Aristida* to obtain 5 kilograms dry matter.

Unlike sheep, which graze for longer periods when the vegetation is poor or when the water/dry matter ratio is so high that they must eat a large quantity of food to get enough nutritious material (Arnold 1964), camels graze 8–12 hours a day no matter what the quality of the pasture. This amount of grazing time is insufficient only under drought conditions. For our hired camels, which carried about 120 kilograms each for 30 kilometers 6 hours a day, 6–7 kilograms dry matter per day seemed a suitable diet for at least 4 weeks at a time. This amount of daily work is equivalent to what the nomads demand of their camels when they are on the move, but the total amount of work of our hired camels was greater because nomads, although

Table 5 Food Intake on Some Typical Feeding Grounds in Southern Algeria and Mauritania (average quantities in kg of dry matter per day of all animals studied)*

Region	Time	Food Intake (kg/day dry matter)	Proportion of Water in Food (%)	Principal Plants Consumed (no. of species present)
Erg, S Algeria	May 1955	13	55	*Genista saharae, Salsola spinescens, Calligonum azel* (10)
Western Erg, S Algeria	Oct. 1955	12	59	*Cornulaca monacantha, Calligonum azel, Genista saharae* (8)
Wadi Saoura, S Algeria	July 1955	12	70	*Traganum nudatum, Atriplex halimus, Imperata cylindrica, Randonia africana* (13)
Hamada, S Algeria	Feb. 1956	11	55	*Gymnocarpos decander, Launaea arborescens, Farsetia hamiltonii* (12)
Western Erg, S Algeria	June 1955	10	62	*Calligonum azel, Genista saharae, Malcolmia aegyptiaca* (11)
Adrar, Mauritania	May 1964	9	74	*Nucularia perrini, Panicum turgidum*
Daya, S Algeria	March 1956	9	77	*Atriplex halimus, Traganum nudatum, Calligonum comosum* (25)
Hamada, S Algeria	June 1955	8	38	*Aristida plumosa, Anabasis aretioides, Farsetia hamiltonii* (18)
Mountain valley, S Algeria	April 1956	8	75	Mostly annuals: *Diplotaxis pitardiana, Matricaria pubescens, Paronychia arabica, Helianthemum lippii, Anvillea radiata* (37)
Hamada, Mauritania	May 1964	7	41	*Panicum turgidum, Ziziphus lotus, Leptadenia pyrotechnica, Chrozophora brocchiana, Capparis decidua* (8)
Mountain valley, Mauritania	Aug. 1970	7	55	*Acacia raddiana, Balanites aegyptiaca, Panicum turgidum*
Mountain valley, S Algeria	March 1956	6	69	*Helianthemum lippii, Farsetia hamiltonii, Savignya parviflora, Farsetia aegyptiaca, Anvillea radiata* (22)
Wadi, Mauritania	May 1964	6	51	*Balanites aegyptiaca, Calligonum comosum* (6)
Zemmour, Mauritania	Aug. 1971	6	50	*Acacia raddiana, Panicum turgidum, Traganum nudatum, Nucularia perrini* (12)
Erg Iguidi, S Algeria	May 1961	5	5	*Aristida pungens*, dry
Western Erg, S Algeria	Aug. 1969	5	50	*Genista saharae, Calligonum azel* (8)
Mountain valley, S Algeria	Nov. 1955	5	43	*Acacia raddiana, Anabasis aretioides, Aristida plumosa* (15)
Zemmour, Mauritania	Aug. 1972	4	45	*Acacia raddiana, Panicum turgidum, Nucularia perrini* (12)
Adrar, Mauritania	July 1973	2	40	*Acacia raddiana and ehrenbergiana, Ziziphus lotus, Leptadenia pyrotechnica* (5)

*Grazing time, including moving from one plant to another, was 8 hours in May–August, 10–11 hours in March, and 11–12 hours in November.

they move camp frequently, are seldom on the move for a whole month at a time.

Despite their low food intake compared with body weight (300–500 kilograms), desert camels are better able to tolerate hard work coupled with food and water shortages than are camels that graze on richer pastures in less arid regions. Indeed, low food intake may increase an animal's tolerance to heat (Schmidt-Nielsen 1964, p. 95). A camel with a marked hump is not always stronger or more resistant than one with a less pronounced hump. What counts is training. In the western Sahara camels have always had to endure difficult conditions, in the past when their owners, the Reguibat, used them on long-distance camel raids and at present when they must travel 100 kilometers or more between pastures on hamadas, wadis, ergs, or sebkhas to find enough varied food. Grazing for nonworking camels involves much travel, which gives them ample exercise. It is easy to recognize unguarded from guarded herds by the good condition of the former (pl. 19); Baskin (1974) has noted this difference in other kinds of livestock in central and eastern Asia.

Camels thrive on hard, dry, thorny plants, so that even in summer, when they are reduced to grazing in dry grass pastures, they often appear to be in good condition, complete with a marked hump. We often observed them browsing on spiny plants by choice, opening their mouths very wide to encompass long thorns, chewing very slowly, and ignoring leaves that to us looked more palatable. When feeding on acacia, one of the preferred common food plants, camels ate between 300 grams and 1 kilogram dry matter per hour, depending on whether they chose fruits, single leaves, green twigs, or dry twigs. In the summer of 1973 the twigs were so dry and thorny that the camels could consume only 150 grams dry weight of acacia per hour. Acacia leaves normally have a fairly high water content, even in summer, so that camels that feed on them are less dependent on water than are camels that forage on drier foods. A number of other more or less thorny plants are also highly palatable to camels. Of the thorny plants, *Balanites aegyptiaca*, whose leaves are rich in protein, has the longest spines. A bite consisting of a 10-centimeter twig may have a dozen spines 2–5 centimeters long, and some as long as 10 centimeters. Weight intake from this tree is similar to that from dry grass or other less spiny plants— about 0.7 kilogram per hour. In drought or under working conditions extra food, in the form of barley, oats, date stones, or corn, is sometimes given to camels.

Although we observed camels under exceptionally hot conditions, when we ourselves had little appetite for food, the camels showed no reduction in grazing activity. Our observations conflict with those of Schmidt-Nielsen, whose laboratory camels almost stopped eating when their water loss reached 20 percent of their body weight (B. Schmidt-Nielsen et al. 1956). In rich pastures and seb-khas when the temperature ranged from 40° to 46° C, our camels ate 10–12 kilograms dry matter per day. Normal grazing continued even after a water loss of more than 20 percent of the body weight. In June, when the temperature was 40° C, a 24-year-old male weighing about 400 kilograms fed normally the day before it drank 104 liters of water at a single session.

Food Selection Camels usually seek out a variety of foods that presumably give them optimal nutrition (table 6). A list of the 114 principal food plants eaten by camels in the northwestern and western Sahara is given by Gauthier-Pilters (1969, pp. 1306–9). Nomads know where different species grow and when each is important in the camel's diet, which helps determine where a tribe or family travels during the year. Preference for a plant species may vary with the season. It is not rare to see a herd of camels move from dense, juicy vegetation to a dried-out grass pasture several kilometers away, or to see a herd cross a green daya without stopping in order to get at some barely visible grass in an otherwise barren, rocky plateau. Seasonal food preferences are often independent of the water content of the plants. Some plants are eaten all the year around at almost the same rate, while others may constitute most of the diet in one or two seasons but be essentially ignored in another.

Palatability of the vegetation may vary with the region. For example, *Haloxylon scoparium* was fairly well grazed in Beni-Abbès during the summer of 1955 but was rarely eaten during the same season in the Zemmour of Mauritania, even though the selection of foods there was much poorer. Similarly, *Randonia africana* was more browsed in the Western Erg near Beni-Abbès than it was on the nearby hamada. In a varied pasture two or three plant species are generally eaten far more than all the others, while a third to a half of the plants present are ignored or barely touched (table 6). For example, in a spring

Table 6 Plants Consumed Most in the Beni-Abbès Region

Month	Biotope	Total No. of Species Present	No. of Plants Consumed Most	Proportion by Volume (as % of species in previous column)	Species Eaten Most (with % of total eaten)
February	Hamada	12	3	87	*Gymnocarpos decander* (40)
February	Wadi	12	2	69	*Traganum nudatum* (47)
March	Mountain	22	3	47	*Helianthemum lippii* (21)
March	Daya	25	2	66	*Atriplex halimus* (34)
April	Mountain	37	1	31	*Diplotaxis pitardiana* (31)
April	Erg	13	4	86	*Calligonum azel* (32)
May	Erg	10	3	84	*Genista saharae* (32)
June	Erg	11	2	88	*Calligonum azel* (72)
June	Hamada	18	3	77	*Aristida plumosa* (43)
July	Wadi	13	3	62	*Traganum nudatum* (28)
October	Erg	8	2	95	*Cornulaca monacantha* (65)
November	Mountain	15	3	65	*Acacia raddiana* (23)

acheb pasture containing 37 plant species, one, *Diplotaxis pitardiana,* made up 31 percent of the total food intake. On occasion a single species (*Calligonum azel*) constitutes 73 percent of the total food intake.

Camels, like other ruminants, are not necessarily entirely vegetarian. Gauthier-Pilters often saw camels eating charcoal, bones, or even mummified young gazelles, heads and all (pl. 20).

Water Content of Food   We calculated the amount of water present in the plant parts eaten by camels in order to estimate what percentage of their total water consumption was ingested in food. Annuals and salty plants at any season contained the most water—up to 80 percent. In general the dune plants in southern Algeria, of which almost half are shrubs, seem to have a more stable water content throughout the year than plants growing on rocky plateaus. Within a species, plants growing in sandy soil have a higher water content than plants growing in rocky soil. The content may vary with rainfall, however. In the wadis the water content of plants is probably always high—70–80 percent (fig. 8).

Even in summer camels often prefer rather dry plants to green ones, in contrast to sheep and cattle, which seek out

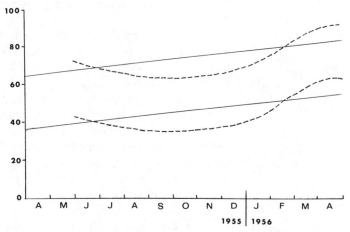

Fig. 8   Maximum (*top*) and minimum (*bottom*) ranges of percentages of water in plant parts consumed by camels near Beni-Abbès, by month. *Dashes* = hamada plants; *solid* = erg plants. The heavier rains in December 1955 (38 millimeters in a few days) than in the previous year (November 1954, 12.8 millimeters; December 1954, 7.5 millimeters; January 1955, 14.7 millimeters) presumably account for the higher water content of the plants in the spring of 1956 than in the spring of 1955.

young green vegetation, which, if it is available, differs in chemical composition from older material (Arnold 1964). Near Beni-Abbès in June 1954, when the air temperature had already reached 40° C, the two driest plants, *Aristida plumosa* (32 percent water) and *Anabasis aretioides* (7 percent water), were eaten far more than other plants by a camel herd that was watered every 4 days. *Aristida pungens,* whose water content is 50 percent during flowering, 40 percent after flowering, and 5 percent as dry stalks, is sought out by camels even in summer after the flowers have been eaten and the plant is dry and brown. The dried remains of this species apparently stimulate lactation and may contain much more mineral, protein, fat, phosphorus, and calcium than when verdant (Adam 1962). According to Rosenstiehl (1959), camels consume certain grasses in the Sahel only in summer, when they are dry.

It is noteworthy that after 18 rainless months in 1961, the water content of consumed plant parts at the Algerian-Mauritanian border was on the whole only slightly less than the water content of the same species growing in the Beni-Abbès region in the spring of 1956, when there had been abundant rainfall several months earlier. The salty plants contained just as much water during the dry year 1961 as they did during years of normal rainfall.

Salty Plants   In many arid regions salt occurring in the soil is taken up by species of plants called *halophytes* or, more commonly, *saltbush,* since most are shrubs, mainly of small size. These plants, whose salt content may reach 10 percent of their wet weight, readily tolerate the salt present in their tissues. The salt of halophytes is usually NaCl, sometimes Na_2SO_4, and sometimes organic sodium salts (Walter 1970). The camel is very fond of many of these plants, which are important for its wellbeing.

Most of the 30 or so Saharan halophytes are of Mediterranean origin, occurring in regions of the north from the Atlantic Ocean to Egypt that receive winter rains (Ozenda 1958). Their tolerance to salt in the soil varies from species to species, and sometimes also with the stage of development; some species, such as *Atriplex halimus,* survive well in salty soils when they are adult but less well when they are young (Planhol and Rognon 1970). The most salt-resistant halophyte is probably *Halocnemum strobilaceum,* which grows in soil with as much as 20 grams of chlorine per kilogram of soil (Ozenda 1958). In the saltiest regions of the sebkhas, species of *Tamarix* and *Suaeda vermiculata* are generally the only plants present. *Arthrocnemum glaucum*, which also tolerates very salty soil, was eaten in small amounts by our camels in the Wadi Saoura. Two often abundant species that camels favored were *Atriplex halimus*, which grows on moist clay soil with a low salt content, and *Traganum nudatum*, which occurs on dry salty soils. In a spring pasture near Beni-Abbès, where 25 different species of plants grew, these two species constituted 35 and 33 percent, respectively, of the total food eaten by camels. Some halophytes grow in relatively unsalty soil, such as the much-browsed *Anabasis aretioides* and *Haloxylon scoparium* in rocky soil (the latter on extensive loose steppes in the north) and *Cornulaca monacantha*, an important fodder plant and purgative, in sandy soil.

Only a few salt plants grow in the salty soils of hyperarid regions and of the southern Sahara, although it receives summer rains (presumably because even halophytes do not adapt readily to the high salt content of the soil that results when continuously high temperatures cause quick evaporation of rainfall). Here the salty soils are generally barren, so camels must either walk great distances to find saltbush or obtain salt from their owners.

According to the veterinarian Leese (1927), about one-third of a camel's food intake should be from saltbush, which is high in protein, generally low in cellulose, and usually green in summer with succulent leaves. The camel will eat large amounts of preferred halophytes such as *Nucularia, Traganum,* and *Atriplex*—as much as 6 kilograms dry weight per hour! The camels of the Zemmour are said to owe their special resistance to plants of the endemic genus *Nucularia*. Indeed, the Arabic verb *zemmer* means to make an askaf (*Nucularia*) cure for camels in the Zemmour (Monteil 1953).

Salty plants together with dry grass, which supplies carbohydrate, form a well-balanced diet for camels. In the northern and central Sahara free-grazing herds make periodic salt cures, alternating between rocky and dune pastures. In the Beni-Abbès region they take place in the spring in the big Wadi Saoura but not in summer, when mosquitoes are said to cause an eye disease in camels, or in autumn because of the danger of sinking into wet mud following a flood. In the central Sahara, as well as in northern and central Mauritania, the nomads take their herds to salty pastures in the summer.

Leese (1927) states that camels should be given a daily ration of 45–60 grams of salt in the absence of saltbush, but practices vary. In Iraq 20 grams of salt are supplied, but only when saltbush or salt licks are not available. In the Sudan camels are given large quantities of salt at infrequent intervals, such as a quarter to half a kilogram in water at the beginning and at the end of the rainy season, enough sometimes to produce symptoms of poisoning (Leitch 1940). Peck (1939), who experimented with different quantities of salt, suggests that 140 grams be given daily to each camel to prevent cutaneous necrosis and other ailments and to prevent arthritis; even with this supplement camels sometimes still eat saltbush. Leitch (1940) feels that "some of the obscure nervous diseases which occur in the camel may be due to chronic salt starvation and dehydration." Cramps occur in camels, as in men, if the salt lost in sweating is not replaced. Camels deprived of salt may eat their own fur and that of other camels (Yakovlev 1945).

Toxic Plants   Some plants in the Sahara are toxic, but few camels are killed by them. Curasson (1939) states that camels recognize and ignore harmful plants growing in familiar pastures, but if they feed in new pastures they may graze on a poisonous plant, mistaking it for a similar harmless species with which they are familiar. Poisoning may also occur when climatic conditions favor abnormally increased densities of toxic plants (Adam 1962).

The most dangerous plants are those whose every part is poisonous throughout the year, whether green or dry. One such species is *Perralderia coronopifolia*, a strong-smelling composite that grows in rocky soils in southern Algeria. Its toxicity is apparently due to the presence of cyanohydric acid (Foley and Musso 1925). A camel that eats 1 kilogram of the plant will die within a few hours (Ozenda 1958). Nomads try to avoid regions where this plant grows, and in certain areas pull up all specimens they find.

A second type of toxic plant is that in which only certain parts of the plant are poisonous, often the fruit. Nomads told us that the fruit of *Pergularia tomentosa*, a very common Asclepiadaceae of the hamadas and wadis on which our camels grazed in small amounts in the spring, was harmful if eaten in larger quantities. Also, parts of *Retama raetam*—the twigs according to Maire (1933) and the fruit according to Trabut (1935)—are said to be toxic. Camels, however, eat the flowers of this shrub, which is one of the most common in the southern Algerian dune massifs. They give an acid taste to the milk (Capot-Rey 1942). Nomads told us that camels of the Reguibat who have moved to the south Algerian ergs browse on *R. raetam*, which does not grow in the Mauritanian ergs, whereas camels of the Chaanba nomads of southern Algeria do not. Certainly the only camel that we saw eating a few bites of *R. raetam* fruit was a Reguibat camel far from its home area.

A third category of toxic plants is those that are toxic only at certain seasons, often during fructification when cyanohydric acid is present (Foley and Musso 1925). In June our camels sampled the hamada grass *Danthonia forskhalii*, which is said to be toxic in spring. The annual grass *Phalaris minor* var. *haematites* kills animals that eat it when green, although McBride et al. (1967) mention that sheep in Australia graze on *Phalaris*, apparently without harm, when the toxic alkaloid content is high.

The shrub *Genista saharae* is so toxic in winter in southern Algeria that nomads keep their camels away from the ergs where it grows. Camels like to graze on this common species, but in winter in the males the twigs cause obstruction of the urethra. Unless a nomad catheterizes the blocked urethra with a slender grass stem, such as that of *Aristida pungens*, the camel will die. *Lotus jolyi*, which grows in wadis and in clay depressions with small sand deposits, is also harmful to livestock. A camel that eats it may become paralyzed and die within 2 months. Such animals are recognized because they become very thirsty; they are sometimes cured when they are forced to eat crushed dates mixed with water. The salty plants *Suaeda mollis* and *Zygophyllum album*, which also grow in wadis, are somewhat less toxic; our camels ate small quantities of each without suffering apparent harm.

One of the most dangerous desert plants is the oleander (*Nerium oleander*), the leaves of which contain oleandrine, a poison almost as potent as strychnine. Camels may consume leaves or seeds that have fallen to the ground (Curasson 1947); 30 grams of fresh leaves and 70 grams of dry are considered toxic doses. Villachon (1962) reports that in two camel corps in Djanet, southern Algeria, 22 camels died from eating oleander during a 5-year period. Cross (in Denis 1970) mentions that a camel that ate 56 grams of crushed oleander leaves died after 36 hours and one that ate twice that much died after 24 hours, suffering from diarrhea and stomach lesions. Poisoning from oleanders is quite common in the central Sahara, India, and Arabia, especially in animals new to a region.

A species of plant growing near watering points which camels do not touch and which is also highly toxic to man—but which sheep, goats, and gazelles eat without harm—is *Hyoscyamus falezlez*, a Solanaceae. Man is said to die even if he eats crickets that have eaten it and therefore contain its alkaloids. The Tuareg poisoned the members of the Flatters Expedition in 1880 by mixing this plant with dates (Ozenda 1958). Its toxicity varies by region, apparently because of differences in the concentration of certain salts in the various soils (Schiffers 1950; Gabriel 1958). Another poisonous Solanaceae is *Datura metel*, which grows at oases.

A group of plants that are quite common in Mauritania are never touched by the camel because they contain a caustic latex, which is much used in native pharmacies. These plants include *Cassia italica*, which was the only flowering plant we encountered in the drought year 1973, *Aerva javanica*, *Euphorbia calyptrata*, and *Calotropis procera*. The latter, a widespread tropical tree 5–6 meters high with large green leaves, looks strange in the desert.

Many camels have been poisoned by plants in Australia, especially by those in flower or in pod. Toxic species include the emu bush (*Eremophila maculata*), ironwood (*Acacia excelsa*), *Acacia cambagei*, and *Gastrolobium grandiflorum* (McKnight 1969). Barker (1972) feels that the most dangerous poisonous plant for camels is ironwood, which, while it kills camels, does not kill sheep or cattle. Camels in Australia also died when they ate bones impregnated with strychnine that ranchers intended for dingos.

Productivity of Pastures

Productivity of pastures in the desert is extremely low, although locally, following a rainfall, it may be temporarily high. In general, productivity increases with rainfall. Our data from the western Sahara, where we estimated the food resources in many monospecific pastures, correspond more or less with those of Walter (in Monod 1963), who found that in southwestern African grasslands for every 100 millimeters of rain per year, the vegetation increased by about 1,000 kilograms of dry matter per hectare. Our data for the food resources in monospecific pastures of *Psoralea plicata*, *Nucularia perrini*, *Aristida acutiflora*, *A. pungens*, and *Panicum turgidum* are given in table 7. The latter two species are especially important as camel fodder because they are eaten throughout the year, both green and dry.

The productivity of *A. pungens* pastures, which cover immense dune areas in the western Sahara, is very high, with a plant cover of up to 10 percent common in arid parts of Mauritania, especially on the edge of large dune massifs (pl. 21). The grass tufts may reach 1.7 meters in height, but they are almost always entirely grazed. In late spring we calculated an average production of 220 metric tons of dry weight per 100 hectares. This represents enough food for 244 camels for 5 months, since a camel eats about 6 kilograms dry weight per day. Thus, 100 square kilometers could feed almost 25,000 camels for a whole summer at an average use of 27 square meters of pastureland per camel per day. However, because camels do not settle in one area and graze it completely, far less food is actually consumed than is available. It is of interest that a relatively dense desert grass pasture, such as the *A. pungens* pastures of the western Sahara, may produce more potential food than a mixed pasture of the same density in the Sahel (see table 7). In northern Chad, where there is 320 millimeters of rain annually, Gillet (1961) estimates a production of 4 metric tons per hectare in a *Schoenfeldia gracilis* pasture and 6.5 metric tons per hectare in an *Aristida mutabilis* pasture. The latter is one of the most common and most productive of the Sahel pastures, and is especially favored by livestock in the dry season, but it requires a fair amount of rain.

Another main food of camels in the western Sahara is *Panicum turgidum*, which grows in sandy depressions and wadis, greening after a rainfall. The grains of this grass have been eaten by inhabitants of the desert apparently since before the introduction of agriculture to the Sahara (Williams and Farias 1972). *Panicum turgidum* occurs in less abundance than *A. pungens* and is about one-third as productive. A 100-hectare pasture with an 8 percent plant cover would produce approximately 80 metric tons of dry matter. Because a camel eats about 7 kilograms dry weight of *A. pungens* each day, 1 hectare would support 114 camels a day, with each camel requiring an average of 88 square

Table 7 Productivity of Some Typical Extended Pastures in the Desert (using average values)

Pasture	Region	Season*	Annual Rainfall (mm)	Vegetation Cover (%)†	Yield Fresh Weight (kg/ha)	Yield Dry Weight (kg/ha)
Aristida pungens, dry	Mauritania	Spring 1964	50–100	9	2,300	2,200
A. pungens, dry	Erg Iguidi	May 1961	<50	2–3	720	684
Panicum steppes	Mauritania	Spring 1964	50–100	8	1,400	800
Nucularia colonies	Mauritania	Spring 1964	50–100	11	2,150	470
A. pungens, flower	Mauritania	April 1964	50–100	9	300	154
Psoralea colonies	SE Tindouf	March 1961	50	7	320	143
A. pungens, flower	Erg Iguidi	April 1961	<50	2–3	116	58
A. acutiflora	Erg Iguidi	April 1961	<50	1–2	80	42
Cenchrus, Cyperus, Leptadenia	Mauritanian Sahel	...	500	8	...	1,680‡

*Measurements were taken in the spring, which in the western Sahara is the dry season.
†Apparent density was measured at the top of the tufts rather than the bottom.
‡From Bremaud and Pagot (1960).

meters of pasture per day. An area 100 kilometers square could theoretically support 7,600 camels during the 5-month dry season, but in practice not all the available food would be eaten.

4 Drinking

Frequency of Drinking Because the camel is exceptionally tolerant of desiccation and has a very slow rate of water loss, it can go without drinking water longer than any other domestic animal. How often a camel needs to drink depends on its age, the work it is doing, the humidity, the environmental temperature (both day and night), and the quality, quantity, and water content of its food. Generalizations about water requirements, therefore, have little value (see table 8).

During the six or seven cool months of the Sahara, camels usually do not drink, even if water is offered to them, because they obtain enough moisture from food plants (which contain, on the average, 50–60 percent water during the cool season), thus giving areas around wells a respite from heavy grazing and browsing pressure. Even working camels can go as far as 1,000 kilometers without water during the cool season (Monod 1958), and in Australia camels can go for long periods without water, even in the summer. In 1883 camels loaded with 350-kilogram packs each journeyed 447 kilometers in 16 days of hot weather and then, after a day of rest, traveled 240 kilometers more, all without water (McKnight 1969). In 1875 camels crossed the Victoria Desert in summer in 17 days with only a drink of 8 liters on the thirteenth day (Macfarlane and Howard 1972). Barker (1972) claims that "a camel worked till it had no hump left, just skin and backbone, would do a longer journey without water than those with a big hump and full of fat."

When temperatures reach 30–35° C, camels can go 10–15 days without water; only when daily temperatures exceed 40° C do camels drink at short and regular intervals. However, such frequent watering is usually only necessary during the six hottest weeks of summer, and even then a few cool nights or a brief, localized shower can extend by several days the period camels can go without water.

Table 8 Amount of Water Ingested by Camels, Directly and in Food, and Number of Days between Drinks

Region	Month	Average Amount of Water Drunk* (liters/day)	Average Amount of Water in Food (liters/day)	Total Amount of Water Consumed (liters/day)	No. of Days without Drinking
Hamada, S Algeria	February 1956	...	13	13	...
Sebkha, S Algeria	March 1956	...	30	30	...
Mountain valley, S Algeria	March 1956	...	15	15	...
Acheb of mountain valley, S Algeria	April 1956	...	25	25	...
Adrar, Mauritania	May 1964	20	6	26	3–6
Wadi Saoura, Algeria	July 1955	26	20	46	2
Western Erg, Algeria	July 1955	22	14	36	5–7
Adrar, Mauritania	July 1973	11	1.5	12.5	2 (working)
Adrar, Mauritania	July 1973	9	1.5	10.5	5–10 (free)
Hamada, Guir	August 1955	27	4	31	3–4
Western Erg, Algeria	August 1969	25	6	31	4–8
Adrar, Mauritania	August 1970	25	5	30	3–7 (guarded)
Zemmour, Mauritania	August 1971	11	6	17	2–3 (working)
Zemmour, Mauritania	August 1972	7	5	12	8–10
Western Erg, Algeria	October 1955	...	17	17	...
Mountain valley, S Algeria	November 1955	...	4.5	4.5	...

*Camels did not drink water during relatively cool weather.

We note below a few examples we encountered in the course of our fieldwork during the hottest temperatures of the year to demonstrate the effect of meteorological and climatic factors on the frequency of drinking in camels.

In the Western Erg in July, when we experienced maximum daily temperatures of 44°–46° C but nights that were cooler than they were in other biotopes such as wadis or hamadas, when the minimum relative humidity was 14 percent, the winds strong, and the sky partly cloudy, we observed nonguarded and free-grazing herds that went without drinking for 4 days. When maximum daily temperatures dropped to 40–41° C and the winds decreased, they drank every 5 days. With the same maximum daytime temperatures but cooler nights (21° C minimum), they came to the well only every 6 or 7 days. On the southern Algerian hamada, when maximum daytime temperatures were between 43° and 46° C, the relative humidity was less than 10 percent, and nights were warm, the herds came to the well every 3–4 days, perhaps because their food was drier then. Although July in the Western Erg was almost unbearably hot, by August the night (but not the day) temperatures dropped significantly, so that the camels only drank every 8–10 days.

In the Zemmour, camels in summer went without drinking at least 5 days, 6–7 days if they ate dry and salty food, and at most 10–12 days, but usually 8–9 days. When they did drink, they consumed less water than did camels farther south and east. In the mild summer of 1972, at the wells of Tourassine 70 kilometers south of Bir Moghrein "lost" camels waited 16 days without being watered, during which time maximum temperatures varied between 32° and 42° C. Such comparatively low water needs are due mainly to less heat stress. The climate of the Zemmour differs significantly from the climate of central Mauritania, that of the Algerian-Mauritanian border, and that of the Beni-Abbès region (as pointed out in chap. 2). The nights are often below 20° C, so that we needed to use sleeping bags. Thus there was often a range of more than 20° C between the maximum and minimum temperatures during a 24-hour period. In the Rio de Oro farther west, where there is an even more marked maritime influence than in the Zemmour, camels drink only every 10–12 days. In areas where they graze at night and where the nocturnal relative humidity reaches 40 percent or more, they might even take advantage of the water in hygroscopic plants, whose leaves gain moisture under such high-humidity conditions (Taylor 1968).

In central Mauritania in summer, when both days and nights are hot (maximums to 48° C and minimums often in excess of 30° C), most camels drink every 5 days. In 1973, however, when food was scarce, many camels went 10 days without water, thus saving the energy needed to walk more often between pastures and wells. (It will be shown later that undernourished camels drink less than well-fed ones.) Aside from the factors of climate and nutrition, there is undoubtedly an individual variation in resistance to thirst, as has been shown for sheep in Australia (Macfarlane, in Lynch and Alexander 1973). Also, the breed and training of a camel may play a role. For example, erg camels are said to tolerate thirst better than hamada camels or camels living on the steppes. In former times camels used for long raids were trained to drink rarely.

In general, free-grazing camels in summer can easily go 8 days without drinking water and can therefore utilize feeding areas that are inaccessible to other domestic animals. A heat-adapted sheep in Australia, for example, will die in temperatures of 45° C if it does not have water for 4 days (Lynch and McClymont 1975). In central Mauritania, except during periods of drought, most herds of camels are guarded throughout the year, so that drinking schedules are determined by their owners. This contrasts with the situation in southern Algeria, where herds are free to roam during the summer, returning at intervals to the wells where their owners are encamped. Called *hmila* in Arabic, this ancient custom of allowing the camels to graze unguarded is practiced where camels are not herded great distances and where their seminomadic owners often have gardens to look after in nearby oases.

Consumption of Water   Information on the water needs of camels is not only of scientific but of practical interest, because it enables efficient wells to be constructed. Natural surface water is almost unknown in the Sahara, so camels have to be watered at wells, where their exact water intake can be measured. Because so many factors affect the amount of water a camel drinks, we measured the consumption of 600 animals of all ages, some of which were guarded and some of which roamed freely. The water consumption of many of these animals was measured more than once, for a total of

800 measurements. Each animal to be studied was separated from the others and given as much water as it would drink in a separate container while the number of liters it consumed was noted.

The camel has a very large drinking capacity, not to store up water for future needs but to replenish water already lost via evaporation, urine, and feces. When the maximum temperature was 40° C or higher, 6 percent of all the adults we studied drank between 100 and 135 liters at their first drinking session. (A drinking session is defined as the time between which a camel begins drinking and walks away voluntarily from the water supply, either to rest or to return to the pasture.) These values often represented 80–90 percent of the total amount of water drunk during the day of the first drinking session (sometimes 100 percent) and up to 70 percent in severely dehydrated camels (those that had probably lost more than 30 percent of their normal body weight). Of two large males that had a water loss corresponding to about 40 percent of their weight (since they each drank almost 200 liters in 1 day), one drank 50 percent of this water during each of two sessions while the other drank 67 percent of the total amount during the first drinking session. By contrast, Macfarlane and Howard (1972) found that in Australia dehydrated camels that had lost 20–25 percent of their weight replenished only 60 percent at the initial drinking session. If a camel has been severely dehydrated, it usually drinks two or three times during the course of its visit to the well to regain its full weight. Of the 249 camels that drank 90 liters or more at their first session (a volume corresponding to a water loss of at least 20 percent of body weight in 350–500-kilogram adults), 75 percent drank a second time within, at most, a few hours and 16 percent drank a third time. The remaining 9 percent drank just the one time. Almost all the camels drank more in their first drinking session than in subsequent sessions, if any. In the summer of 1955, camels in southern Algeria drank as much as those in central Mauritania in 1970, where temperatures were similar but the vegetation quite different (table 8).

Only animals in good condition are capable of replacing their water loss in a single watering (100–130 liters consumed in a few minutes), which gives them more time to graze. This gain in feeding time increases their food intake and in turn their capacity for drinking. In the summer of 1970, when most camels in Mauritania were in good condition, 20 percent drank 100 liters or more in a single session, whereas in 1969, when the camels had been poorly nourished in the degraded pastures of the Western Erg, only 12 percent did so.

B. Schmidt-Nielsen et al. (1956) calculated that a camel would be severely dehydrated if it lost 20–25 percent of its body weight. However, many of our camels that had had enough to eat (at least 7 kilograms dry matter a day) drank 150 liters of water over a period of several hours after they had gone 5–7 days without water, and some up to 200 liters (pl. 22). They weighed at most 500 kilograms, so a water loss of this magnitude represents approximately 40 percent of the original weight of the animal.

To summarize, a camel that goes for 3–5 days under extreme heat stress without drinking water needs an average of 20–30 liters of water a day, with older animals and lactating females needing the most. In northern Mauritania, where heat stress is less, they need about half as much. Water drunk by free-ranging camels that visited the Tourassine wells in northern Mauritania during the summer of 1972 after an exceptionally long period of dehydration (10–16 days) averaged no more than 6–8 liters per day, in part because of the decreased water loss per day with increasing dehydration and in part because they had insufficient food. These low values approached those we measured in the drought summer of 1973. In Australia, where heat stress was not extreme at 40° C, Macfarlane and Howard (1972) found that cattle lost 7–8 percent of their total body weight per day, sheep 4–6 percent per day, and camels 1–2 percent per day.

Various authors have emphasized the increased water needs of working animals when the food supply is adequate. During a 1-month trip we undertook through northern Mauritania to survey the available food and water resources for camels, we were able to measure the total amount of water drunk by four rented camels under working conditions, namely, daily walks of 30 kilometers carrying 120-kilogram loads each. During the first 2 weeks the maximum daily temperature always exceeded 40° C and the camels usually drank every other day, averaging 10–20 liters of water per day. Later, when the days were slightly cooler, they averaged 8 liters per day. On our August 1972 trip into the same region, our four pack camels only drank once during an 8-day trip, averaging 16 liters per day. These values are lower than those obtained farther south and east because of the difference in climate and because the camels, which were working, ate less than free-grazing camels. Working camels in the Western Erg that obtained much more water in their food drank an average of 20–30 liters per day in summer, an amount similar to that given by Leitch (1940): 45 liters every other day during a forced march. Undernourished camels, however, working under extreme heat stress will only drink an average of 10 liters per day.

The more dehydrated a camel becomes, the more it conserves water (B. Schmidt-Nielsen et al. 1956; Charnot 1958; Clair 1962). Under natural conditions, with air temperatures of 40° C or more, the average daily amount of water consumed (which corresponds to the amount of water lost) diminished only after 4 days of dehydration, and was reduced by half when a camel had not drunk for more than 7 days. By contrast, water loss of sheep in arid lands diminished by one-half after 4 days without drinking and with poor food, and of stall-fed *Bos indicus* by one-third after 3 days without drinking (Payne 1966).

The state of dehydration in camels can be deduced from the shape of the hollow in their sides behind the ribs (pl. 23). Diagnosis by this hollow is so accurate that nomads can tell almost to 10 liters how dehydrated an animal is.

Camels prefer to drink clean water, as Barker (1972) also observed in Australia, so nomads are always anxious to keep dirt out of the drinking basins. Indeed, water for our drinking and cooking was taken from these basins only after the camels had been watered at them. Muddy water that collects on the ground around poorly constructed wells is not drunk by camels, and water in unequipped waterholes soiled with urine and feces is drunk only reluctantly.

Drinking in Undernourished Camels In the summer of 1973 we were able to study camels under conditions of extreme drought. In that year many camels died from lack of food or illness (we counted 15 corpses in the immediate vicinity of each of two wells, plus many others away from wells), and the herds had been allowed to wander free, unguarded by their owners, with men stationed at the wells to draw water for any camels that came by. Despite the high temperatures, the extremely scarce and dry vegetation, and the long periods between drinking, camels that came to the wells drank little. This confirmed our observations in the summer of 1969 in the depleted pastures of the Western Erg that when camels are undernourished they drink less water than when they are well fed. This same correlation between inadequate nourishment and reduced water intake has been found in domestic sheep in southern Australia (Clark and Quin, in Macfarlane and Howard 1972). The daily average consumption of water by 37 camels feeding freely was 5–10 liters. The total consumption by our four pack camels during a 12-day trip, on which they usually drank every other day, was 120 liters each (10 liters per day), no more than many well-fed camels would drink in one or two sessions after going 4 or 5 days in similar temperatures without water. In general, the camels seemed unable to drink a quantity of water greater than 20–25 percent of their weight.

When better food is available, resistance to dehydration seems to be greater. Even the experimental animals of B. Schmidt-Nielsen and her colleagues (1956) which ate dry dates and hay were able in summer to tolerate a loss of water equal to 27 percent of their body weight.

Rapidity of Drinking　All large prey species drink quickly in order to spend no unnecessary time at waterholes, where they are especially vulnerable to predation. Although the camel is now domesticated and can generally drink in the desert only if the water is drawn by man, it continues to suck up water fairly rapidly at wells. A well-nourished camel usually drinks 10–20 liters or more per minute. The maximum speed we recorded during more than 180 measurements was 27 liters per minute. Camels sometimes drink a small amount of water quickly and then a large amount slowly, or vice versa, but there is no correlation between thirst and speed of drinking. Of 27 camels that drank 90–120 liters at one session, 19 drank at a rate of 13–16 liters per minute. The camel gulps three or four times in drinking 1 liter of water. While drinking, it raises its head at frequent short intervals, often shaking its head and lips. We rarely saw a camel drink longer than 2 minutes at a stretch. In the drought summer of 1973 undernourished camels drank more slowly than usual and with more frequent interruptions.

We also recorded drinking speeds for 20 or so free-grazing donkeys and cattle. The donkeys drank 20–30 liters at the same rate as the camels, while the cattle drank 45–95 liters at variable speeds, but faster than camels and with fewer interruptions. One cow drank 80 liters in 3 minutes without once lifting its head, while camels drank at the most 60 liters during the same period.

5 Adaptations to the Desert

As we have already seen, the camel has adapted in a number of ways to help it survive in the desert: (1) it eats a wide range of plants; (2) it samples plants over a wide area instead of overgrazing and thus destroying desert vegetation in a small region; (3) it can utilize the thorns, dry vegetation, and saltbush that other mammals avoid; (4) it can go for long periods without water, which frees it to graze on pastures far from wells; and (5) it can drink large quantities of water in a short time, and thus spends minimal time at usually overgrazed well areas.

In this chapter we discuss the many other ways in which camels are suited to the desert, including: their ability to conserve water by producing little urine and dry feces; eyes that are adapted to excessive light and are protected against sand; nostrils that can close to keep out sand and that have cavities where inspired air is moistened and exhaled air can be cooled, reducing water loss; the localized storage of energy as fat in the hump; the diurnal rise in body temperature in hot weather to conserve water; fur that provides insulation to some extent during hot ambient temperatures; sweat glands that provide evaporative cooling when necessary; behavior that minimizes exposure to heat; the ability to endure extreme dehydration without serious effect; a low metabolic rate, which reduces the need for water; and the ability to recycle urea when food protein is limited.

The adaptive physiology of the camel was first studied in 1954–55 by the Schmidt-Nielsens and their colleagues at the research station in Beni-Abbès, southern Algeria, under the auspices of UNESCO and various American scientific agencies. Their findings were so intriguing that further basic work on camel physiology was undertaken in Morocco by Y. Charnot, in Australia by W. V. Macfarlane, in Kenya by F. M. O. Maloiy, and in Israel by R. Yagel and G. M. Berlyne. Most of this research, however, involved a small number of animals kept in or near a laboratory where they were fed a more or less artificial diet.

In our research, we studied free-ranging camels in western and northwestern Africa under a variety of conditions for a total of 32 months between 1954 and 1973. We made our last five expeditions to the Sahara during summer in order to determine how camels exist in times of extreme stress caused by high temperatures, scarce food, and limited water. Conditions were exacerbated in 1973 when the western Sahara was suffering the worst drought in more than 50 years.

The free-ranging and working camels that we studied in their natural environment were subject to many variables, including contrasting day and night air temperatures and variable humidity, wind, and solar radiation; distance and speed at which the camels walked; what loads they carried; what they ate; and how much and when they drank. Unfortunately, there was no way for us to weigh the camels. Still, the data we obtained are of interest because no other physiological studies have been made of camels subject to normal desert stress. In all, water output was measured for a total of 120 hours during the cool green season and a total of 140 hours during the hot dry season.

Elimination of Feces and Urine   Researchers who have studied the water metabolism of the camel have all emphasized the camel's low water loss in hot weather through evaporation and the production of urine and feces. The loss through evaporation, which includes respiration and sweating, accounts for at least 50 percent of the water loss during the cool season and much more than this during summer. When a camel is dehydrated in summer, evaporation accounts for about 65 percent of total water loss; when it is hydrated or drinking freely, evaporation accounts for about 85 percent of total water loss (B. Schmidt-Nielsen et al. 1956). The Schmidt-Nielsens and their colleagues calculated evaporative loss indirectly by weighing camels existing under apparently stable conditions, collecting urine and feces to analyze their water content, and then subtracting the calculated value of the water in urine and feces from the total water loss (i.e., loss in body weight) to obtain the amount of water lost through evaporation.

Quantity of Feces Produced   The quantity of feces produced depends on the quality, quantity, and digestibility of the food eaten. Camels produce more feces when food is tough and woody rather than soft and moist, so it was important to note what was eaten as well as how many fecal pellets were produced by each camel. To measure the water content of an animal's feces, we collected in a cotton bag at least 40 freshly produced pellets and weighed them immediately. Then we dried them, either in an oven at 105° C during the cool season or in the open air during the hot season, until they reached a constant weight. The difference in weight equaled the water content of the pellets.

We noted the total pellet production of a camel in terms of its walking, grazing, and resting activities, as well as in terms of the amount and kind of food it ate, although camel activities were not necessarily related to fecal production; rather, feces were a reflection of what the animal had eaten perhaps the day before. As an exceptional example, although a female ate normally on the day we studied her activities, her fecal production was low because she had given birth 3 days earlier and had not eaten normally for several days after she had given birth. The variation in pellet production was greater in 1955–56, when there were a large number of different pastures, than in 1973, when food was uniformly scarce.

The total weight of feces was calculated from the number of pellets produced during a period averaging 5 hours per day (range 3–11 hours) times the average weight of the pellets (2.2–3.4 grams dry weight). In good pastures camels defecated about twice each hour, producing on the average 200 grams dry weight of fecal matter in distinctively shaped pellets for each individual. In poor pastures they defecated on the average only once an hour, producing not quite 100 grams dry weight of feces.

The food input and fecal output of the camels varied sharply with the quality of the pasturage. During the extremely dry summer of 1973 when only woody and spiny food was available, the weight of the dried feces was roughly 80 percent of the weight of the dried food eaten, indicating that little of the food was digested (table 9). This was the same in autumn even though the food was greener and more varied, but the dominant plants were dry and rich in cellulose. By contrast, in spring the digestible proportion of the plants rose markedly and there was proportionately much less fecal matter. The proportion of food digested was greater in February than in March, because although there were many more green grasses and annuals in March, there was also a very woody plant, *Helianthemum lippii*, which the camels ate more than the other plants.

The average input and output of solid materials of 20 camels feeding on four types of pastures are given in table 9. Our fecal values for camels in their natural environment, even in extreme drought, are higher than those of B. Schmidt-Nielsen et al. (1956) and of Maloiy (1972a), who report 370–500 grams dry weight per 100 kilograms body weight per day for their experimental animals. Values for the ass in Somali were closer to ours; it eliminated 500–2,000 grams of feces per 100 kilograms body weight per day (Maloiy 1970).

Loss of Water via Feces If the amount of water present in the feces and the number of pellets produced by a camel each day are known, the volume of water lost daily through the feces can be calculated. This volume is small in camels compared with other ruminants, like cows, which may lose via the feces as much as 20–40 liters of water per day, along with large quantities of undigested material. The pellets of camels are tacky to the touch when they are first produced, but they quickly dry out.

The water content of the feces of free-grazing camels was between 40 and 66 percent, depending on the quantity and quality of the food ingested, which varied greatly. In November 1955 the water content of feces was as low as it was in July 1973 (40 percent), although the camels ate two and one-half times as much and the water content of the food was three times as great. In November 1955 the camels drank rarely and only a few liters at a time, even though the food was mostly woody and dry. In February 1956 the water content of feces rose to 60 percent; although the vegetation supplied less water than it did in March, much of the vegetation consisted of salty plants and the feces usually contained slightly more water than in March. Pellets collected in April in acheb pastures contained 66 percent water. Under summer drought conditions, the feces of our pack camels, which drank every 2 or 3 days, apparently contained no more water than the feces of camels that had gone 10 days without drinking, but these results should be verified, as B. Schmidt-Nielsen et al. (1956) found that under laboratory conditions a dehydrated camel produced drier feces than camels watered every day. The water content of summer feces increased slightly about a day after drinking.

Although camels feeding in green spring pastures lost 6–7 liters of water per day in their feces, and in salty pastures even more, in July 1973 our pack camels, which weighed about 250 kilograms each, lost 1.3 liters per day (table 10). This 1.3 liter value is similar to that of B. Schmidt-Nielsen et al. (1956), who calculated a 0.5-liter water loss via feces per 100 kilograms body weight for camels eating dry food. Our values for hydrated and dehydrated camels are similar to those found by other workers studying camels in other countries (table 11). In a nonruminant, the donkey of Somali, the feces are less dry than in the camel, and because it eliminates relatively more nondigested food than the camel, it loses two to three times as much water via its feces (Maloiy 1970).

Loss of Water via Urine   Under experimental conditions Charnot collected camel urine in plastic containers, Macfarlane and Schmidt-Nielsen and co-workers catheterized their females, and Maloiy placed buckets under camel cages. We used two methods to measure the amount of urine produced in our free-ranging animals: either we collected it in a measuring container, which was the more accurate method, or, when this was not feasible, we timed the flow after ascertaining approximately how much was produced each second. Because males, unlike females, produce a slow, steady stream which varies little in rate, about 5 milliliters per second, the figures for males are probably more accurate.

In July 1973 the heat was so great in the middle of the day (up to 60° C in direct sun) that we were usually unable to observe our camels, as they moved from plant to plant, for more than a few hours at a time; our two longest observation periods lasted 7 and 8 hours. Our observations enable us to make the following comments:

1. The amount of urine produced was small during the summer of 1973, when the camels were undernourished, even though these animals drank every 2 or 3 days. It averaged about 1.1 liters per day, which is similar to Siebert and Macfarlane's (1975) findings.

2. During our two longest observation periods in July 1973, two male camels each urinated only once during each

Table 9 Average Weight of Food Eaten and Fecal Matter Eliminated (both as dry weight)

Pasture	Month	No. of Species	Hours of Grazing per Day	Food Eaten (kg/day)	Feces Produced (kg/day)	% of Feces to Food
Dry grass, *Acacia*	July 1973	5	8	2.2	1.8	81
Mostly *Acacia* and *Anabasis*	Nov. 1955	15	11–12	5.9	4.8	81
Green, in part salty	Feb. 1956	15	10	11.5	4.4	38
Green, mostly *Helianthemum*	March 1956	22	10–11	8.2	4.2	51

Table 10 Average Quantities of Water Ingested (directly and in food) and Lost via Feces in Different Pastures

Pasture	Month	Water Ingested (liters/day)	Water Lost via Feces (liters/day)	Ratio of Loss to Gain (%)	Approximate Weight of Camels (kg)	Maximum Daily Temperature (°C)
Dry grass, *Acacia*	July 1973	11.2	1.3	12	250–300	40–47
Mostly *Acacia* and *Anabasis*	Nov. 1955	4.2	3.1	74	400–500	20–24
Green, in part salty	Feb. 1956	15.3	6.7	44	400–500	15–18
Green, mostly *Helianthemum*	March 1956	16.6	5.7	34	400–500	17–24

Table 11   Percentage of Water Present in Feces of Experimental
Camels Receiving Dry Food

	Hydrated Camels	Dehydrated Camels	References
Algeria	52	43	B. Schmidt-Nielsen et al. (1956)
Australia	58	43	Siebert and Macfarlane (1975)
Kenya:			
At 22° C	57	46	Maloiy (1972a)
At 40° C	53	44	Maloiy (1972a)
Morocco	73	63	Charnot (1958)

period, as opposed to approximately once an hour in green spring pastures.

3. Quantities of urine eliminated during any one urination for any one animal varied greatly, as Charnot (1958) also noted for both day and night. In July 1973 quantities varied from 50 to 650 milliliters, the most frequent amount being about 250 milliliters.

4. Among our four camels in 1973, the one female produced more urine than any one of the three males. At the same time, she lost less water than the males via her feces and drank only slightly more than them.

5. The female produced the single largest quantity (650 milliliters) and she did so only once, 1 day after drinking. This exceeded the maximum of 450 milliliters noted by B. Schmidt-Nielsen et al. (1956), who collected 400 samples of urine over a 9-month period. During this high-volume urination, the urine was emitted more forcefully than usual and was clear and odorless, unlike the urine usually produced in summer, which has a strong odor and dark color. She did not urinate again during the next 3½ hours.

We can only estimate from our data how much urine camels produce in 24 hours. In March 1956 the average quantity produced during 2-, 3-, and 5-hour periods of observation was about 300 milliliters per hour, so the average daily amount could have been about 7 liters per day during a period when the camels were obtaining almost all the water they needed from vegetation.

Our values for urine production of camels are similar to those of other camel researchers, who also found that far more urine is produced by camels that eat fresh green food rather than dry food, and slightly more by hydrated camels compared with dehydrated ones (table 12). For

Table 12   Amount of Urine Produced in 24 Hours (in liters) by Experimental Camels Fed Dry Food

	Hydrated Camels	Dehydrated Camels	Reference
Algeria	0.75	0.5	B. Schmidt-Nielsen et al. (1956)
Australia	2.9–8.6	0.7–1.7	Siebert and Macfarlane (1971)
Morocco	5	1.5	Charnot (1958)
Kenya:			
At 22° C	0.7	0.4	Maloiy (1972a)
At 22° C–40° C	0.8	0.2	Maloiy (1972a)

example, B. Schmidt-Nielsen et al. (1956) noted that animals that had browsed in the erg in winter produced about 7 liters of urine per day, while Leroux (1960) calculated that camels that drank regularly and grazed freely in green winter pastures produced 5–7 liters of urine per day. This is as much as cattle in temperate zones produce. After 6 days without drinking, camels produced about half as much urine per day. In summer, camels drinking regularly and eating green vegetation produced 4–6 liters while dehydrated animals foraging in dry pastures produced only about three-quarters of a liter.

As might be expected, experimental camels fed on dry food produced little urine (table 12). Siebert and Macfarlane (1975) found that camels that were given hay and lucerne and had free access to water in summer (35–42° C) produced as much as 9.3 liters in 24 hours, but that after only 1 day without drinking generally produced less than 2.8 liters in 24 hours. Compared with sheep foraging in summer in the same habitat, the camels lost 10 times less water through their urine in proportion to their weight. The low volume of urine that camels sometimes excrete may be a function of high tubular reabsorption in the kidneys and high sensitivity of the kidneys to the antidiuretic hormone vasopressin (Macfarlane et al. 1971).

Maloiy (1972a), who studied renal function in camels, found that if they were given salty water (0.25–5.5 percent NaCl) they drank two to four times as much water as usual and the quantity of urine increased from 0.7 to 3–9 liters per day, and ate more food as well. Maloiy reports that camels can tolerate for some days drinking water containing 5.5 percent NaCl while eating only dry hay. By contrast, cattle can only tolerate water with 1.0 percent NaCl and sheep 1.3 percent NaCl (Macfarlane and Howard 1972).

Input-Output Results, 1973

As the foregoing indicates, we were able in the summer of 1973 to make a rough estimate of the water input and output of our four 250-kilogram camels, which carried 100-kilogram packs for 100 kilometers, walking about 10–15 kilometers a day and resting little during the daytime (table 13). Maximum daily temperatures were 40°–47° C and minimums were 25°–32° C. The difference between output and input (8.8 liters) represents water lost through evaporation. This is similar to the evaporation figure given by B. Schmidt-Nielsen et al. (1956), who calculated a loss of 3.4 liters per 100 kilograms body weight. It is a remarkably low rate of water loss for animals carrying loads under extreme desert conditions.

Anatomy

So far we have considered the physiological adaptations of the camel to the desert which we could study directly. There are other ways in which the camel is adapted to the desert, among them features of its anatomy. In hot, dry regions native mammals are generally either small or large. The small ones venture abroad only at night, returning during the day to their burrows, where the microclimate is relatively cool and humid. Without such burrows they would quickly die. Nonburrowing mammals must survive each day in full or shaded sunlight where they have to tolerate great heat. Aside from the camel's relatively low dependence on water sources, its long legs enable it to cover large areas in its search for food while its large size allows it to use less food and water per unit mass than is the case for smaller animals. The adult camel's head

Table 13   Water Input and Output per Day (in liters) for Working Camels under Drought Conditions

Input:	
Water drunk	10
Water present in vegetation	1.2
Total input	11.2
Output:	
Water lost via feces	1.3
Water lost via urine	1.1
Total loss	2.4
Difference (water lost by evaporation)	8.8

is about 2.5 meters above the ground, but with its neck stretched upward it can reach twigs and leaves 3.5 meters from the ground (see pl. 17) that are inaccessible to most other animals. Its height also enables it to see distant pastures.

In most respects, the camel has anatomical features similar to those of other ruminants, as a perusal of many of the references listed in the bibliography will indicate. But it differs from other ruminants in that its long neck has a peculiar arrangement of nerves to the neck and shoulder muscles (Kanan 1969) and a special arrangement of the cerebral arteries (Kanan 1970). The latter ensures that the blood pressure at the brain will not fluctuate to any extent when, for example, the camel is reaching high for food or drinking from a low basin on the ground.

The large veins of the camel's legs and neck have valve cusps arranged one above the other along the axis of the veins (Amoroso, Edholm, and Rewell 1947). These are found in the jugular and femoral veins and prevent the backflow of blood into large tributaries when there is a sudden rise in pressure in the main vein. The camel, which often lowers its head to browse, can do so without the blood in the jugular vein flooding the brain.

Unlike smaller ruminants such as goats and sheep, the camel has a bone in its diaphragm which not only prevents compression of the blood stream while the camel is active but which distributes the forces of muscular pull of the diaphragm over a proportionally larger tendinous surface area (Maskar 1957; Etemadi 1966).

The eyes of the camel, which are protected both by a skeletal postorbital bar and by thick, long eyelashes, are arhythmic in that they can see well both by day and by night (Walls 1963). At night the eye uses a choroidal tapetum to enhance its vision. In the daytime when light is intense, the fringed margins of the iris (*corpora nigra*) shield the pupil so that only a small amount of light strikes the retina. The eyelids are somewhat translucent, enough to permit a camel to continue walking during sandstorms with its eyes shut (Barker 1972).

The camel, which is exposed to dry air and sometimes blowing sand, has a constant and large flow of lacrimal secretions that keep the conjunctiva and corneal epithelium from drying out (Abdalla, Fahmy, and Arnautovic 1970; Awkati and Al-Bagdadi 1971). The puncta lacrimalia is absent, so tears often overflow the eyes of the camel, wetting the fur of the cheek underneath. The lacrimal glands of other mammals have many excretory ducts that open separately at the conjunctiva, but the camel has only two, and they are too wide to become blocked with sand.

The camel has a number of cavities in the rostrum that moisten inspired air. A pair of blind sacs that open into the anterior part of the nasal cavity are lined with mucous membrane that apparently secretes fluid (Arnautovic and Abdalla 1969a). The sacs can also be depressed by the action of adjacent muscles to produce a vacuum that sucks in secretions from the nasolacrimal duct for reabsorption. The turbinates, which have a total surface area of about 0.1 square meters, can cool the air from the lungs so that, although the expired air is fully saturated, because of its lowered temperature some water from it is recondensed in the nose and therefore conserved (Langman et al. 1978).

The lateral nasal glands are active sites of mucous secretion because of their abundant goblet cells and laminar mucous glands (Abdel Magid and Abdel Razaq 1975). Ciliated cells in the mucous membranes of the sacs produce currents that move these secretions toward the nasal cavities, where they moisten the dry air. It is possible that the lateral nasal glands could excrete concentrated salts as they do in some birds and reptiles, but this is unlikely.

The long, paired vomeronasals, or Jacobson's organ, in the camel also secrete mucous, which undoubtedly moistens the inspired dry air of the desert (Arnautovic, Abdalla, and Fahmy 1970). There is no information concerning this structure in the camel and its possible relationship with the behavior pattern called "flehmen" (see chap. 6) (Dagg and Taub 1971; Estes 1972).

The external nares of the camel are slitlike, with muscles that can almost completely close the openings against blowing sand. The nostrils are lined on each side with short, soft hairs that filter inhaled air. Barker (1972), who worked extensively with camels in Australia, stated that camels could smell other camels 11 kilometers away.

Water Storage   Because of the camel's almost unique ability to survive for days without drinking water even in the hottest deserts, early workers assumed that water was stored for use in the camel's body. The self-appointed task of these researchers was to determine where camels stored their water, not whether they stored it at all.

Pliny the Elder (ca. A.D. 23–79), in his *Historia naturalis,* was the first writer to declare that camels stored water in their stomachs. Other authors accepted this theory, even though as early as 1806 Sir Everard Home proved it could not be so by a careful dissection of a camel's stomach, which showed that there was not room to store much water in the stomach and that the structure of the stomach was unsuitable for this purpose (Home 1806). As recently as 1950 Hegazi agreed with Pliny, describing in a scientific paper three separate groups of water sacs at the side of the rumen, each sac with a holding capacity of between 200 and 300 milliliters (Hegazi 1950).

During the 1950s the Schmidt-Nielsens and their colleagues undertook to discover how camels could exist for weeks without drinking in a hot, desert climate. Their first task was to determine whether camels did indeed store water. Their study of the carcasses of 13 butchered animals showed that there was moisture in the rumen diverticula, or "water sacs," but that they were mostly filled with particles of masticated food (K. Schmidt-Nielsen et al. 1956). The contents of the rumen proper were more fluid, but were a digestive broth rather than stored water, a fluid present in quantities in the rumens of all ruminants. For camels, the average quantity of rumen contents was 11 kilograms per 100 kilograms body weight, a quantity similar to that found in cattle.

One stomach plus parts of others were sent to Copenhagen, where Anker Hansen examined their structure, both grossly and histologically (Hansen and Schmidt-Nielsen 1957). The diverticula of the rumen contained large numbers of glandular cells, but whether their purpose was to absorb fermentation products from the stomach or to secrete fluid to help digest the food was not known. The "water sacs" also contained muscles, but in no way could these be described as "sphincters" that could contract and close off the sacs from the main area of the rumen, as earlier writers had suggested. In general, the camel stomach differs significantly from those of true ruminants, so there seems little doubt that the camelids and other ruminant lines of evolution independently developed the faculty of ruminating and that camelids are not closely related to the true ruminants (Bohlken 1960).

K. Schmidt-Nielsen et al. (1956) in Beni-Abbès also analyzed the chemical composition of the rumen fluid in camels. It was largely composed of water but had a relatively high sodium and a low potassium and chloride content, which made it similar to the rumen fluid of other ruminants and to the composition of saliva. When a camel that had been deprived of water for 17 days drank 62 liters of water, the rumen fluid as monitored with a stomach tube was at first diluted, but its ionic concentration soon began to increase, and continued to do so despite repeated ingestions of water. Within 2 days the water was distributed throughout the body. None was stored as pure water.

Many laymen still claim that water can be stored not only in the camel's stomach but in its hump too. In reality, however, the hump contains mostly fat stored when vegetation is plentiful. When food is scarce, the 10–15-kilogram hump almost disappears. Although it is true that when fat metabolizes it produces a large amount of water, the process requires oxygen from respiration. However, while oxygen is breathed in, air saturated with water vapor is breathed out, so that in the case of camels in the desert evaporation of water from the lungs in dry air exceeds that which is produced from oxidation of the fat. Because fat is not stored subcutaneously over an extensive area of the camel, but rather in the hump, body heat flows unimpeded to the surface of the skin to be dissipated (Schmidt-Nielsen 1964).

There is no anatomical evidence that camels can store water anywhere else in their bodies either, despite the fact that a camel can drink as much as 100 liters after going several days without water and that, if it were stored for future use, there would have to be some detectable place for it to go. Nor is there evidence that the overall water content of the camel is higher than that of other mammals, as was ascertained through careful testing by Macfarlane, Morris, and Howard (1963) in Australia.

Body Temperature   In the summer desert, water loss in camels is slowed by their fluctuating body temperatures and the good insulation provided by their coats, both of which reduce evaporation through the skin. Because of the camel's relatively high temperature during the day and its relatively low one at night, water that would otherwise be lost as sweat is conserved in two ways: first, through toleration of stored heat in the body so that water need not be dispersed by evaporation and, second, through minimization of the heat difference between the ambient temperature and body temperature so that less evaporative cooling would be necessary than if the camel's temperature were lower. K. Schmidt-Nielsen et al. (1957), who studied this phenomenon at Beni-Abbès, found that in summer camels deprived of drinking water had rectal temperatures as low as 34.2° C in the early morning and as high as 40.7° C in the afternoon. When the camels were watered regularly, the diurnal variation of their rectal temperatures was much less extreme, ranging between 36° and 39° C, with an individual variation of about 2° C, similar to temperature variations in winter. Other large desert mammals that show marked diurnal temperature variations when dehydrated are the donkey, oryx, Grant's gazelle, and the Dorcas gazelle (K. Schmidt-Nielsen et al. 1957; Taylor 1970; Ghobrial 1974).

Insulation and Evaporation   The hair of camels, like that of other mammals in hot climates, has the dual and contradictory function of simultaneously protecting the animal against high ambient temperatures while allowing the dissipation of body heat to the surrounding air. During the winter most camels have thick, fairly long wooly fur, which in the USSR weighs up to 2 kilograms for females and 4 kilograms for males (Donchennko 1956). In the spring, desert camels either shed their winter fur or it is shorn by their owners, who use it to weave cloth for waterproof tents. The summer fur of one unshorn camel was about 30 millimeters long on the flanks, 50–65 millimeters on the midline, and 110 millimeters over the hump, with some of the coarse hairs as long as 140 millimeters. On the ventral surface and the legs, the hair tends to be straight and generally 15–20 millimeters long (Schmidt-Nielsen 1964). In northern Kenya and the Sahel, where winters are not cold, camels have short hair and it is not shed seasonally. The fur is of two types: long cover hairs, which occur singly, and shorter wooly hairs, which grow in groups of about 10 (Appleyard 1967; Ghobrial 1970). Each group has an associated erector pili muscle, one to three sweat glands, and sebaceous glands beside each hair follicle.

The sweat glands, which are present in all areas of the body except the upper lip, external nares, and perianal region (Lee and Schmidt-Nielsen 1962), are more deeply set than in other mammals, which may explain why they were missed by early histologists (Dowling and Nay 1962). They average on the midbody about 200 per square centimeter, a density similar to that in man. (Cows, by contrast, may have four to eight times as many sweat glands, depending on the breed.) Above black bulb thermometer readings of 35° C, the evaporation from an area of a camel's shoulder was observed to increase linearly with heat load (K. Schmidt-Nielsen et al. 1957). In total, a camel may produce each hour up to 280 milliliters of sweat per square meter of skin for evaporative cooling (Macfarlane et al. 1963).

The sweat of the camel evaporates under the fur at the surface of the skin itself, where the process provides maximum cooling of the camel's body. Thus camels do not appear to sweat unless one looks under the saddle or other load, where the fur is wet because evaporation cannot take place. Schmidt-Nielsen (1964) illustrated the importance of the camel's fur by comparing the rate of sweating in summer of shorn and unshorn animals. Their total water expenditure per day was 3 liters per 100 kilograms body weight in the shorn animal and only 2 liters in the unshorn camel. Thus a shorn camel with fur 0.5–1 centimeters long would evaporate 50 percent more water than would an animal with unshorn fur. The temperature at the fur surface was as high as 70°–80° C, so the temperature gradient through the fur was more than 30° C. In winter the camel expends water at a rate corresponding to less than 1 percent of its body weight per day, with slightly more being produced in hydrated than in dehydrated camels. In summer the rate is more than two times as high in dehydrated camels and nearly four and one-half times as high in hydrated camels (B. Schmidt-Nielsen et al. 1956).

On hot summer days evaporative cooling in camels occurs either via the skin or via respiration, but the latter is apparently relatively unimportant because the respiration rate is highly variable, ranging between six and 18 breaths per minute, and does not increase substantially as ambient temperature rises, as one would expect to find in other animal species under similar conditions. An increase in respiratory evaporation probably accounts for less than 5 percent of the total increase in evaporation due to heat regulation (K. Schmidt-Nielsen et al. 1957). The rate of respiration in later experiments was found to decrease with dehydration (Schmidt-Nielsen et al. 1967).

Certain behavior minimizes evaporation in both hydrated and dehydrated camels. They may rest all day in the same place to avoid exertion, always facing the sun as it moves across the sky (pl. 24); if they move at all, it will be only slightly, to take up as little heat as possible from the ground. During hot periods they often huddle in groups, because there is less heat flow between two camels than between a camel and the air (pl. 25).

Dehydration Camels can survive extreme desiccation. While a man will be near death if he loses body water equal to about 12 percent of his body weight, a lean camel can survive a body water loss equal to 40 percent of its body weight. We have seen that the camel dehydrates slowly because of its reduced urine output and very dry feces. When Macfarlane et al. (1963) deprived three camels of water at ambient temperatures as high as 41° C, the camels lost weight at a rate of only 19–23 grams per kilogram body weight in a 24-hour period because of the small losses of sweat, urine, and respiratory and fecal water, and a lowered metabolism. This was half the rate of weight loss noted in Merino sheep under the same conditions. Of the weight the camels lost, the interstitial fluid yielded 9.3 percent, the plasma 5.2 percent, and the cells and gut 81.2 percent. Indeed, the markedly gaunt abdomen of a dehydrated camel fills out immediately when it drinks large quantities of water. The alimentary tract can hold large quantities of fluid: the rumen holds 110 grams per kilogram body weight and the rest of the tract holds 180 grams per kilogram body weight, of which more than 80 percent is water (Macfarlane et al. 1967).

Under normal conditions, the water in the plasma of camels (and man) constitutes about 16 percent of the total body water. In a camel that has lost 25 percent of its body water, the blood volume will drop by less than a tenth, while under the same conditions a man's blood volume will drop by a third; his blood will thus be too thick to carry his body heat to the skin, where it can be dissipated, and he will quickly die (Schmidt-Nielsen 1959)

The unusual ability of the camel to undergo considerable dehydration (a loss of, say, 20 percent of its body weight) without sustaining a proportional loss of water from the blood (only 5 percent of its total body weight) may be a function in part of its capillary system. When examined under an electron micrograph, typical skin capillaries of a camel had extremely thick walls and narrow lumina, with room in cross section for only one red blood cell (Montgomery, Ashworth, and Fontaine 1964). There was no fenestration in the capillary walls in any of the sections, indicating that fluid movement from the lumen to the interstitial space is accomplished by the transcellular route. Thus the capillary walls may help prevent loss of water from the blood vessels during periods of substantial loss of total body water.

The erythrocytes of the camel may also be adapted to desert conditions: they are oval shaped and small, but numerous, with as many as 12.5 million per cubic millimeter (Sharma, Malik, and Sapra 1973). Perhaps the narrow width of the red blood cells (cross section ca. 4.5×2.5 microns) enables them to continue circulating through the body even when the blood viscosity has increased somewhat because of dehydration. The total amount of hemoglobin in camel blood is similar to that found in other mammals, with the hemoglobin highly concentrated within each erythrocyte. Camel hemoglobin has a high affinity for oxygen, so that camels can take up more oxygen per unit volume of cells than can many other mammals (Bartels et al. 1963). Camel blood is also unusual in that the plasma possesses a relatively large amount of albumin, which is highly resistant to dehydration (Siebert and Macfarlane 1975).

Rehydration   When a dehydrated camel drinks a large amount of water, the water in the rumen reaches the blood plasma slowly, with 25 percent of the equilibration value attained in 1 hour (Macfarlane et al. 1963). (By contrast, tritiated water moves rapidly from the rumen to the plasma in cattle, where plasma levels as high as 90 percent of the equilibration value are reached in 1 hour.) When a large quantity of the water reaches the blood and tissues of camels, they are diluted to an extent that could not be tolerated by other mammals, whose blood cells would hemolyze in less hypotonic solutions. The erythrocytes of camels can swell up to 240 percent of their initial size without breaking (Perk 1963, 1966).

Metabolic Rate   The metabolic rate of the camel, like mammals in general, increases with increasing body temperature (i.e., fever) and decreases with decreasing body temperature (i.e., hypothermia and hibernation) (Schmidt-Nielsen et al. 1963, 1967). During the summer, therefore, its metabolic rate increases each day with its diurnal rise in body temperature, thus adding substantially to its heat load. Dehydration per se, however, leads to a reduction in the metabolic rate. A low metabolic rate has probably evolved in the camel over millions of years because of its desert habitat. The metabolic rate of the camel in the desert and subdeserts of Australia is 50 kilocalories per metabolic kilogram each 24 hours, about half that of a cow living in a similar environment (Macfarlane et al. 1971). The camel's turnover of water is also low, 82 milliliters per kilogram each 24 hours for animals grazing in summer—about half the rate of cattle in the same region. The turnover rate for camels in summer is double that in winter, and it is higher in lactating than in nonlactating females.

The Kidney   The kidney of the camel has other adaptive features besides excreting diminished amounts of urine when necessary to conserve water. Unlike most mammals, the camel can produce urine with a concentration of salt almost twice that of sea water (Charnot 1960), and if it is fed a diet low in protein, it can produce urine extremely low in urea (about 0.3 grams of urea nitrogen per day) (B. Schmidt-Nielsen et al. 1957). In the camel, urea formed during protein metabolism is not necessarily excreted, but may enter the rumen from the blood plasma via the saliva as well as the rumen wall. Bacterial urease in the rumen produces ammonia from the urea that is immediately used in protein synthesis by the extensive microbial flora present in the rumen. The bacterial protein then passes to the intestine, where it is absorbed into the bloodstream. This conservation of urea occurs when food is low in protein or when a camel is growing or pregnant.

Despite a low rate of urine flow in camels, B. Schmidt-Nielsen et al. (1956) found that the concentrations of solids in the urine of their experimental camels was not exceptionally high, rarely reaching values of 2–2.5 osm even in periods of extreme dehydration. At these concentrations the urine flow may vary between 0.5 and 1.5 milliliters per minute (Siebert and Macfarlane 1971). However, camels grazing in wadis, possibly on salty vegetation, had urine concentrations as high as 3.17 osm.

Mortality   Mortality of camels is greatest in the very young, especially in areas such as northern Kenya, where heavy milk consumption by the nomads limits the supply available to the young camels. Of 205 camel calves born in India studied by Bhargava, Sharma, and Singh (1963), 40 (19.5 percent), 26 males and 14 females, died before they reached 3 years of age; 33 of the 40 (82.5 percent) died before they reached 6 months of age. The female calves remained in the herd longer and often suckled longer, which probably explains their higher survival rate. Left alone, most Indian camels mate from November to February, but there camel men tried to arrange breeding so that the young were born in February; it was their experience that foals born in December usually did not survive because of the severe cold. Camels can live as long as 40 years (Barker 1972), but are usually slaughtered for food long before then.

6 Behavior

**Unguarded
Herds** Camels are generally maintained in a semiwild state in
which they choose their food from wild vegetation but are
watered by man. In some parts of the Sahara, such as
southern Algeria, Tripolitania, and Tibesti, herds are
allowed to roam freely during the 4–5 hottest months but
are guarded again as the rutting season approaches. The
unguarded camels return at regular intervals to a familiar
well, where their encamped owners draw water for them.
Such camels form stable groups comprising a few animals
to over 30. Table 14 shows that the average herd size of 28
herds that came to a well in southern Algeria in spring and
summer was 11. Of these 28 herds, 13 consisted of male,
female, and young; 6 of male and female without young; 5
of females with young; and 4 of males only. Old males
were occasionally solitary. These herd compositions are
not unlike those found in giraffes (Foster and Dagg 1972).
Yearling camels, however, are never seen without females,
as young giraffes occasionally are. When camels are re-
grouped or are forcibly separated, they often give a loud,
deep roar.

The herds listed in table 14 were formed when food was
plentiful. In the drought summer of 1973, when Mauritanian herds were unguarded, we encountered only very
small groups. Even 2-year-olds, which normally stay with
their mothers, sometimes came alone to the wells.

In Turkmenistan, free-grazing camels form bachelor
herds and mixed herds of perhaps one male plus 10–15
females and their young. In Australia, feral herds usually
consist of 10–30 animals, although 300 have been seen together in some years, and 500 in periods of drought. Outside the rutting season males may form bachelor groups
(McKnight 1969).

On their way to and from wells camels walk in single file
(pl. 26), usually with a female leading (observed also by

Table 14   Composition of Unguarded Herds Coming to a Well in Southern Algeria

Month	Herd Size	Adult Males*	Adult Females	Juvenile Males (1–3 yr)	Juvenile Females (1–3 yr)	Foals under 6 mo
May	33	5	15	4	4	5
	20	5	11	2	2	...
	18	3 (2+1)	9	1	1	4
	16	1 (1+0)	11	...	2	2
	13	2	8	...	3	...
	12	5 (1+4)	7	...	...	...
	11	5	3	...	...	3
	10	2	6	1	1	...
	8	1	5	1	1	...
	5	5 (3+2)	...	...	...	...
	5	2 (2+0)	3	...	...	...
July	24	3	7	4	3	7
	20	11	7	...	...	2
	15	6	5	3	1	...
	14	2	10	2	...	...
	11	3	6	1	1	...
	10	10 (10 + 0)	...	...	...	...
	10	5 (3+2)	5	...	...	...
	9	5 (3+2)	4	...	...	...
	8	3	5	...	...	...
	7	7	...	...	...	...
	6	2	4	...	...	...
	4	...	2	...	...	2
	4	...	2	...	...	2
	4	...	2	...	...	2
	2	2	...	...	...	...
August	6	...	3	...	...	3
	4	...	2	...	...	2

*Where intact and castrated males were noted, these are indicated, respectively, in parentheses.

Baskin [1976] for camels in Turkmenistan), the young staying together, and an old animal sometimes trailing far behind. Camels crossing a reg or hamada often follow 30-centimeter-wide winding paths, which may be very old, avoiding rocks or stones that might injure their soft feet. Such trails are numerous near wells, fanning out in all directions. In dunes, camels tend to follow men's or goats' paths when they go up and down hills. In Australia, also, camels use trails when they are available and approach wells in single file. Barker (1972) reports that in Australia camels followed a vehicle track all day long, choosing the most distinct route when the track forked. In Kenya, camels traveling single file follow the trails used by game such as giraffe and zebra.

Like most ungulates, camels confronting moving vehicles often try to run ahead and cross in front of them. In Mauritania, camels have been killed when part of a herd has rushed in front of a train to join the rest of its members on the far side of the track. If an entire herd is grazing on one side of the track when a train approaches, they tend to run away from it. A small group of camels that we once pursued by car fled in a compact group.

Guarded Herds   During the mating season, which lasts from December to May, all herds are guarded, so their composition is then determined by man. Most of the males in the areas we visited had been castrated between the ages of 3 and 5, but even so they were sometimes attacked by a breeding male if they tried to approach his females. Two rutting males in the presence of females have been known to fight to the death, showing an aggressiveness uncommon in uncaged ungulates. During the cool months there are three types of herds: herds with one male and up to 30 females with their 1- or 2-year-old young, generally guarded; herds consisting of males only, both castrated and intact, not permanently guarded; and herds of females and their newborn foals. If nomads want to keep a herd nearby, they tether by the fetlock the leading animal of the herd. In the first type of herd, the breeding male keeps his females together from a position at the rear of his harem, often uttering a continuous deep call, thus facilitating the herder's task, which consists in part of keeping the various herds separated. Baskin (1976) found that a breeding male remained on one side of his herd for most of each day, crossing briefly only once or twice to the other side. Camels become attached to their group; we have seen individuals separated from the herd to do work wait several days at a well for their companions' return, despite the lack of food there. A newborn foal may leave its mother to join a passing herd, but it quickly returns to her when she calls to it. Barker (1972) reports that camel herds in familiar country might wander off in different directions in the evening to feed but apparently keep track of each other because they are together again the next morning.

In the western Sahara most herds are guarded all year

around, except in periods of drought, because wells are few and pastures often widely dispersed; migrations thus are continuous and take place over far larger areas than is the case in southern Algeria. There is also the chance that unguarded camels might be stolen, which was not uncommon in earlier times. Rich nomads in Mauritania, who until the recent drought owned 1,000 camels or more, kept only lactating females near their camps. These females were milked each evening to provide the main source of nourishment for the nomads. The rest of the camels sometimes grazed several hundred kilometers away, guarded by a few herders and their families. The constant search for new feeding grounds requires high mobility for men and animals, which is impossible for a large tent community.

Similar herd management is practiced in northern Kenya, where frequently only milking camels and a few strong pack animals are kept near a settlement while the other camels are herded from a bush camp. These bush camps, where up to 1,000 camels may be supervised by warriors in the dry season, are moved constantly so that the animals will not have to go far to find food. The camels that are kept at the settlement, however, are managed differently from the way they are in Algeria and Mauritania. In Kenya they are herded to the pastures about 9 A.M., after the goats, sheep, and cattle have gone, and are marched along by their herders, sometimes for 3 hours, before they are allowed to stop. Then they browse for about 6 hours while they slowly head back to the settlement; again they are hurried along for the last few kilometers so that they will not arrive too long after dark. They spend less time feeding than do desert camels, presumably because the vegetation is more abundant. Each evening the foraging camels, which are kept together by the herders so that thieves or predators cannot prey on them, readily follow the lactating mothers whose young have been kept all day near the settlement.

Since the general scarcity of vegetation cannot support large herds, a wealthy nomad in the western Sahara farms out most of his camels to a number of poor relatives, who care for them and in turn use them for transportation, milk, and wool. Such an economical arrangement, called *menhia* in Arabic, was adopted as early as biblical times because it diminishes the risk of camels getting lost or stolen, reduces possible government taxation, and increases the hope of the owner, by providing for poor relatives, that he will go to paradise. This custom was unknown to the Berbers and was probably introduced into the Sahara by Arab invaders.

In the western Sahara, where settlements and economic development are scarce, camel breeds are especially hardy and can cover great distances without food and water. Even in summer Mauritanian camels may travel 80 kilometers or more from the nearest well. By contrast, in the Algerian Sahara, where seminomadism prevails, herds rarely move more than 20–30 kilometers from a well. In northern Kenya, where wells are scarce, camels often stay 6 days on pastures 80 kilometers from a well, walk 3 days to the well while feeding, stay 1 day at the well, and then return to the distant pastures. Cattle, which must drink every 2–3 days, stay within 10 kilometers of a well.

Fidelity to Home Area   Camels retain an affinity for the region where they are used to living (and probably also to the group to which they belong), which we call, for want of a better name, the home area. No one knows how large a home area is, or how many such areas live in the memory of a herd, but both nomads and former members of the French camel corps (which have been disbanded) have testified that displaced camels will travel long distances to return to the home area, even though they have been away for many years. Such areas do not always have superior pastures; for example, we observed camels near Beni-Abbès, where the food supply was excellent, try to return to the west despite the inferior pastures there. Gauthier-Pilters worked with a nomad of the Western Erg who had sold some camels to a man from Timbuktu, over 1,400 kilometers away. Three of these animals escaped from their new home and were found 3 months later, in the autumn, near the place where they had been sold. Barker (1972) also related that unguarded camels in South Australia found their way back to their home station over 1,600 kilometers away. Females are likely to return to the region where they first foaled, so camel men try to buy females before they give birth for the first time if they are to be moved to another region. Sometimes the front legs of camels grazing away from their home area are tied together to prevent them from running away. Camels that we hired for our field trips were always hobbled during the 4-hour midday stop and at night so that they could be easily recovered when it was time to move on. Even so, our camel men sometimes had to track them for many kilometers before they found them and brought them back to camp.

Camels also remember good pastures and wells, even when they are outside their home area and the pastures and wells are several hundred kilometers away. An Arab proverb says that a foal knows the well where its mother came to drink before she gave birth to it. Knowing their camels will return to the same well at frequent intervals, tribes in southern Algeria graze their local camels unguarded in summer.

No one knows how camels are able to return to home areas across vast tracts of desert—whether by sight, smell, a special sense of orientation, or a combination of these. They can do so quickly by walking steadily at 5 kilometers per hour, 100 kilometers per day. Camels can detect pools of water and fresh pastures at a considerable distance if the wind is favorable, so undoubtedly smell is important (Denis 1970). On some of our trips, camels constantly turned their heads toward rain clouds on the horizon when the wind blew from that direction, and tried to go toward them. We, too, could sense the moisture in the air. Rosenstiehl (1959) reports that it is not uncommon to see a whole herd of camels rushing toward distant rains.

The risk of camels escaping is especially great after a rain, when, if pools of water have collected, the camels are temporarily liberated from their dependence on wells. The errant camels are usually located only when they again need water and must approach a well. Lost camels at wells are usually not watered by other nomads, because, if they were, they would abandon the area and be much harder for their owners to find. We found it distressing to leave thirsty camels clustered at a well for days without water to facilitate their owners' finding them. Nomads are helped in recovering their lost camels by the "Arab telephone"; by the identifying brand marks on their necks and trunks (pl. 27); and by their footprints. Some nomads spend several months each year hunting for lost camels, a diversion that gives them a welcome opportunity to visit distant friends and relatives.

Camels are easily frightened, so sometimes a strange person, luggage slipping from a saddle, or the approach of a car or other unusual object may frighten an individual, which may in turn stampede the whole herd. Even an unusual movement by a rider may panic a camel, although they are said to be unperturbed by gunfire and have been used in military barricades (Farias 1967).

Camels that have roamed free for months are very difficult to approach. Four escaped males that we encountered in spring in western Algeria fled when we got within 100 meters of them on foot. Feral camels in Australia also flee from man, but once one has been captured, it soon becomes docile (Macfarlane, personal communication, 1977). In northern Kenya camels left unguarded for only 2 weeks flee from men. Foals that become separated from the herd remain in the same area for several days, but they only tolerate men on camels, not those on foot (Denis 1970). Barker (1972) found that in Australia pigs frightened camels more than did any other animal, but their "first sight of a mine battery or railway train or motor car [did not] frighten them in the least."

Body Care Behavior   Common comfort movements of camels include rolling on the ground, rubbing, and scratching. The most frequent type of scratching is with a hind leg against a foreleg, the brisket, the neck, or the head. They scratch their flanks or their forelegs with their lower incisors, and can even reach their withers and tail. All camelids rub the metatarsus from up to down on the exterior side of the other hind leg, and camels also rub their forelegs in this way. They may rub chin, neck, flanks, and shoulders in a slow rhythm against bushes or tree trunks until the latter are polished smooth. Rubbing is contagious, so several camels will spend many minutes rubbing themselves, especially where trees are rare. Since rubbing surfaces are scarce in the desert, camels will also rub their head and neck against another camel or on their own hind knee callosity as they lift it. Sand bathing occurs in all camelids and is also contagious, with camels sometimes forming a line at sandy "rolling places." In the dune areas these are usually in the interdune valleys. These activities remove ticks from the body and otherwise soothe the camel. Camels dislodge flies and other insects in a number of ways: by raising the head quickly, shaking the raised head and the flaccid lips, flicking the ears, throwing the head down and back against the side of the body while simultaneously blowing out, bending a front leg quickly so that

1 Campsite fortified against the midday sun. Guide
   Mokhtar is at right.
2 Guide Mokhtar (*right*) being entertained by visitors while
   he prepares the food.

1

2

3 The camels in the foreground have been separated from the others so that their drinking capacity can be measured individually.

4 Gauthier-Pilters drinking tea in the tent of a family of Mauritanian nomads.

3

4

5   Well-fed camels from northern Kenya
6   A healthy Kenyan camel herd and its many young

5

6

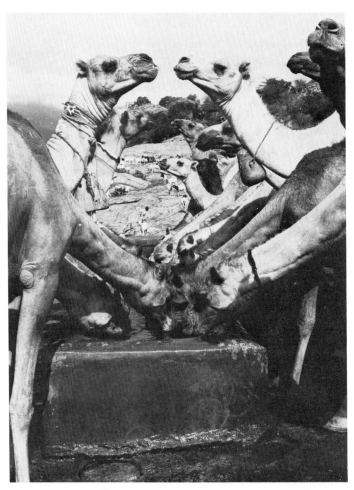

8

9

10

11 Sandy reg in the Zemmour with no vegetation in sight
12 Small thalwegs on a mountain collect rainwater which is funneled to a wadi in the Zemmour. Note the concentration of trees on the dry riverbed.

11

12

13 Inselbergs in the Zemmour
14 *Anabasis aretioides,* a typical hamada plant of the northwestern Sahara. The plants look, and feel, like rocks.

13

14

15 Wadi in the mountains near Beni-Abbès, with relatively dense vegetation of ephemerals, shrubs, and trees.

16 A sandy wadi near a mountainous region with the shrubs *Lasiurus hirsutus* (*left*) and *Retama raetam* (*right*) in the foreground and an *Acacia raddiana* tree on the left.

17 A camel stretching its neck can reach vegetation 3.5 meters above the ground.

18 Camel feeding on an *Acacia* twig with long thorns

15

16

17

18

19 Guarded camels (*left*) meeting unguarded camels, which are in better condition (note their larger humps) because they have had more time to feed.
20 Camel munching on a camel bone. Bones supply calcium and phosphorus and help keep a camel's teeth ground down.
21 *Aristida pungens* steppe with *Acacia ehrenbergiana* tree. Concentration of camel pellets indicates that the tree is a favorite food species.
22 Camel in good condition immediately after drinking

19

20

21

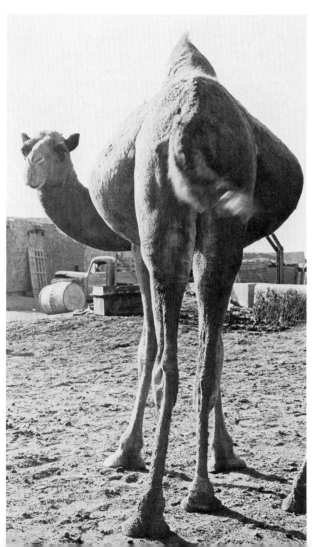

22

23

24

25

23 The hollow behind the ribs of these well-fed camels indicates they are dehydrated and need watering.
24 Camels face the sun during the hottest part of the day, thus exposing as small a surface as possible to the sun.
25 Camels huddling together in a partially shaded area to keep as cool as possible (which also minimizes evaporation).
26 Camels walking single file toward a well in a small oasis
27 Owners usually brand their camels on the neck, face, or hindquarters. Many of the marks represent letters from the Arabic alphabet.

26

27

28 A rutting male in typical posture, grinding its teeth and salivating strongly, approaches some females.

29 Male rubbing his occiput glands on his shoulders—a behavior pattern in aggressive or sexually excited animals.

30 Rutting male beating its tail during urination and standing crosswise to a rival male.

31 With increased excitement, a rutting male spreads its hind legs farther apart and lifts its head higher.

28

29

30

31

32 A camel can open its mouth wider than other ruminants
33 An aggressive male may take a rival's head into its mouth
34 Fighting males attacking each other from the front
35 Fighting males trying to pin each other down by the neck while other camels watch.
36 Fights may end with both camels being asphyxiated if they cannot be separated by camel men.

32

33

34

35

36

37 Rutting male flehmens the urine of a female, lifting his head high and raising his upper lip.

38 Camels copulating

37

38

39 Parturition in a 4-year-old female
40 Newborn hunting for its mother's teats for the first time

39

40

41   A 2-year-old isolated male hybrid shows affection toward Gauthier-Pilters.

42   A 3-day-old foal follows researcher Roswitha Hartung

43   Feet and legs of a camel. The feet have toes instead of hooves. Five callosities are visible, two on the front "knees," two on the upper part of the back legs, and one on the chest.

44   Bactrian camel walking quickly with a pacelike step

41

42

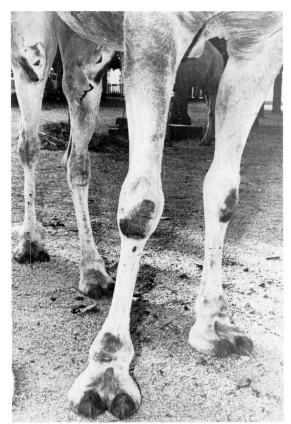

43

44

45 A loaded camel climbing up a steep slope is helped if its head is stretched forward.

46 A Reguibat tribesman with camel stick sitting on a *rahla* saddle.

45

46

47 Mauritanian camel with a typical *rahla* saddle

48 A Tuareg *terik* saddle, which is fastened in front of the hump, gives the rider better control than the *rahla* saddle, in which the rider sits farther back.

48

47

49   A Chaanba woman's saddle
50   A hybrid *Camelus dromedarius* × *C. bactrianus* showing
     the elongated hump.
51   A nomad father sitting with his son after dark
52   Men waiting for tea in the shade of a nomad tent
53   Thousands of nomads come from as far away as 1,000
     kilometers to attend a *shouffan,* a yearly assemblage of
     nomads in southern Morocco for trading and selling
     goods and camels. The nomads feast on camel meat dur-
     ing these gatherings.

49

50

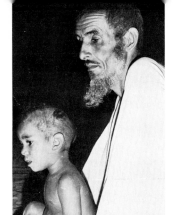

51

52

53

54 Our guide Mokhtar dries camel meat bought at the Char oasis.

55 Camels transporting the gear of a nomad camp during a migration.

56 A camel loaded with goods from a nomad tent

57 The lead rope of a loaded camel is usually tied to its nose ring. The rope around its neck is used to hobble it during rest periods.

54

55

56

57

58 Nomad tents form an oasis of shade in the barren desert
59 A nomad woman sitting in her tent beside her elaborate saddle.

58

59

60 Camels that have died of starvation are usually found in this bizarre position, with their necks bent far back.
61 An Algerian well with a vertical drawing system for use by man rather than camel.

60

61

62

63

64

62 A Mauritanian nomad using a hard wooden pulley to draw water.
63 A slanting tree trunk and pulley in use at a crumbling well.
64 Two pulleys being used simultaneously to draw water
65 This well mouth is so large that sand readily blows into the water; a camel or person could also fall in and drown.
66 All the camels at this well must be watered from a single metal tin.

65

66

67 So many camels can drink at once from a basin this wide that water cannot be drawn fast enough to keep it filled.

68 This camel man must hoist manually in his dellou water he empties into the basin for his camels.

67

68

the foot touches the chest, rubbing the legs against each other as described above, jerking the hind foot forward so that it touches the front legs, and by swishing the tail, either slowly and horizontally or quickly and vertically.

Marking Behavior
It is not surprising that a migratory species such as the camel deposits its urine and feces at random; camels are constantly on the move to find food and water, a practice which does not correlate with territorial behavior. By contrast, South American camelids defecate and urinate in communal piles only at certain places, which is presumably important in identifying the territory of the herd. Vicuñas show a specific "defecation ceremony" (Pilters 1954; Koford 1957). They approach a dung pile, sniff at it, put their forefeet on it, tread up and down alternately, and then turn around and defecate. After defecating they urinate, the females squatting down more and producing a larger stream of urine than the males. They may then turn, sniff, and tread the pile, and turn and void again before walking away. Vicuña-alpaca hybrids and occasionally alpacas show the same behavior pattern of pawing the dung before or after defecation, but llamas, guanacos, and vicuña-llama hybrids do not react to dung piles in this way.

Camels defecate and urinate not only at random places but when standing, walking, feeding, or lying. They have no particular display posture for defecation and—except the rutting male—none for urinating either; they merely raise their tails and perhaps spread apart their hind legs, which tend to be stained with urine. The male urinates backward and more frequently than does the female, producing urine in a thin stream. Urine also plays an important role in his intimidation display during the rutting season. The female either urinates in a trickle or in a gush.

It is possible that the occipital, or poll, glands (which in *Camelus* occur only in the male) play a role in the camel's marking behavior. These glands, situated 5 centimeters below the apex of the head on each side of the midline, are composed of small, independent, curled tubules (Purohit and Singh 1958; Mimram 1962). They increase at puberty and double or triple in size during the rutting season, when the dark, greasy secretion is especially abundant. If a male is castrated, the glands decrease in size and function little. Baskin (1976) noted that rutting males in the Turkmenian deserts show territorial behavior in the well areas, where they are given extra food, by rubbing their heads against vegetation to deposit a strong-smelling secretion. Baskin shows in a photograph a male rubbing his head against the sandy soil while kneeling on his carpal joints. Baskin also saw the male marking with a mixture of sperm and urine while rubbing his abdomen against the soil, sometimes stretching one hind leg backward as if to enlarge the marked area. In Australia, too, Barker (1972) noticed that domesticated rutting males rubbed the back of their heads against posts, depositing a secretion that smelled for days.

We were unable to detect any marking behavior in free-ranging Saharan camels foraging over large areas, perhaps because we mostly studied castrated males and herds outside the rutting season or because trees or other surfaces for rubbing were scarce. We saw camels rub their occiputs against trees when their heads apparently needed scratching, but did not notice any deposits of secretion. In the Iguidi, where there are no trees or bushes in the dunes, camels spent hours rubbing their flanks, shoulders, chins, and occiputs against tamarisk trees growing near wells whenever they came to drink. However, an adult Bactrian male at the Vincennes Zoo in Paris, which was kept alone during rut, frequently rubbed its occiput against the wall near the door leading to the outside enclosure. This whitewashed area became dark brown and smelled strong. When Gauthier-Pilters rubbed her finger over the secretion and held it up to the nose of a tame, nonestrous female, the animal immediately snapped at the finger and gave a cry. Gutknecht (1975) believes the secretion activates estrus in the female.

Aggressive Behavior

Threatening. Except among male rivals during the breeding season, there is little aggressive behavior in free-ranging or in captive camels. In contrast, llamas, at least in captivity, frequently show a number of threatening behavior patterns, such as an aggressive posture with the ears well back, spitting, kicking, jumping, chasing, and making various vocal noises to drive other individuals away from food, a foal, a favorite resting or rolling place, or a rubbing post. Camels in similar situations usually just cry out or snap at an interloper without biting. An adult camels pushes another camel with its lowered head and neck or with its whole body to get it out of the way, seldom jumping at it or kicking it with a foreleg as a lamoid would typically do to a conspecific (in this book we adopt the word "lamoid" to refer to any of the four New World species belonging to the genus *Lama*). Dromedaries may blow out cud when they are excited and cry out, even when they are not ruminating, but unlike llamas and Bactrian camels they do not deliberately spit. Barker (1972) claims that a badly treated camel or one with a sore back might blow out in distress over a liter of partially chewed food.

Camels have a more conspicuous intimidation display than lamoids, employing visual, acoustic, and olfactory signals. If a rutting male sees a rival, he walks toward him, making himself as tall as possible and frequently uttering the rutting cry, a repeated "blo-blo-blo" sound. At each call he lowers his head, then lifts it above the horizontal and bends it backward to display the bushy hair under his chin. (This hair is not present in castrated males or in females.) He does this even if the other male is 100 or more meters away. At the same time he grinds his teeth loudly, perhaps to indicate his predisposition to bite, and salivates heavily (pl. 28). Occasionally he blows the skin bladder or *dulaa* out of his mouth, an activity sometimes seen outside the rutting season. The dulaa is a reddish balloon structure arising from the oroventral part of the soft palate which fills with air from the trachea when the anterior nares are closed (Arnautovic and Abdel Magid 1974). It is present in all adults, but is small and never extruded in females. It increases in length in males during the cool season, being longest (up to 36 centimeters) when the testicles are heaviest (up to 253 grams) (Charnot 1963*b*) and thus undoubtedly is of sexual significance. The Bactrian camel does not seem to have a dulaa (Cauvet 1925–26); during the rutting season it utters a sound similar to the blo-blo-blo of the dromedary while its nostrils and cheeks vibrate strongly. A threatening male also rubs the back of his head against his shoulders (pl. 29). In a region where rubbing surfaces are rare, this behavior pattern has presumably evolved from a body comfort gesture and may also be correlated with marking behavior. It was seen particularly often in captive Bactrian males during the rutting season. After these males sniffed at a male dromedary's mouth through the crack in a door, they rubbed their heads against their shoulders, ground their teeth, and salivated copiously. The youngest camel we observed rubbing its head against its shoulders was a 16-day-old

Bactrian male. The secretion of the occipital glands seems to play an important role in encounters between rivals, because it increases with excitement (Baskin 1976).

When two or more rival male dromedaries approach each other, they stop several meters apart, spread their hind legs wide, and urinate on their tails, which they hold forward between their legs. (The camel's penis directs urine backward, facilitating this action.) Then they swing their wet tails upward so that their tails repeatedly strike their backs with an audible noise, dispersing urine in a radius of several meters (pl. 30). The more excited a male is, the wider he spreads his legs, the more he bends his knees, and the more frequently and intensely he beats his tail following urination (pl. 31), and sometimes defecation. Tail beating sometimes occurs without urination or defecation. This intimidation display usually ends with one of the males retreating.

If a member of a bachelor herd approaches a rutting male and his females, he is generally chased by the male without being given any threat display or warning. The male stretches his neck forward as he pursues the presumptuous rival, and only after he returns to his females does he give the complete, and sometimes only a partial, intimidation display—if he does so at all. Perhaps this acts as a release mechanism for the male. During the breeding season rutting males tolerate young males in their herd until they are 2 years old. However, if the young males play-fight at this time, a mature male approaches them in the typical display posture and the young immediately stop their game. In zoos, guanaco and llama males must be separated from their fathers by the time they are 2, and vicuña males before they are 1.

Fighting. Barker (1972) noted that a rutting male looking for a fight paces in circles with his chin close to the ground, frothing at the mouth with his lips spread out at the side. After two rutting males have found and threatened each other, and neither retreats, they will fight. Relatively few fights occur in the field, because herds are guarded during the rutting season; if males start quarreling, the herders immediately separate them with whips and yelling. However, there may not always be enough men to control the camels. Fights among males may also occur outside the rutting season; in fact fights between nonrutting males, together with intimidation behavior, were observed more often than the rutting fights, usually at wells, where males from different groups were likely to encounter each other.

All the efforts of fighting camelids, except thrashing actions with forefeet, are aimed at toppling an opponent and crushing him, preferably at the neck to asphyxiate him. Two males usually first snap at each other's front and hind legs, less often at the head, neck, or throat, while at the same time they try to force down the other's neck. A camel can open its mouth wide enough to take its rival's head between its jaws (pls. 32 and 33). Occasionally camels snap at each other's flank, hump, tail, or testicles. Their bites can cause serious wounds because of the sharp upper incisors and upper and lower canines, a complement of teeth not present in noncamelid ruminants. Between attempts to bite, camels roar loudly.

Lamoids tend to attack each other from the front, jumping at each other simultaneously. We observed this fight pattern only in young camels when they were play-fighting and in adults in only a tentative way. Camels not only attack each other from the front (pl. 34), but also work their way to a side position where each tries to lean with his chest or to reach with his neck over the other's neck or back to bite at his legs. The "under" male retaliates by withdrawing his legs, bending them, and pushing. In all but one fight we observed, the males eventually broke away or one retreated.

The one serious fight was observed by Gauthier-Pilters in July in southern Algeria, between two males of equal strength. They belonged to different groups, which met at a well where several herds had gathered, including mixed groups, bachelor groups, and small groups of females with young. This contest showed clearly that fights can be serious enough to kill not just one but both combatants (pls. 35 and 36). Male A, while biting at the carpal joints of male B, unbalanced B, and before A could withdraw his head it was pulled down under the neck of B as B fell. Male A was pulled down and in falling caught the neck of B under his chest, so that neither animal could move once they were sprawled on the ground. While they struggled for air, their dulaas protruded. Fortunately six men were able to separate the animals before they suffocated.

Public camel fights are still organized in some countries, such as Tunisia, Turkey, and Afghanistan, but because the camels are valuable they are either muzzled or the fight is stopped before serious injury occurs. According to the nomads, rutting camels can also be dangerous to man, biting him, pushing him to the ground, and even crushing him to death. In the Mulhouse Zoo a keeper was seriously hurt by a male that seized his head with his teeth, crushing the man's maxillary sinus and injuring his facial nerve (Gutknecht 1975).

We never saw fights between female camels or between males and females. In the lamoids a high-ranking female in the wild or in captivity may attack a young male by kicking him with both front legs alternately and then chasing him away; such behavior has not been observed in camels.

Little quarreling occurs among castrated males, especially if they are working camels. In a group of 40 nonworking castrated males, one individual approached another to usurp its resting place for sand bathing. The lying male immediately jumped to his feet and snapped at the intruder, which reacted by leaning over the back of the other and snapping at his legs, thus showing a typical fighting behavior pattern. When meeting another male, a castrated male sometimes protrudes its dulaa and utters the same sound a rutting male makes.

Courtship During the rutting season, and outside it as well, a male camel often sniffs at the genital region, urine, or feces of a female, then performs the typical flehmen gesture of artiodactyls by lifting his head and curling back his upper lip (pl. 37). In addition, he may bite the female, either on the vulvar lips or at the back of the hump, sometimes hard enough to draw blood (Khan and Kohli 1973c). Flehmen occurs also in females and castrated males in response not only to urine and feces but also to the smell of such things as tobacco, ether, or a person's breath; it is usually followed by yawning. These latter stimuli have provoked flehmen in 1-day-old camels, but feces and urine do so only when the young are about 3 weeks old. Flehmen is more marked in camels than in lamoids, where in the former it occurs more frequently and each sequence lasts longer. In lamoids captive females flehmen less than captive males, and in both sexes the reaction is only provoked by urine and feces.

We never saw a male switching his tail up and down while urinating as a prelude to copulation, but this may be because we observed few copulations in the field. Gutknecht (1975), however, observed pre-copulation tail switching in captive Bactrian camels. When a dromedary male approaches a female, he may utter the same blo-blo-blo sound with his head lifted high as he does when meeting a rival, eventually protruding his dulaa and rubbing his occiput against his shoulders. One captive dromedary separated from his herd during the rutting season protruded his dulaa merely on hearing the call of a female he could not see.

Unlike lamoids, female camels often spread their hind legs apart and, while urinating slowly, present their genital region to a male. They may also rub their sides against him. A captive female that was ignored by a male cried out, rolled on the floor, pushed him, urinated at frequent intervals, pawed the ground, jumped, kicked, and lay down repeatedly in front of him.

Copulation   Camelids are the only ungulates that copulate in a couched position. A female in estrus generally lies down spontaneously if a male approaches. If she does not do so, the male forces her to lie down by (1) passing his nose along her head, neck, and side to the genital region, where he noses and rubs his neck against her vulva; (2) putting his neck on the neck or lumbar region of the female and pushing her down with his full weight; and (3) if she is still erect, biting her on the stifle joints, which keeps her from walking and causes her to lie down. If a female runs away, he will chase her with his neck stretched forward, as he does when chasing a rival.

Copulation has been described by Gauthier-Pilters and by other zoologists (Singh and Prakash 1964; Khan and Kohli 1973c). The male mounts the female by placing his front legs on either side of her shoulders and his hind legs on either side of her pelvis and then sits on her so that his sternal callosity rests on the rear part of her hump (pl. 38). His front legs thus remain extended, feet on the ground, while his hind legs are completely folded, with the area from the heel to the hock resting on the ground. His head and neck are stretched straight and held high above the neck of the female. The total copulation time lasts about 10–20 minutes, with ejaculation occurring three or four times during that period. During copulation the female grunts occasionally and bites playfully at the male's neck. The male also cries out in a muted voice, dribbles saliva from his mouth, and blows out his dulaa. After copulation the male generally falls sideways from the female before standing up. Khan and Kohli (1973c) not only observed copulation in eight male camels as noted above, but collected semen from males for artificial insemination (1973a).

Mathur (1960) found a small number of male camels exhibiting satyriasis, or excessive sexual desire. During the rutting season these males made every effort to service receptive females, even killing other animals or men who stood in their way. They rubbed their heads often in disseminating the profuse discharge of the occipital glands, tried to escape from captivity or their work, frothed, grunted, blew out the dulaas, and ate so little that they became weak and emaciated. Such males may service as many as 70 females in a season.

Copulation of camels is rarely seen in the wild; indeed, nomads claim that camels rarely mate when people are near. However, if a rutting male encounters new females, he tries to copulate right away; after the long recent drought period, when most females had not been in heat for at least 2 years, Gauthier-Pilters in 1976 often saw camels copulating in the midst of people and other animals. A mating couple stimulates other conspecifics, which surround the mating couple and nuzzle at their mouths and anal regions. In Turkmenia, female camels have been observed to lie down close to a mating pair or to try to mount one of them (Baskin 1976), a behavior pattern also noted in young lamoids and in female lamoids in heat.

In regions where both dromedaries and Bactrian camels live, mating between them is hazardous. If the male is a dromedary, he may injure the second hump of the female, thus causing her to roll onto her side and risk being injured further by the male; if the male is a Bactrian, he may lose his balance during copulation because his legs are shorter than those of the dromedary.

The rutting season varies with region and is apparently correlated with the wet season; in North Africa it falls largely between December and May. In Mauritania we encountered newborn foals in August, so mating also occurs in the summer (the gestation period lasting about 13 months). According to Curasson (1947) and Leonard (1894), mating may occur at any season if the food supply is good, although in zoos it usually takes place in the spring. In 1969 the *International Zoo Yearbook* conducted a survey of breeding in captive camelids (Schmidt 1973). For 47 births recorded for the dromedary in 11 zoos in the

Northern Hemisphere, 72 percent fell between February and May, with other births in small numbers occurring in all other months but November. In the Pretoria Zoo, in the Southern Hemisphere, most births were recorded between August and November, 6 months out of phase (Brand 1963). Asdell (1964) records that, of 166 Bactrian camel births, 66 percent occurred in April and May, with none occurring from September to December—a more limited mating season than for dromedaries, even though the domesticated Bactrian camel in the USSR has estrous cycles all year around. Three hybrid camels were born in March and April. Most mating occurs in India from November to February; in Pakistan from December to March; in Israel from January to March; and in Somalia in April and May (Novoa 1970; Schmidt 1973). Foaling in winter or spring would seem to promote survival, coinciding as it does with periods of maximum vegetation. Captive South American camelids gave birth to young in all months, but especially in the summer and autumn.

Male camels become sexually mature when they are 4 or 5 years old, and females when they are 3 or 4, although they are often not bred until they are older. Females may continue to produce young until they are 30 (Novoa 1970).

Gestation   During the rutting season, a female camel is receptive for 3 or 4 days or more, followed by 10–20 days of anestrus. If she does not conceive during one period of heat, the cycle is repeated (Novoa 1970). Studies of camel viscera in Cairo showed that the ovaries changed seasonally, with the greatest ovarian activity between December and May, although there was a sudden drop in activity in February (Shalash 1965). Corpora lutea apparently only occur with pregnancy or pseudopregnancy, so it may be that ovulation is stimulated by copulation. Females in heat often stay near the males and are restless, with swelling of, and discharge from, the vulva. Males are sexually active throughout the rutting season, when their testes increase greatly in weight (Charnot 1963*b*; Bodenheimer 1957; Abdel-Raouf, Fateh el-Bab, and Owaida 1975).

The fertility rate of camels is low compared with other domestic animals—only 43 percent or less in one study (Yuzlikaev and Akhmediev, in Novoa 1970). Sources of infertility include the failure of follicles to develop, embryonic mortality, and anatomical abnormalities in the female (Shalash 1965; Novoa 1970). However, in a study of

227 pregnancies in India, only 22 fetuses were aborted. Of the 205 live births, 101 were males and 104 females (Bhargava et al. 1963; Sharma et al. 1963). There was no twinning.

The gestation period of camels varies considerably according to various zoo keepers, perhaps correlated with the state of lactation of the mother (Hediger 1952). It is difficult to predict when parturition will occur because a female copulates many times during the rutting season. In one study in which 33 females were serviced only once, the mean length of pregnancy, including the day of mating and the day of calving, was 389.9 ± 2.1 days (Mehta, Prakash, and Singh 1962). Gestation period did not vary significantly with sex of the calf, sequence of calving, or month of parturition. Extremes given in the literature are 308 days (Schmidt 1973) and 440 days (Grzimek 1968). The average gestation period for 850 Bactrian camel births was 406 days (Novoa, in Schmidt 1973). Pregnant, unlike nonpregnant, females curl up their tails when a man or a male camel approaches; the male camel may sniff at them or only utter a call from nearby.

In the northwestern Sahara most females give birth in January, February, or March, more rarely in April, and only exceptionally in December. They usually become pregnant every 2 years, although on very rich pastures they may conceive again a month or so after parturition. This was true in Australia where abundant mulga and saltbush provided excellent fodder (Barker 1972). Females may also conceive shortly after the death of a newborn. This was observed by a zoo keeper at the Vincennes Zoo, who noted that a female was mounted by a male the same day she gave birth to a foal that died. She gave birth again 391 days later, after a pregnancy during which no other copulations were observed. In the Sahara females with newborn foals are usually kept apart from the breeding male and his harem.

Parturition Just prior to parturition the female's vulva and udder swell, the latter extended with milk so that the teats point down and forward. The sacrosciatic ligaments on either side of the root of her tail relax, forming two grooves. During contractions the female is restless, eating little or nothing. At intervals she may lie down on her sternum or on her side with her legs extended (Prakash and Singh 1962). Gauthier-Pilters assisted in the field at the birth of a foal to a 4-year-old primipara (pl. 39). The evening before parturition, the female moved about 300 meters away from the guarded herd. The next morning, with the help of the herder, she gave birth to the foal in a few minutes while standing, without making any vocal noises. The waterbag appeared first, followed by the forelegs with the foal's head between them. Even before the foal had dropped to the ground, breaking the umbilical cord, it made a humming noise as it was eased from the vulva by the herder pulling on its leg. Prakash and Singh (1962), who observed 45 females giving birth in India, found that unassisted labor lasted a mean of 336 minutes (range 120–600 minutes). The average time required for expulsion of the fetal membranes and diffuse placenta following birth was 117 minutes (range 65–300 minutes). In only one case did a female require human assistance during labor. Along with suids, the camelids are the only artiodactyls that do not lick their young following parturition, but only sniff them extensively. They do not eat the afterbirth.

Newborn Camels   Camels are large at birth. The mean birth weight of 134 newborn calves at Bikaner, India, was 37.3 kilograms (range 26.4–52.3 kilograms), with males not weighing significantly more than females. The height of the top of the hump from the ground in a standing calf averaged 123 centimeters in 40 males and 118 centimeters in 40 females. Bhargava, Sharma, and Singh (1965) made 15 other measurements of these calves. Like the adults, the young can be all shades, from white to dark brown.

Behavior of Newborn   The following motor patterns appeared spontaneously in the neonate whose birth Gauthier-Pilters witnessed: chewing at 10 minutes; grinding its teeth and shaking its head at 18 minutes; shifting on the ground at 74 minutes; vacuum-activity sucking at 100 minutes; kicking at 156 minutes; yawning at 160 minutes; urinating at 185 minutes; tail beating at 198 minutes; rubbing its neck against its mother at 294 minutes; body shaking at 304 minutes; and rolling on the ground at 85 hours. In the first hour it emitted five different vocalizations. Other motor patterns, such as scratching, nibbling, snapping, jumping at others, and mounting, appear at variable times.

When it was 8 minutes old, the foal crouched upright, and 2 minutes later it attempted to stand, although it was unable to do so. After nearly 1½ hours it tried again, this time performing the second phase of getting up by lifting its back several times while resting on the carpal joints. The third phase soon followed: it put one foot on the ground and 5 minutes later it stood for the first time, but it fell down again a few seconds later. After this, the mother periodically sniffed at her young, at which times it tried to get up, but it succeeded in balancing itself with wide-spread hind legs only after another 45 minutes. Thus, 2½ hours elapsed after its birth before it could stand for 2 minutes. It took a few uncoordinated steps at 3½ hours, fairly regular steps at 5 hours, and was able to pace normally on its second day of life. If a young is born to a female during a journey, it is carried on a camel's back until the evening's rest, and is expected to follow its dam the next day (Jennison 1928).

When the foal was 3 hours old, it got up fairly quickly and started to search for the udder, first under its mother's neck, then in the angle between her neck and forelegs, then in the angle between her forelegs and sternal callosity, shortly after that in the angle between her abdomen and hind legs, and finally in the correct place (pl. 40). However, it only sucked for the first time 1 hour later, nearly 5 hours after birth. A neonate may suck sooner when it is helped by man. Instinct probably directs the young to search for the teat at some angle, as neonates in zoos sometimes search extensively in a corner, or between the head and neck or arm and body of a human observer, even if the mother is present. Of the 12 neonates Gauthier-Pilters observed almost all searched for the teat in the same places and in the same order, without any help from the mother. Lynch and Alexander (1973) observed that newborn sheep and goats are attracted to any tall vertical surface and to the shade under a low object, and that they will follow the nearest large moving object. In one zoo a newborn camel was removed from a wet, unheated stall and kept from its experienced mother for 3 days while it was bottle fed with the mother's colostrum (Davidson 1974). The mother then accepted the young, despite its 3-day absence, and raised it successfully.

While the young sucks, its mother nuzzles and licks its anal region, a behavior pattern present in many mammals which stimulates defecation and urination. She does this not only when she is suckling but at any time when the young is ready to defecate. The mothers of all camelids also nibble at their young's mouth with their lips, tongue, and teeth, flicking their tongue in and out. This "gesture of affection" is made by the mother soon after her young is born, and is first reciprocated by the young when it is 2 or 3 days old. An isolated 2-year-old hybrid camel at the Rotterdam Zoo made a similar gesture each time it nuzzled Gauthier-Pilter's face or hands at the fence of his enclosure (pl. 41).

On its first day of life, a newborn camel may make a scratching gesture with its hind foot toward its foreleg without actually making contact. Scratching and nibbling are less frequent in camels than in lamoids, whose motor patterns mature more quickly although not always in the same order. Even a 2-month-old camel may occasionally scratch "in the air" with its hind foot toward the foreleg, whereas a lamoid will routinely be able to scratch its foreleg with the hind foot at 1 week.

On its second day of life, a newborn camel observed in the field sucked every hour or two and urinated about every half-hour, often while lying down. During its first few days a young will suck all sorts of objects (Baskin 1976), and even foals a few months old will suck a person's fingers held near the foal's mouth, or the penis of another foal. On the morning of one neonate's second day, its mother moved as much as 50 meters from the foal, and in the afternoon as much as 90 meters. They called to each other rarely, but when the young cried out the mother immediately joined it, smelling it all over. The young followed its mother, but it still followed people, too, which it had done for the first time when it was 10 hours old (pl. 42). Baskin (1976) also commented on this following behavior in 2- and 3-day-old foals. At 2 days the foal is fairly active, jumping about, stretching itself as adults do, often kicking with its hind legs, rubbing its head and flanks against its mother, and rolling on the ground. Mostly, however, it lies down, yawning even more than it did the day before.

On its third day a foal first jumps playfully at its mother, then at people, snapping its jaws in the air. They do this quite often. The mother will now feed 100 meters or more from its young and does not pay much attention to its calls, unlike the previous day, unless there seems to be some "danger," when she again joins it. When the mother of one foal we observed wandered almost out of sight of its resting young, the foal got to its feet spontaneously and lay down close to Gauthier-Pilters. Thus, unlike many ruminants such as the wildebeest, the young camel does not always stay close to its mother, and in fact may lie a considerable distance from her, as a deer fawn will, even though in the desert a young camel is not well camouflaged. It has been thousands of years since camels have had to deal with predators, which may account for the young's behavior. At night, when the mother lies down to rest, her young lies down beside and parallel to her. If there is possible danger, the mother will stand in front of her young and paw lightly at its back, which brings it to its feet. The foal also stands up if she paws the ground next to it or comes close to it and gives a long, low cry. When the foal is a few days old, it lies down for the first time facing the sun, as adults generally do. Unlike adults, however, it holds its neck straight up.

When mother and foal rejoin the herd after a few days, the yearlings come to inspect the foal extensively. Mother and foal then join in the normal activities of the group, keeping in touch with each other when they are apart mainly by voice. If the foal becomes completely separated from its mother, it will emit loud and continuous distress calls with its mouth open, one call lasting perhaps 5 seconds or more, while running from one animal to another, often exciting other young to run about too. Its mother does not always answer. Even when she is standing nearby her foal may not recognize her, and may run in the opposite direction until it is alerted by her call. If the mother approaches her young without making a vocal noise, it may flee as it would from a strange camel. One-year-old camels may also search for their mothers by calling loudly. A mother and young deliberately separated by men may call to each other for days. In fact, herding of mother camels in Turkmenistan is facilitated by separating the foals from their mothers; the mothers always return from pasturing to the place where their young last sucked (Baskin 1976), just as they do in northern Kenya.

In Kenya, where the nomads make extensive use of camel milk, the mothers are taken to pasture without their young a few weeks after parturition. At this time the mother will give deep roars and hang back on the way to the pasture, often looking behind her. She will continue to do this for about 6 weeks. The mother and young remain together during the night for the first 4–5 months, and then for only part of the night after that. When a mother and young come together at a well, the nomads put mud on the female's udder to prevent the young from sucking.

Even on their first day of life, camelids show interest in food by smelling and nibbling at plants; we observed a 1-day-old zoo camel chewing with grinding noises on a stalk. The camel foal in the desert starts feeding at 2 weeks of age and by the time it is 1½ or 2 months old it is eating regularly. When camels in the Sahara are born, the herds are not yet being watered, so it is difficult to tell when a young would start drinking water. A zoo camel drank when it was 25 days old, but it may well have drunk sooner.

Duration of lactation in camels varies with the individual, the breed, the food supply, and the milk demands of the nomads. The daily production is about 6 liters over a 9–18-month period (Frädrich-Leupold 1971). The young are generally weaned by man completely when they are 1 year old, earlier than they would be naturally, so that their owners can have more milk for themselves. When the young are 7–10 months old, the nomads of the western Sahara prevent the young from sucking during the day by wrapping the mother's udder in a straw net. Later they put a piece of wood into the lip of the foal so that it will hurt its mother when it tries to suck, and the mother will chase it away. Despite man's precautions, a camel will occasionally still try to suck when it is 2 or 3 years old. A female will always chase away foals that are not her own. At the London Zoo, young camels first begin to eat vegetation when they are about 3 months old and are weaned when they are 1–1½ years old (personal communication from zoo official, 1977). In northern Kenya, where most of the camel milk is used for human consumption, the young grow very slowly during their first few months, only reaching normal species weight after the rainy season, when most of them are 10 months old. The mortality of these young is very high.

Playing   Young camels play less than young lamoids, which often race about during their first few weeks. However, camel foals will try to mount their mothers on their first day of life, whereas this behavior was first observed in 11 captive lamoids when they were 6 days old. Before sexual maturity, both male and female young often try to mount their mothers as soon as they lie down after grazing, and try to mount other camels too, which usually chase them away. Sometimes female captive adults try to mount other females, behavior that is rarely seen in captive female lamoids.

When they are only a few days old, young camels are already snapping and jumping at their mothers; real play-fighting with their peers begins at 4 or 5 weeks. In lamoids such play-fighting is usually intense, with frequent jumping against each other and quarreling accompanied by spitting and threatening gestures, but in camels it consists usually of snapping at each other's legs and bodies, pushing, and scrambling about. Play-fighting was most often seen in yearling males, but it also occurred in 5- or 6-year-old adult males outside the rutting season. It differed in intensity from serious fighting, with one male perhaps holding the other's leg between his teeth for a few seconds instead of actually biting the leg. During the rutting season, the vocal cries that accompany play-fighting in the young annoy the rutting male, which hurries forward to stop their activities.

Camels in zoos as well as in the field chase and play not only with each other but with people as well, pushing them, jumping toward them, and snapping at them. Barker (1972) saw Australian camel foals playing with donkeys. The foals tried to catch a donkey by the ear, and reached over its back to nip its front feet. Some old camels even went to sleep while goats and children climbed up and down their necks. A neonate that Gauthier-Pilters observed in the field began to play with her when it was 3 days old. Older foals, which often stayed together in the pasture, also liked to gather around her to nibble at anything they could reach, or take her hat, pencils, or notebooks away. One 7-month-old female that had lost its mother 2 months earlier came to Gauthier-Pilters when its herd visited the well and spontaneously lay down beside her with its head on her legs, obviously enjoying being scratched. None of the female camels in the herd would let the motherless foal suck. One 2-year-old captive male hybrid tried to play with Gauthier-Pilters almost every time he saw her approaching his enclosure, jumping at the fence, snapping at her arm, and playfully biting at her face.

7 Locomotion and Loads

Camels are unique because they are the only species that generally paces (i.e., the foreleg and hind leg on one side—"unilateral legs"—move forward simultaneously and alternately with those on the other side) rather than trots (the foreleg on one side moves forward simultaneously with the diagonally opposite hind leg) when moving at a moderate speed. Other mammals that can pace are horses, dogs, and bears, but they more commonly trot. Indeed, in bears the pace is generally a transitional gait occasionally used when going from the walk to the lumbering gallop.

The camel is not among the fastest mammals known, but it is famous for its great endurance in the hot, arid regions in which it lives. Denis (1970) gives numerous examples of its prowess in the Sahara: if necessary, camels can travel 150 kilometers in 15–20 hours; they can cover the 300 kilometers between Cairo and Gaza in 2 days; they have journeyed alone 640 kilometers in 4 days and 160 kilometers in 16 hours; camels carrying passengers have traveled 80 kilometers in 6 hours and 150 kilometers in 13 hours; and they have been clocked at more than 5.5 kilometers in 14 minutes and, in one instance, at 80.5 kilometers in 4 hours and 20 minutes. Denis also cites the 1913 expedition of Captain Charlet, who led a company of 70 meharistes more than 800 kilometers in 11 days without losing one camel. After all such feats of exertion and endurance, camels need a long period of rest.

In Australia, where in the past mounted camels often traveled 80–90 kilometers in 1 day, record performances were 144 kilometers in 10 hours and 448 kilometers in 3 days. In a 1-day horse-versus-camel race in the 1890s over a 176-kilometer course, a horse won by a narrow margin, but on the following day the horse died while the camel returned to the starting point of the race (McKnight 1969).

Feats of endurance are not always forced on camels. Barker (1972) reports that once, after his camels had worked all day hauling goods, he freed them for the night. Rather than feed and rest, they walked off down the road unattended and were found the next morning grazing in good pasture 40 kilometers away. We noticed similar behavior in 1973 with our four hired camels, which sometimes, even when their front legs were tied loosely together in the evening after they had worked all day, were found the next morning at a well or in a pasture 10 kilometers or more away.

Legs and Feet   The legs and feet of the camel are not like those of other ungulates. Although the camel belongs to the order Artiodactyla, whose other ruminating members all have cloven hooves, the camel's feet are not hooves but rather large pads with two anterior toenails (numbers 3 and 4 of the basic pentadactyl limb). The front feet (about 18 centimeters long × 19 centimeters broad) are larger than the hind feet (about 16 × 17 centimeters), probably because, given the long neck of the camel, they support a greater proportion of the animal's weight. Both are large, which helps prevent the camel from sinking deep into soft sand. The stance of the camel is plantigrade to digitigrade rather than unguligrade, as in other ruminants, with cushions and elastic structures under the diverging phalanges, which adapt the foot well for soft ground (Arnautovic and Abdalla 1969b) (pl. 43). The sole is placed down flat on the ground during a stride as the camel shifts its weight onto the foot, but it pushes off from each foot with the toes. The sole of the foot is thick and flexible enough that the camel can step without much discomfort on small pebbles, but it prefers to follow winding trails where there are no loose stones. Camels are almost helpless in mud, but their feet are not adapted to rough, hard ground either; if they have to walk long distances on such surfaces, their soles may crack and bleed so that leather patches have to be sewn over them for protection (Pond 1957). The extra-tough feet of some breeds of camels, such as those of the Hoggar, are adapted to stony ground.

Adaptation is evident not only in the camel's feet but in its long legs too. The fibula is reduced and the radius and ulna are fused proximally, while the metacarpals and metatarsals are fused partially into a cannon bone resembling an inverted Y.

Gaits   Dagg's original reason for coming to the desert was to study the camel's three gaits, walk, pace, and gallop, in order to compare them with those of other artiodactyls, especially the giraffe—the mammal most like the camel in shape and habitat (Dagg 1974). With their long legs, both the camel and the giraffe put the hind foot on the ground ahead of where the front foot on the same side was planted (fig. 9). By contrast, in the tracks of most ungulates, the hind hoof lands more or less on top of the front hoof-mark, thereby obscuring it.

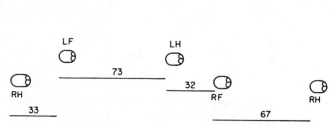

Fig. 9   Pattern of footprints of a walking camel, with distances between the prints in centimeters. R = right; L = left; H = hind; F = front.

At first, Dagg's field research on camel gaits involved mainly filming camels from the side as they walked, paced, or galloped. She saw camels pacing only when men whipped them away from wells, and galloping only when the whipping was especially violent. Most of the time at the wells, and always away from the wells, the camels moved from place to place at a slow steady walk. This walk was of interest because, like the giraffe, the camel swings the legs on one side of the body forward more nearly si-multaneously than other mammals (Dagg and de Vos 1968) (pl. 44). This type of movement is very different from that of the white-tailed deer (*Odocoileus virginianus*), which begins to move the front leg on one side forward as the hind leg on the same side is about to land on the spot the front leg is leaving (fig. 10). This is illustrated in figure 11, which gives the percentage of time an animal spends on each combination of supporting legs during a stride.

The walk. Dagg was able to film and later analyze hun-dreds of strides of camels walking, more than had ever before been analyzed during research on a single species' movements. With such a wealth of material she was able

Fig. 10   Walking camel and white-tailed deer at the instant the right hind foot is placed on the ground. (Drawing by D. Leach.)

to compare the walks of our four hired camels, loaded and unloaded, both among themselves and with other camels. The walking patterns of the adults were statistically similar, but they were different from those of animals pulling water at wells and of young camels (table 15). Support of the body by lateral legs was employed most by the young (to 6 months) camels (44 percent), which had proportionally the longest legs, second most by the yearling camels (41 percent), and next most by the adult camels (33 percent). This type of walk, which is particularly suitable for long-legged individuals because the legs on one side never hit each other as they swing forward, is shared by the other camelids (Dagg 1979). Camels pulling water used the unilateral stance least because they needed firm traction to carry out their work. Unlike the other camels, camels pulling water used diagonally supporting legs a significant amount of the time, and used three supporting legs even more. The use of four supporting legs for balance during a walking stride was fairly common in young but not in adult camels.

Working camels walk at a speed of about 5 kilometers

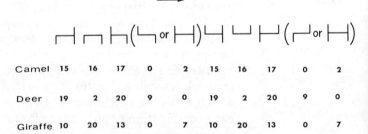

Fig. 11   The sequence of supporting legs in three walking artiodactyls, with the numbers representing the percentage of time spent on each combination of legs. Horizontal lines represent the body, vertical lines the legs. Arrow indicates the direction of motion. Deer and giraffe data from Dagg and Foster (1976, p. 96).

Table 15   Average Percentage of Time during a Stride Spent on Supporting Combinations of Legs for Various Types of Camels Walking on Flat Ground

Combination of Supporting Legs	Camels under 6 mo	Yearling Camels*	Adult Camels*	Adult Camels Pulling Up Water from Well*
Unilateral legs on ground	44	41	33	22
One front leg off ground	25	28	34	37
Four legs on ground	9	5	3	†
Diagonal legs on ground	0	0	†	7
One hind leg off ground	22	26	30	34
Number of strides analyzed	39.5	58	387	55.5

*Yearling camels, adult camels, and adult camels pulling up water from wells have statistically different types of walks (p<.01, χ^2 test).
†Value less than 0.5% but greater than 0.

per hour, or 40 strides per minute, but nonworkers walk even more slowly. When the support pattern of adult camels was analyzed for changes with speed, it was clear that in relatively fast walks unilateral supporting legs were used for much longer periods than in slower walks, while three supporting legs were used less. The faster any animal goes, the less time it has its feet on the ground and the less support it needs.

The significant use of unilateral supporting legs in a camel's walking stride is probably related to its habitat for two reasons. Most important, because of the open desert in which camels live, there is little danger that they will be ambushed by predators, so they can use a walking pattern that is not particularly stable but is very effective, allowing the muscles on one side of the body to work almost in unison to pull the legs forward. This contrasts with the diagonal, very stable walk of the woodland deer, which allows it to spring away at the first sign of danger. Second, because the ground is flat, the unstable but effective walk of the camel is no great hindrance. With rough terrain, as is sometimes found in the deer's habitat, a stable gait is important to enable it to keep its balance. It has been wrongly said that riding a camel can make one "seasick," for in reality the camel's walk is very smooth. An untried rider may, however, develop saddle sores at the base of the spine.

The camel's main force of locomotion is in the forequarters, rather than, as in the horse, the hindquarters, so that when a camel comes to a hill it "pulls" its body up slowly, instead of accelerating and pushing itself up quickly as a horse does (Fraguier 1955). The camel takes smaller rather than fewer steps as it climbs (pl. 45). If a sandy hill is very steep, a pack camel may drop to its front knees so that its load remains more or less level. Coming down a steep hill, a camel may lower its hindquarters so that its hind legs are half folded, and may go faster than a horse.

The pace. The pace is the common fast gait of the camel, with which it can move at a steady speed for many hours. In the French camel corps, Denis (1970) records that three different pacing speeds were recognized. In the footprints of a camel moving at a *slow pace*, the hind foot fell behind the front one on the same side of the body, which indicated that the camel was traveling about 7–9 kilometers per hour. If it was lightly loaded, it could continue at this speed for 10–20 hours. At a *medium pace*, in which the camel's hind footprint covered the front footprint, its speed was 10–12 kilometers per hour. At a *fast pace*, in which the hind footprint fell in front of the front one, the camel traveled 16–20 kilometers per hour. The fastest speed was about 25 kilometers per hour, but this could only be sustained for 1 hour or at the most 2. After that time the animal had to rest and recuperate.

The pace is a symmetrical gait in which the camel's legs move unilaterally in much the same rhythm seen in trotting horses, whose diagonal legs, however, move together (fig. 12). A pacing camel is usually supported by two lateral legs at a time, but at a slow pace it may also be supported for a short time by all four legs, and at a fast pace it may be unsupported by any legs for a fraction of a second at a time (fig. 13). In Dagg's study, 83 percent of the time of each stride of a pacing camel was spent on unilateral legs, 1 percent on all four legs, and 2 percent on no legs at all. The rest of the time was spent either on one or on three legs. The hind legs were on the ground more than the front legs, perhaps because slightly more propulsion for the gait came from the hindquarters than from the forequarters. The faster a camel paced, the less time it spent on three or four legs and the more time it was supported by only one leg, or none. In the pace the body swings noticeably from side to side as the weight of the animal is supported first

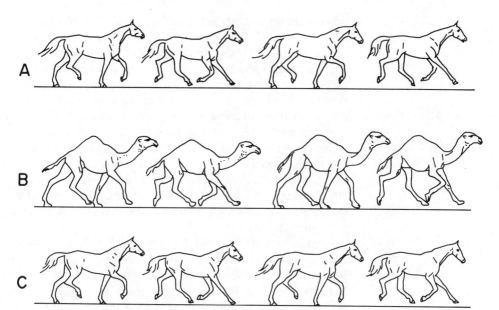

Fig. 12 Sequence of supporting legs of trotting and pacing horse and pacing camel. *A* = trotting horse; *B* = pacing camel; *C* = pacing horse. (Drawing by R. A. Alexander.)

by the legs on one side of the body and then by those on the other side, but this lateral movement is checked somewhat by the weight of the neck and head, which are carried fairly low. The pace does not allow an animal to turn as quickly as it can during a trot, but in open country where visibility is good, maneuverability is not so important.

The gallop. An asymmetrical fast gait in which the body is supported during a stride by any number of legs or by none at all, the gallop is almost never employed by camels, except for the playful young, which is not surprising since camels have few or no predators and since the temperature is often too hot for excessive activity. We only saw this gait

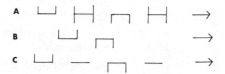

Fig. 13 Usual combinations of supporting legs used by camel in pacing stride. *Horizontal lines* = body; *vertical lines* = legs; *arrow* = direction of motion; *A* = slow pace; *B* = medium pace; *C* = fast pace.

when a man viciously whipped a camel away from a well; then the animal soon slowed to a pace, and then to a walk. In the galloping strides analyzed by Dagg, the camels usually were supported by at least one leg, so their speed was not very fast, but they were not supported by three or four legs to any extent, so their strides were not unduly slow either. In the galloping strides, which lasted 0.4–0.7 seconds each, the feet were placed on the ground in rotary order rather than in the transverse order used by horses; the camel's footfall was thus right hind, left hind, left front, right front, and so on. In the fastest galloping strides, front and hind feet were never on the ground simultaneously, although they sometimes were during slow galloping strides.

It takes an excellent rider to stay on a galloping camel, because not only does the rider lack stirrups and reins but he must give his mount great leeway with the nose rope so that its head can move up and down with each stride. Mounted camels have been whipped into a gallop for as much as a kilometer, but this is rare (Denis 1970).

Evolution of Gaits

The primary gait of the camel in the desert is the walk, with which it covers great distances to find food. Under natural conditions it seldom uses a faster gait, because of the excessive heat and the lack of predators. The pacelike walk motion of the camel, in that it sacrifices maneuverability and stability for freedom of swing for the legs and hence length of stride, is well adapted to the desert, where the terrain is flat and visibility is great. The pace evolved instead of the trot presumably for the same reasons and as a faster version of the pacelike walk. The pace and the trot are comparable in speed, although horses, which can perform both gaits, pace marginally faster than they trot. Webb (1972) claims, on the basis of its fossilized tracks, that the Miocene camelid *Protolabis* also paced, but it is impossible to demonstrate this conclusively from such evidence.

Lying Down and Getting Up

When it has a choice, a camel chooses a smooth place on which to lie down. It does so more or less slowly and jerkily, first falling on both carpals, then bending its hind legs, and then settling its forequarters down so that the bent forelegs extend symmetrically forward from its trunk. A camel can spend many hours in this position, exposing minimal body surface to the sun's rays, supporting its chest weight on its sternal callosity, ruminating, resting, sleeping, or even feeding if there is any food within its reach. If the camel is tired, it may stretch its neck forward along the ground, in line with its body, and fall asleep in that position (Barker 1972).

The camel also gets up in three distinct movements, first hoisting its forequarters so that its radial-ulnar bones are vertical, then straightening its hind legs, and then putting its front feet on the ground one at a time and straightening its front legs. Camels have difficulty rising if one of their legs is injured, so if they are not being worked they may lie in one place for as long as a week until the leg is strong (Barker 1972).

Camels have callosities on the sternum, elbows, knees, and stifles, which help support the weight of lying camels. These callosities are not seen or felt in the neonate and are barely perceptible in animals 1 month old, but are plainly visible in camels 2½ months old. In older camels, in which the hair has been entirely worn off by contact with the ground, they are hard, discolored areas 5–10 centimeters in diameter on the legs and 15–20 centimeters in diameter below the sternum (pl. 43).

To mount a camel that has been saddled with a Mauritanian *rahla* saddle, a rider puts his left foot on the couched animal's front upper leg and then his right foot on the shoulder of the camel, turning so that as he slides down into the saddle he faces forward. Mauritanian camels generally rise as soon as the rider begins to mount, so that a good sense of balance on the part of the rider and a well-fixed saddle are essential to counteract the backward-forward-backward motion as the camel unbends and rises. Would-be riders are occasionally injured when they are thrown over a camel as it stands up. Once aloft, the rider holds the head rope, guiding his mount with the rope or by a touch of his foot or stick on the camel's neck. The head and neck of the camel are more sensitive than the rest of its body (Barker 1972).

Camel Loads   Because of the arch principle, the camel, with its convex back, can carry a heavier load than a horse can. A camel's load, however, is limited by the weight it can rise with. If its packs are too heavy, a camel may not be able to raise its hindquarters. Once its hindquarters are up, though, it can always get up on its front legs.

The camels of nomads generally carry maximum loads of

150 kilograms each, but they can carry up to 300 kilograms
for a short distance. In the French camel corps the weight
limit was 150 kilograms, and in the British camel corps
about 200 kilograms. Leitch (1940) found that heavy bag-
gagers weighing around 600 kilograms could carry 200–325
kilograms for a normal march and up to 475 kilograms for a
short distance. A record load of 865 kilograms was carried
by a male in Australia (Barker 1972). Camels are more
often used for work in the Beni-Abbès region than in the
west, carrying wood, straw, and charcoal from the desert
to oases. Camels are occasionally hired for scientific trips,
as ours were, or for tourism.

Camels are ridden to a greater extent in the western
Sahara than in the Algerian Sahara. The Reguibat, who
live largely on camel milk and therefore do not need to
carry extensive food provisions on migrations, usually
ride their loaded camels. The Chaanba, who carry larger
loads and more food on their journeys, usually walk rather
than ride their heavily laden camels. In Australia, Barker
(1972) found camels particularly useful because they carried equipment (such as tools for repair work) that a horse
would not carry. Camels were also more useful than horses
in crossing rivers because they could wade through water
nearly 2 meters deep without getting their loads wet.

Camel saddle design has always been a problem because of the camel's hump, which cannot support a heavy
weight without deforming and which may change shape
depending on the season and availability of food. A heavy
load can only be carried if it is distributed such that the
camel's skeletal structure, either through the front legs, the
hind legs, or the rib cage, or all of these, bears the brunt of
the burden. Several types of saddles are used in the Sahara. In the west the Maures and the Reguibat use the
rahla saddle (pls. 46 and 47); in the central Sahara the
Tuareg or *terik* saddle is used (pl. 48, fig. 14); and from
Tibesti eastward, including Iran and Pakistan, the *terké*
saddle is used, but as a pack saddle only (Monod 1967). (In
fact, the Somali consider mounting a camel ridiculous
[Bulliet 1975] and, like the nomads of northern Kenya,
never ride camels.) The rahla saddle is concave and larger
than the terik, with a leather cushion underneath which
places the rider so high that he needs a stick to guide his
mount. The flat terik saddle, which is the easiest saddle on
which to mount a camel, allows the rider to guide his
camel with his feet. The women's saddle is large enough to

Fig. 14   Tuareg saddle

hold a woman plus several children and small animals. Chaanba women drape their saddle, called *bassour*, with carpets and cloth so that men cannot see them (pl. 49). The more emancipated nomad women of the western Sahara never hide their faces, so their saddle, called *amshaqeb*, is open. Its frame is made of *Balanites* or *Capparis* wood.

Swimming   There is contradictory evidence about the swimming ability of camels. When Colonel Earle in 1884 wanted to cross the Nile with 620 camels, he had to tow them one by one on a short lead while they floated passively along behind his boat (Denis 1970). Some tried to swim, but did so awkwardly, their long necks tending to sink under the water while their hindquarters rose to the surface. Three of the camels drowned. (The longer-necked giraffe, by the way, is one of the few mammals that cannot swim at all.)

Despite Earle's experiences, other writers claim that camels are good swimmers. Twenty-five camels were driven from Texas to California in 1857, and they swam the Colorado River without trouble, although 10 mules and two horses drowned (Lesley 1929). Camels have been observed swimming well in Australia (Barker 1972) and on the Niger and Wadi Halfa rivers (Denis 1970). It is important that the river banks be solid, for camels tend to lie on their sides on soft ground and, if they get mired in the mud, may break a leg while struggling to free themselves.

Part 2

Relationship to Man

Domestication   It is generally assumed that the camel was first domesticated in central Arabia, where prehistoric rock paintings of them as game and riding animals have been found (Epstein 1971). Walz (1956) hypothesizes that this was the center of domestication, from where domestic camels spread to the north and to Africa, but Mikesell (1955) and Bulliet (1975) believe that the center was more likely southern Arabia, where early man presumably lived on the coast or along river valleys such as the Wadi Hadhramaut. A refuse dump from 3000–2750 B.C. shows that early inhabitants of this area mainly ate sea cows or dugongs but also wild camels. The transition from hunting wild camels to taming them may have been facilitated by the camels' early lack of predators and by their dependence on the limited number of watering places, which were also used by the human inhabitants. Perhaps the natives lured them with bait of dried shark and sardines, which are still added to camel fodder today in southern Arabia but nowhere else in the world. Once domesticated, camels in southern Arabia were probably used to some extent as pack animals and for riding, but mostly for milk, as they are today.

The domestication of the camel occurred relatively recently compared with other animals, such as sheep (10,000 B.C.), goats (8000 B.C.), pigs (6500 B.C.), and cattle (5000 B.C.) (Planhol and Rognon 1970). However, opinions on when camels were first domesticated differ widely, which is to be expected where evidence must be gleaned from ancient texts of uncertain dating, on artifacts that may or may not portray camels with harnesses or saddles, and on circumstantial evidence relating to camel technology and saddle types. Authors such as Free (1944), Zeuner (1963), Ripinsky (1975), and Bulliet (1975) believe that camels were domesticated before 2000 B.C. Epstein (1971), taking into account the earliest Egyptian and Mesopotamian archaeological evidence, dates domestication as early as the fourth millennium B.C. Walz (1956), however, believes that camels were domesticated perhaps during the thirteenth or twelfth century B.C., but not before 2000 B.C. (Camels are mentioned in the Bible [Genesis, chap. 12] as being used by man in Abraham's time, about the eighteenth century B.C., but Walz [1956] and Albright [1942, 1961] hypothesize that priests from a later period may have tampered with earlier texts and included camels in their reworked version of Genesis.)

Because most of Arabia is cut off from mainland Asia by the great expanse of desert called the Empty Quarter, the indigenous culture of southern and central Arabia based on domestic camels was confined to that area for centuries. Northern Arabia had little knowledge of the camel, while southern Arabia had no direct contact with the pack asses and animal-drawn plows and wagons of the north. The impetus for the northward spread of the camel was undoubtedly the overland incense trade in the second millennium B.C. Before that time, goods had been transported almost entirely by water, so there was little need for pack animals beyond local agricultural areas.

The first documented use of domesticated camels on a large scale was by Midianites invading Syria and Palestine in the eleventh century B.C. The first recorded use of camels in Mesopotamia was in the ninth century B.C. during the Assyrian campaign against the Arabs (Walz 1954). Camel breeding undoubtedly became important in northern Arabia and the Middle East after the twelfth century B.C. When the Semites took over the overland incense trade, they encouraged the use of camels as herd animals, primarily in order to breed them for transport. Efficient saddles were developed which were either secured behind the hump or were constructed in the shape of a doughnut or horseshoe to surround the hump. The latter seems to have been used in warfare, where its higher and more forward position gave the rider more control of the camel's head and placed the rider in a position higher than that of opposing horsemen. Even so, camels made poor fighting mounts because camel saddles were relatively insecure platforms from which to fire arrows and, later, to wield lances and because camels were no match for horses, with their superior speed and power.

Camels were important as pack animals during early

historic times. Herodotus reported that the Persian king Cambyses, whose troops all perished in 525 B.C. in a sandstorm in the Libyan desert, used camels to transport water on his campaign to Egypt, and that in the battle of Sardes in 546 B.C. soldiers of the Persian king Cyrus mounted their pack camels, which terrified and routed the horsemen of his opponent Croesus (Zeuner 1963). Xerxes too used camels around 480 B.C. both for transport and for cavalry in protecting his borders (Zeuner 1963). In 331 B.C. Alexander used camels in his journey to Siwa in Libya (Epstein 1971), as did King Juba of Numidia in his fight against Julius Caesar in 46 B.C. Caesar, who won the battle, captured 22 of them. At that time this species was still virtually unknown in North Africa.

Early Domesticated Camels in North Africa

There is no doubt that camels have been used on a large scale in North Africa from the first centuries A.D., but controversy surrounds their origin. One theory, held by Gautier (1950) and Gsell (1914), is that the camel was introduced into North Africa during the Roman period, but archaeological and textual evidence (as above) indicates that the camel was present before the arrival of the Romans (Charnot 1953; Demougeot 1960). It is generally agreed that domestication of camels in large numbers first occurred in Africa in what is now Somalia and Eritrea. Bulliet (1975) reasons that camel herders in Arabia decided about 4,000 years ago to migrate to the horn of Africa, perhaps lured there by tales of dhow owners describing a rich land from where frankincense and myrrh were shipped to Egypt. Coastal tribes would have had no trouble transporting themselves and their camels on dhows propelled westward by the northeast monsoon. These camels and herders would have thrived in the insulated area, bordered on the west by the Ethiopian highlands, on the north and east by salt water, and on the south by disease barriers. Even today, Somalia, with over 2 million camels, is one of the richest camel territories in the world.

In Egypt, the country in Africa closest to Arabia and the Middle East, it is widely accepted that domesticated camels were present for many centuries before Christ, but only in small numbers. Archaeological material indicates with certainty that camels were not continuously there in prehistoric times (Midant-Reynes and Braunstein-Silvestre 1977). Domesticated camels probably entered

Egypt during the early incense trade, but the first histori-
cal reference to camels in Egypt is in the seventh and sixth
centuries B.C. in connection with the Assyrian and Persian
invasions of Egypt. Camels were probably not bred there
until much later, but before the second and first centuries
B.C., when there was trading by camel between the Nile
and the Red Sea in an 800-kilometer-long area south of the
delta. The camel breeders were apparently not Arabs,
although they got their camels, breeding skills, and
technology from the Arabs. The evidence suggests that the
camels and the expertise came from beyond the Red Sea
via the Sinai Peninsula and then southward, but not via
the heavily cultivated Nile delta, where camels die of
insect-borne diseases and where nomads are held in low
esteem. Camel breeding, which at first was centered in the
desert east of Thebes (now Luxor), where camels were
bred for both trade and warfare, gradually spread southward into the eastern desert of the Sudan (Bulliet 1975).

Camels may have spread westward from Egypt to central and western North Africa, although people usually
preferred to travel west by sea rather than by land, or they
may have moved north and west from the southern Sahara
(Demougeot 1960). When the Romans moved into western
Libya and southern Tunisia, from the first century B.C.
onward, camels were already present there although they
cannot have been numerous because Pliny (ca. A.D. 23–79)
did not mention them as inhabiting North Africa. By the
second century A.D. there was a Roman camel corps under
Hadrian, and by the third and fourth centuries A.D. camels
were numerous; Ammianus Marcellinus, for example,
mentions a requisition of 4,000 camels imposed on the city
of Leptis Magna in A.D. 363.

When the Romans in North Africa finally were able to
acquire camels in some quantity, they did not use them for
milk or for riding, as some tribes did, but as pack animals
and for agricultural work. There was little trade across the
Sahara until the Islamic conquests centuries later, so
camels were used mainly for plowing fields and pulling
carts. Single draft camels are still seen in Tunisia and
Morocco.

Although one thinks of the invention of the wheel in
terms of progress, as the camel culture became widespread
in the increasingly arid Sahara, the use of wheeled vehicles died out. Judging from rock pictures found deep in
the Sahara of chariots pulled by horses, vehicles were

widespread at one time. Chariots were important for military use until about the eighth century B.C., but then were eclipsed by mounted cavalry. One of the last occasions on which they were used was by the Carthaginians in the fourth century B.C. In Roman North Africa wagons were depicted in mosaics from the first three centuries A.D. onward, and roads were built in the first and second centuries, but by the second century the number of wagons and carts was decreasing. By the seventh century A.D., carts and wagons were more or less completely replaced by pack camels, which were 20 percent more economical to use.

Aside from the camel's physiological superiority in the desert, transport by packed camels was superior to transport by horse- or oxen-drawn wagons for a number of reasons (Bulliet 1975): camels could go farther in a day than Roman oxcarts (24–32 vs. 10–14 kilometers); harnesses were primitive, which diminished the effectiveness of horses and oxen; camels did not need roads; ancient wagons were heavy and cumbersome, even without loads; wagons were more likely to break down than camels; one man could lead three to six camels, but could drive only two horses or oxen yoked to a wagon; and wagons were expensive in wood-poor areas (although camels were hardly cheap; in Egypt in the second century A.D., a camel cost twice as much as an ox and four times as much as an ass).

Domesticated camels accompanied Arab invaders deep into the Sahara; indeed, camels made the invasions possible. The Arabs probably reached the Atlantic by A.D. 700, although the real domination of the Sahara by the Arabs did not begin until the eleventh century, when they moved in from the east on camels, bringing their families and flocks of sheep and goats.

The early North Africans used camels for fighting, both defensively and offensively. Procopius described Mauri tribesmen arranging their camels in 12 concentric rings, with the women and children in the center, during invasions by the Vandals in North Africa (fifth century A.D.) and in battles with the Byzantine army (Farias 1967). Camels could be marshaled in this way because, unlike horses, they are phlegmatic rather than nervous and temperamental. Some of the Almoravides, a Berber dynasty that extended over the western Sahara, Morocco, and Spain in the eleventh and twelfth centuries, rode camels when waging war. Primarily, however, camels became important for transport across the Sahara.

Trade Routes and Caravans   Long before the domesticated camel reached the Sahara, horses were crossing the Sahara along routes that are still in part followed. The horse apparently appeared in the Sahara about 1600 B.C., when the climate was less dry than it is at present. The Garamantes, a warlike, powerful people who lived in Libya well before 1000 B.C., used two-wheeled chariots pulled by two or four horses to reach the Niger (Lhote 1958). These chariots were primarily used in waging war. Hundreds of rock paintings and carvings found in the Atlas Mountains, Mauritania, the Adrar des Iforas, the Hoggar, Tassili, and the Fezzan indicate that there were two important trans-Saharan routes, one in the western Sahara and one in the central Sahara. They bypassed difficult terrain and waterless regions so that horses could follow them.

The Garamantes nation, which occupied the Sahara before the arrival of the Arabs, had disappeared as a cohesive group by about the seventh century, when the Arabs started invading North Africa. With the Arabs came camels, which quickly replaced horses for transport. Camels depended less on watering points than did the oxen, mules, donkeys, and horses used before them, so that hitherto impenetrable regions were now open to exploration.

Although camels had been used to some extent for transport in the desert in the first centuries A.D. (e.g., the wealth of Leptis Magna in the fourth century A.D. is attributed mainly to commerce by camel), the importance of the camel greatly increased with the arrival of the Arabs. An important but difficult route ran south from east Morocco. Another old, but shorter, route, from Libya to Chad via Murzuk in the Fezzan, was used as recently as the last century by African explorers heading south. The most easterly north-south trade route—and one of the oldest caravan routes in the world—was the *darb el arbaïn*, the road of 40 days, which forged a link between the Nile and El Fasher in the Sudan. This route has been completely superseded by the railroad and by shipping routes, but visible remnants of the large network of subsidiary routes and the main route attest to its former importance.

The goods brought from the south to North Africa were manifold: ivory, ostrich feathers, gum arabic, skins, and wool, but especially gold, slaves, and salt. These commodities were exchanged for arms, cloth, and trinkets. The main routes for the important gold trade that flourished in the fourteenth and fifteenth centuries were the western one crossing Mauritania and that going from eastern Morocco along the Wadi Saoura to the Niger River (Capot-Rey 1953). The gold, which was refined in several towns before being shipped north, was carried in guerbas (goat skin waterbags), each camel transporting about 130 kilograms (Gaudio 1967). At that time there were important empires in black Africa south of the Sahara, the oldest of which was probably Ghana, situated between the mouth of the Senegal River and the loop of the Niger. In the eleventh century most of the goods of the trans-Saharan trade were stocked there. It was so rich that even its dogs wore gold collars and the king was called King of the Gold (*Journal Million* 10 [1972]: 165). Other empires by turn rose in importance and wealth, but none could withstand the invasions of the Arabs. In the fourteenth century, Mali, whose emperor paid 10 metric tons of gold to go to Mecca, was preeminent. In the sixteenth century, the Sonrai empire, whose capital was Gao, provoked the envy of the sultans of Morocco. Pasha Djudder of Morocco sent 8,000 camels as well as 5,600 men and 1,000 horses against Gao and Timbuktu. Most of the camels died on the way. Timbuktu, which was fabled both for its trade and, in the sixteenth and seventeenth centuries, for its intellectual activities, was a town of little importance by the time Europeans reached it, in the early nineteenth century.

In the sixteenth century the gold trade of the Sahara declined, to be replaced by the infamous slave trade. Slaves were captured in many parts of central Africa and sold throughout the Mediterranean, but most were sent north in camel caravans along the Chad-Fezzan-Libya route. Many slaves died on the way, especially the men, who had to walk in chains. Slaves in North Africa were used as servants, gardeners, herdsmen, eunuchs, and concubines. A man in good health cost 10 camels, a woman twice that much, as her future children would belong to her owner. Although the slave trade was officially abolished in the Sahara by the French in 1848, it only disappeared gradually with the military occupation of the Saharan oases; around 1850, 5,000 slaves were still being shipped out of Kano, Nigeria, each year. For centuries the principal work of the nomads and of oasis dwellers was done by slaves. Today their descendants often still work for nomads. Although they are legally free, they are still called *captifs* and do most of the work around a camp in exchange for food and perhaps clothing. In 1964 Gauthier-Pilters traveled for a week with a Reguibat family and its 300 camels; the 30 Reguibat were mounted, but their 15 black servants walked. With industrialization in the Sahara, many such descendants of slaves are able to leave their "masters" and work for wages.

For many centuries the salt trade was one of the main sources of profit for the nomads. In the twelfth century salt was transported from Sidjilmassa in southeast Morocco (a town destroyed 200 years later by Arab nomads) to Ghana, where it was exchanged for its weight in gold (Capot-Rey 1953). Salt was as important south of the Sahara as gold was north of it. Later, a slave could be exchanged for a piece of salt no bigger than his foot. Some people even gave their children away in exchange for salt!

A caravan generally consisted of a few hundred to a few thousand camels. These huge caravans made for safe traveling, involving, as they did, many nomads. These nomads had to pay taxes to the tribes whose regions they passed through, and the tribes in turn protected the nomads. Along the route the camels were changed once or twice, where the vegetation changed (camels cannot easily adjust to new kinds of vegetation). Changes occurred in oases such as Tindouf and In Salah, which thus became flourishing centers. Caravans sometimes got lost; in 1805, 2,000 people and 1,800 camels all died of thirst when their caravan missed the route between Timbuktu and Taoudeni (Capot-Rey 1953).

Exportation of Camels   With the increasing use of domesticated camels for transport, they traveled to distant countries, where records of them may give an overly generous idea of their maximum distribution as a breeding species (Bulliet 1975). For example, there is archaeological evidence of the spread of the Bactrian camel westward from Turkmenistan into the Russian steppes, and possibly even into Czechoslovakia. From here, some camels were taken even farther west by Germanic tribes such as the Goths, whose word for camel was clearly indigenous. Bones found in Roman ruins in Switzerland are probably those of camels used by a Germanic tribe, but it is unlikely that camels were bred to any extent this far west. There are also early records of camels in France, Spain, and Poland and, much later, in the United States and Peru, where their use was probably discontinued because of the widespread availability of Indian slaves as a source of cheap labor.

There were two successful early breeding experiments outside the camel's usual habitat. One took place in the Canary Islands in 1406, when a colony of French people from Morocco settled there with their camels. The camels thrived, thanks to the careful attention given them, and their progeny were used centuries later in further exportation operations. They are still a tourist attraction.

The second experiment was sponsored by Ferdinand II de Medici. In 1622 camels were transported to San Rossore, near Pisa, from Tunisia, mainly to carry wood. The fortunes of this herd varied; they numbered as few as six in the early 1700s to as many as 196 in 1789, and their descendants were all slaughtered for meat during World War II. A number of camels from this herd were used to start further breeding colonies.

With these two exceptions, importation of camels until the 1800s tended to be sporadic and unplanned, with little thought given to setting up breeding herds. In the 1800s, however, with the increased travel of Europeans to many foreign countries, camels were used extensively for general labor and military transport. No thought was given to the camel as a source of meat or hair. Geoffroy Saint-Hilaire founded in 1854 the active Société Impériale Zoologique d'Acclimatation with the express purpose of exploring the uses to which various animals could be put in the French colonies (Saint-Hilaire 1861). Europeans shipped general-labor camels to eastern Europe, Spain, southern Africa, Java, Brazil, Cuba, Jamaica (where chiggers were a major problem), and Venezuela (where many were bitten by snakes), but most died before long.

Although the importation of camels into the United States was first discussed in 1836, there was no action until 1856–1858, when a total of about 120 camels, all but a few dromedaries, were shipped to Texas (Lesley 1929; Greenly 1952; Emmett 1932; Fowler 1950). These camels were used as pack animals for the army and to help subdue Indians along the Mexican border. Some, however, were not needed by the government, and were set free to fend for themselves, eating plants such as prickly pear, thistles, hackberry, wild grapes, and sagebrush. Many of these were subsequently killed by stockmen, who found that they competed for food with their animals and frightened their horses into stampeding by their large size and strong smell. The last feral camels of this group were spotted in 1891 near Kingsville, Texas.

In 1857 some of the Texas camels were used by the government to survey a wagon route to California. At the end of the Civil War, when the government was no longer able to care for the camels, they were dispersed: some were sold to circuses, some as transport animals in Mexico, some to a mine in Nevada, while others were freed in Arizona, where their progeny roamed wild until at least 1905. The last survivor of this herd was a female named Topsy, captured in the Arizona desert and sent to the Los Angeles Zoo, where she died in 1934. In Nevada the memory of the camels is kept fresh today with the annual camel races in Virginia City.

Following the lead of the Texas camel importers, in 1860 a San Francisco company imported 90 Bactrian camels from the Orient, half of which died on the Pacific. They were sent to mines in Nevada and in British Columbia, but they were no more successful in working alongside horses than were the dromedaries. The Canadian camels were soon freed on the Thompson Flats east of Cache Creek, where feral animals were seen until 1905 (Hutchison 1950).

The Camel in Australia   The most successful camel transplantation has been to Australia, an undertaking described in detail by McKnight in his book *The Camel in Australia* (1969), from which the following information is taken. The first serious discussion of importing camels to Australia occurred in 1836, the same year parallel talks took place in the United States, when the government of New South Wales launched an inquiry into the practicability of importing camels from India. Enough settlers and explorers had ventured across the Blue Mountains to realize that although the east coast of Australia was fertile and lush, the dry lands beyond the mountains, which covered most of the continent, might best be settled with the help of camels. A few camels arrived in Australia in 1840, but the first major importation occurred in 1860, when 24 dromedaries were shipped to Melbourne from Karachi, Pakistan. Some of these animals were used almost immediately in the Burke and Wills expedition into the interior, the first group to make a south-north crossing of the continent. Although the party reached the Gulf of Carpentaria successfully, of the six camels on the return journey, two became so fatigued that they had to be abandoned (the first of many feral camels in Australia), two were eaten when the explorers ran out of food, and two, which were in a badly weakened physical condition, were shot when they became mired in mud. The McKinlay relief expedition, which set out in 1862 to rescue Burke and Wills, found camels invaluable even on stony ground and in mud. Unlike horses, they were able to find sufficient food from local vegetation to sustain themselves.

Because of John McKinlay's success in exploring with camels (although not in finding Burke and Wills), the prospect of commercial importation of camels on a large scale became feasible, not as a government scheme, as in the United States, but under private enterprise. Soon hundreds and then thousands of dromedaries were being shipped to Australia, along with camel men from various countries of Asia to look after them. Light riding camels, medium-weight hill animals, and heavy Kandahar camels capable of carrying heavy packs and producing much wool were all imported so that selective breeding could produce camels ideally suited to their new homeland. Their major health problem was mange, which killed many animals before their keepers learned to combat it—with an ointment made of Stockholm tar.

Camels in Australia were bred for riding, as pack animals, or as draft animals, with the native-bred animals superior to the imported camels for all three uses. Riding camels, which were the most valuable, were generally females, which were lighter and had longer legs than males. They were sometimes called "skyscrapers of the gibbers" because their height allowed the rider to see above desert boulders and expanses of bush, an advantage the horse rider did not share. Camels routinely covered 90 kilometers per day with their steady pace, but they could go much faster if necessary—up to 224 kilometers in 1 day. Riding camels were widely used by outback police, mail couriers, ranchers, and graziers. The saddle of the riding camel consisted of a pair of X-shaped crosspieces, one in front and one behind the hump, connected by horizontal bars. Sometimes the rider sat in a saddle depression suspended in front of the hump, but usually he was supported at the rear of the framework, behind the hump, Indian style. With the latter type of saddle, the rider steadied himself with stirrups and could read or write as his mount plodded along.

Australian camels were mostly bred for and used as pack animals. The normal load for such camels weighed between 180 and 280 kilograms, depending on the size and condition of the animal, food and water supplies, and the type of terrain to be crossed. Although many loads, such as bales of wool, were conveniently shaped, some, such as petrol drums, lengths of pipe, and fencing material, were decidedly unwieldy. During a journey, a string of two or three dozen camels, supervised by at least two camel men, walked single file at a speed of about 4.5 kilometers per hour, covering 15–30 kilometers a day.

By the 1870s, a few camel men were experimenting with wagons or drays, whose improved design doubled the weight a camel could move. In addition, draft camels did not have to be unpacked each night, and several camels could be used to haul extra-heavy loads. Occasionally as many as 12 pairs were hitched together to pull heavy mining machinery.

As Australians came to realize how useful camels were, they were pressed into service throughout the country, so that by the 1880s camels were common in the interior. The first major use of the camel was in the exploration and survey expeditions to map areas and routes suitable for ranches, mines, and communication lines. The second was in the construction industry, where they transported heavy loads either by pack or by wagon in areas where food and water were scarce. They were used in the building of: the Overland Telegraph Line (1870–72); numerous outback exclusion fences against dingos, rabbits, kangaroos, and emus; many wells; and the few railway lines that penetrated the desert. Camels excelled in mine work, primarily for packing minerals to railheads or depots and carting supplies back to the mines. If a mine did not have its own camels, it might hire them for temporary work, paying a rate commensurate with the weight of the load and the distance it had to be transported. In times of drought, which lessened competition from oxen or horses, rates increased.

Barker (1972), who drove cartage teams in Australia for many years, found camels to be better work animals than horses; if a team of camels in harness could not at first move a heavily laden wagon, unlike horses, they would try again and again. On ordinary roads a team of 14 camels could pull a wagon load weighing 14 metric tons, but if the road was very good they could pull 20 metric tons. In dry weather they covered 50 kilometers with an empty wagon and 30 kilometers with a loaded one. Barker used both castrated and intact males in his teams, but he preferred the castrated males because they pulled as hard as the others but did not fight as much or smell as bad. Barker found his animals to be quite responsive. They answered to their own names, although if two names were similar, both camels would respond. None of the animals liked wearing blinders and used all sorts of tricks to keep them from being fastened on—stumbling of the shaft, holding their heads high, and turning their heads away. The camels in a team came to know a road once they had been over it. They also knew their own teammates and usually ate together. If a new camel was added to the team, it was bitten at first and not fully accepted by the others for several weeks. The camels were not afraid of machinery, steam, loud whistles, and strong lights.

In all, probably between 10,000 and 20,000 dromedaries were imported into Australia in the 25-year period beginning in the early 1880s, over half into South Australia, especially in the early days, and the rest to the arid state of Western Australia. Although the data on domesticated camels are limited, there were perhaps somewhat more than 5,000 in all of Australia in the mid-1890s, about 10,000 at the turn of the century, and a peak of about 20,000 in the early 1920s, most of them at this time in Western Australia. With the increase in railroad construction and use, and motor vehicles after that, the number of domesticated camels declined drastically, although the number of feral ones increased more or less proportionately. The last use of domesticated camels was for exploring around 1939, for cartage at mines around 1945, for outback police patrols around 1950, and for patrol work along barrier fences in the early 1950s. Domestic camels are now almost gone in Australia, except for a few preserved on cattle stations for general work or sentimental reasons, and some kept by Aboriginals, mostly in central Australia, for personal transport, for collecting wood, and for the tourist trade.

When it was no longer economical to use camels in the outback, owners often released them in the wild. There has not been a market for camel hides or meat in Australia, although the flesh is edible though not tasty to the Western palate. The wild camels were no bother to ranchers as long as they stayed in the arid, unexploited regions of Australia, but in times of drought they seek water on the ranches, knocking down fences that get in their way. In South Australia, a Camels Destruction Act was passed in 1925, which allowed "occupiers of any land" to destroy any camels on that land.

Despite control measures, the feral population probably increased to between 30,000 and 100,000 during World War II, but after that, with the increased human use of the land and of supplies of water, and with more roads into the outback and more people willing to hunt camels, their numbers have declined and are probably still declining. There are at present perhaps 15,000–20,000 feral camels in herds of 10 to mobs of up to 500 in the deserts of Australia, about 40 percent of them in Western Australia, 30 percent in the Northern Territory, 20 percent in South Australia, and 10 percent in Queensland. They forage on many species of eucalyptus and acacia, especially on mulga (*Acacia aneura*) and to a lesser extent on saltbush (*Atriplex* sp.) and the succulent parakelia (*Calandrinia balonensis*) near Alice Springs (Williams 1963). Like Saharan camels, they range widely in their search for food, never staying long enough in one area to overbrowse it. The camels have no real predators, although individuals are sometimes killed by snakebite, poison plants, dingo bait, or droughts, and, occasionally, when they become bogged down in mud.

Although damage to fences is the major complaint against feral camels in Australia, a survey conducted by McKnight pointed up other problems: camels have broken water tanks, troughs, pipes, and pumps during droughts in their desperation to obtain drinking water at cattle and sheep stations; they have fouled, by defecation and trampling, natural watering places sometimes used by cattle or sheep; horses are frightened and sometimes stampeded when feral camels come near them; camels sometimes compete with livestock for food, but this is rare because camels tend to eat leaves above the reach of cattle and sheep; they have destroyed bushes used by sheep for protection against sun and wind; they have been known to bite or kick sheep, but only rarely, when males are in rut or both species are concentrated at a watering point; they have chased cattle away from water sources; and males in rut can be dangerous to men.

In summary, the successful acclimatization of camels in Australia was due to three factors: the large nucleus of breeding animals, the realistic understanding of their work capabilities, and the willingness of an adequate cadre of experienced camel men to accompany the camels to their new home. Where these factors were absent, as in the United States, the camels usually died out.

Domestication of the Bactrian Camel   The Bactrian camel was domesticated entirely independently of the dromedary, but owing to the paucity of records we do not know exactly when or where domestication first occurred. Evidence indicates that it was before 2500 B.C. and possibly at one or more centers in the mountain and plateau regions of what are now northern Iran and southwestern Turkestan (Walz 1954; Bulliet 1975), which were part of the ancient kingdom of Bactria. From here, the breeding of these camels spread outward to parts of Iraq, India, and farther east to central Asia, covering an immense area. The oldest records of domesticated Bactrian camels in Mesopotamia date back to 1500 B.C. (Walz 1956). Domesticated Bactrian camels were common in northern China in the second century B.C. From the beginning of the Han period they were often represented in Chinese art, sometimes pulling carriages or plows. During the Mongol Dynasty they were used mainly as pack animals and for military expeditions (Epstein 1969). Unlike the dromedary, which became the focus of entire cultures, with millions of people dependent on it for sustenance, the Bactrian camel was generally herded only in small numbers and utilized mainly as a stud and, because of its strength, as a work animal.

Camels prefer to mate with conspecifics (Baskin 1976), but when both one-humped and two-humped camels came to occupy the same areas, probably during the second half of the second century B.C. under the Parthians in the Tigris-Euphrates Valley, the two species interbred. The hybrid proved to be an ideal pack animal, larger and stronger than either parent, with a single long hump sometimes indented toward the front (pl. 50). When a hybrid and purebred camel mate, the progeny resemble the purebred parent, so selective breeding has to be carefully carried out, with no mixed herd allowed to breed on its own. Recent experiments have shown that the crosses can occur in either direction, with the hybrid having a diploid chromosome number of 70, as in both parental species (Gray 1972).

At first, the Parthians used Bactrian camels in their trade caravans, which extended across Asia, notably along the Silk Route, but in time they were supplanted by the stronger hybrid camels. By the early Islamic period, Bactrian camels in Iran and Afghanistan were used solely as breeding stock. Only in central Asia proper were Bactrian camels still bred extensively, because there the climate was too harsh even for hybrids. Camel-breeding people such as the Kirghiz evolved a camel culture similar to that of the nomadic Arabs, with milk an important item of food.

Well into the Islamic period, experimentation in camel breeding resulted in the production of a type of dromedary that was long haired, resistant to cold, and well adapted to the Iranian Plateau. Even though this new breed was not as strong as the hybrid, it gradually replaced it, in part because the new breed was entirely independent of the Bactrian line. The vast range of the Bactrian camel had diminished drastically in recent times, although one still sees Bactrian camels in northern Iran, Turkmenistan, and northern Afghanistan.

Some authors believe that wild Bactrian camels still exist in the trans-Altai Gobi Desert (Antonius 1922; Montagu 1957; Bannikov 1958, 1975, 1976; Dementiev and Zevegmid 1962); Bannikov (1976) thinks they now number about 900. These animals have a slender build, short brown hair, short ears, small conical humps, small feet, no chest callosity, and reduced leg callosities. On occasion they are joined by, and interbreed with, feral Bactrian camels.

9 Nomadism

No study of the ecology of camels in the western Sahara is complete without an analysis of the role of their owners—the nomads and seminomads. Nor can these people be understood without reference to the ecology of their camel herds. Both are part of the desert ecosystem. In the Sahara there are many large and small tribes and groups of peoples who, despite their different origins, have a common way of life based on camels, which supply them with milk, meat, wool, and transport. In return, they water the camels, which otherwise would die of thirst in summer. The camels depend on the desert vegetation for food, which in turn depends on the soil and climate. Talbot (1968) calls these interdependent factors the vegetation-herbivore-nomad complex.

There are various forms of pastoral nomadism, ranging from pure nomadism, which excludes any agricultural activity, to the more common seminomadism, in which a family or some members of the family settle down for part of the year to grow crops (northern Sahara) or look after palm trees (northern and central Sahara). Sometimes seminomadism is an evolutionary step toward permanent settlement—but it is also an original way of life that for some north Saharan tribes has not changed in centuries.

Nomadism in the Sahara
While nomadism is disappearing in other parts of the world, it is still a way of life in the Sahara, especially the western Sahara, where economic development and human settlements are scarce. Here the appellation *ahel el bel*—people of the camel—signifies a prestige that cannot be equaled by any other social position or material wealth. In Mauritania the possession of camels still determines the prestige of anyone, be he nomad, worker, or government minister.

It is generally admitted that domestic livestock contribute to desertification, with no distinction often made between sheep and goats, on the one hand, and camels on the other. However, there is a fundamental difference between these animals in relation to the desert environment: goats, which are very hardy and nonselective grazers, tend to destroy the desert vegetation; sheep are selective grazers but tend to bunch closely together and stay near wells, thus degrading the vegetation in those areas. By contrast, camels remain in balance with the desert habitat. (Because cattle require large quantities of water, move slowly, and do not eat salty plants, they do not play a significant role in desert ecology; they are, however, the main domestic animal of the Sahel.) The fewer wells and pastures there are, the more hardy the camels and nomads must be. Freedom of movement is essential for the camels' wellbeing and for the sustenance of the vegetation, so nomads must constantly follow their herds as they move from pasture to pasture. The hard living conditions that this entails forge a close bond between animals and men, probably closer than that in any other culture.

Nomads must remain on the move throughout the year in order to guard their herds, but they do not regard this as a hardship. Indeed, they are proud of their ability to withstand hunger and thirst better than anyone else. They are fiercely independent and extremely self-confident, knowing that any error in judgment or in orientation could lead to death. They are willing to do without material goods to preserve this independence. Indeed, they seldom enter houses, where they feel imprisoned.

Desert nomads in winter as well as summer wear long flowing robes of cotton cloth. During hot weather they often cover their mouths, to reduce evaporation, with part of the long strip of cotton (chèche) they wear as a turban. When they rest during the midday heat they may wrap themselves entirely in a woolen blanket, an astonishing sight at 45° C.

The nomad's way of life has greatly sharpened some of his faculties. He can distinguish his own camels by their footprints, and often those of other nomads too. From a set of tracks he can tell whether the camel that made them was loaded or not, was tired or fresh, was lame or had only one eye, had been watered recently, and the day and time it passed. He can recognize individual men by their tracks, too, and whether tracks of the same kind of sandals were made by a native or by a European.

Nomads possess a virtually perfect sense of orientation. A man can walk for 300 kilometers over flat and barren soil without deviating more than 3 kilometers from his destination. Many times our guides led us, without hesitation, for an entire day across monotonous regs or hamadas, which to our eyes had no distinctive features, right to a well that was visible only from a few meters away. They could do this even in a sandstorm. In the desert, where landmarks as most people know them are nonexistent, nomads remember the smallest detail—a certain species of plant or association of plants, a barely perceptible depression, a change in the color or composition of the soil. They have terms for all such variations in the environment. At night, when geographic details are virtually invisible, they tell directions by the stars. Nomads also know the importance of the various desert plants they encounter—which ones are good for camel food, which ones have curative properties for man, and so on.

Nomad children learn such things when they are young. Each day they lead herds into the desert so the animals can graze. If an animal escapes they must retrieve it; if a sandstorm strikes they must find their way with their flocks back to camp. They can go days without food, water, or shade, but they do not complain of suffering. Who among them would sympathize? The nomadic life is incredibly hard. Yet nomad men are very fond of their children, carrying infants about and entertaining them for hours (pl. 51).

Even with his knowledge of the desert, amassed from centuries of experience passed from generation to generation, the nomad must be fatalistic, knowing as he does that unforeseen events and hazards are part of life. One's own will is of little importance in the desert, where long sandstorms make all projects vain, where the camel carrying the waterbag may suddenly escape, where rain clouds on the horizon dictate a complete change in direction from the one planned. When a nomad finds a water hole dried out, he cannot afford to despair, but must act immediately to save his life, no matter how tired he may be. Only an absolute confidence in Allah keeps a nomad free from worry and enables him to live without fear. Indeed, his confidence in God and in his own ability often make him careless in a way that annoys the stranger. We were particularly upset on one occasion when the owner of a Jeep we had hired to drive us 400 kilometers across the most arid part of Mauritania neglected to bring sufficient oil or gas for the trip. Halfway on our journey we were forced to tent for 2 days with an isolated nomad family until a passing truck agreed to take us to our destination. Nomads often waste water, expecting Allah to supply more when it is needed. A camel owner will search for weeks or even months for lost camels, taking with him nothing except some water. He goes from camp to camp, sure to be given food and drink at each tent he visits. But camps are often far apart, so that he may have to walk for days without food. He does not worry about this, however, or regret his actions.

The perpetual struggle with life makes a nomad hard on himself and others. He knows no pity. When we wanted to give presents to Mauritanian women with children who looked especially poor, our Arab companion was disgusted; he felt that such poor people did not deserve gifts. He insisted that anything we wished to give away should be given to him; he would then decide who should have the old sandals, or torn shirt, or water canteen, which offended our ethical conviction that those who had the least deserved to be given the most. The nomads observe a strict hierarchy, which has undoubtedly been essential to the survival of families and tribes in such a hostile environment. Without raising his voice, the man orders his family about, the guide his helpers. There is never any discussion or argument about the commands; they are carried out immediately. A strong man morally and physically despises a weak man, but admires another strong man, even though he may be a potential enemy. Nomads can be very touchy, but they soon forget their anger. Their temperament is often a mixture of stoic calm and childish enthusiasm.

Nomads are invariably polite among themselves. They never criticize other people or ask indiscreet questions. The old, both men and women, are highly respected because of their experience, and their advice is always considered. In the desert, where each meeting is a special event, salutations have evolved into a ceremony of ritual remarks that allows each member to study the others in a detached manner before the real news about rains, herds, camps, and friends is exchanged. Because such meetings are rare, they are accompanied by long talks and tea ceremonies. Green tea was introduced into Mauritania in the nineteenth century and soon became the national drink. Three small glasses are always drunk at each tea ceremony, with some nomads enjoying seven sessions a day. When nomads run short of milk, tea is their principle "food," as it is drunk with a great deal of sugar. Milk is of much greater importance, however, and nomads are proud to be able to offer it to their guests. "There was plenty of milk" is the most favorable description the nomads can give a year. Although we visited with many nomads in 1972 and 1973, the drought was so severe and extensive that the camels were not breeding and we were offered milk only once.

Visiting and talking with friends are such important activities to nomads that when possible their migrations focus around them (pl. 52). Even during periods of drought, when nomads may be forced to abandon their migrations to settle down beside wells and must depend on government handouts of food for survival, they take any opportunity to go by local transport to visit friends. Hospitality is not only a virtue but a necessity, without which life in the desert would be impossible. It is also the nomads' sole contact with the rest of the country.

Because nomads enjoy company and take advantage of any occasion to stop and make a pot of tea, they have often been called lazy by people who have never shared their lives. These observers do not realize that mere survival in the desert requires endless effort, such as gathering firewood in the blazing sun where there is little vegetation of any sort, looking after widely dispersed animals, fetching water from wells as far as 20 kilometers away, rebuilding tents after the frequent sandstorms, and watering large herds of animals 5 months of the year.

Camels are an immense source of prestige to nomads, who value them both materially and aesthetically. They are mentioned in many Arabic proverbs and poems, where they are compared to the most beautiful women, the most precious jewels, and the finest weapons. To lyrical nomads the camel's cheeks are as soft as silk, its walk as fluid as that of a young girl, its long neck as slender as a minaret, its ears as well formed as two falcons, and its gentle eyes as clear as mirrors. Nomad poetry is filled with such imagery.

There are almost 700 camel-related words in the rich vocabulary of the nomads (Leborgne 1953). There are words that refer to the shape of the camel's tail, its legs, and its hump, and words to describe its temperament—whether it flees from man, gets up quickly, tries to dislodge its packs, refuses to rise, or cries excessively. There is a word for every age and 40 words to describe its coat color, such as white, beige, gray, reddish brown, piebald, black, whether one color predominates, and where, for example, a white spot is present on its body. The word that describes an individual's color is often its name.

White camels are favored the most. Piebald females are also appreciated because they are supposed to give much milk and luck, but piebald males are considered weak and hard of hearing—good enough only for the despised castes of blacksmith and musician.

In most years camel milk is the main source of nourishment for the nomads. We stayed 1 month with a nomad family in the western Sahara whose only source of food was camel milk. They drink it morning and evening, but not during the hottest hours, when it increases thirst. The all-important milk is wrapped in superstition. Blowing on milk brings bad luck, so foam must be removed with a stick. Milk must never be left uncovered lest it be attacked by bad spirits. Milk chases away all evil, and helps women attain the ideal corpulence.

In northern Kenya, where the use of camel milk exceeds that of cattle milk, two milk camels can supply one family (Spencer 1973). Kenyan nomads sometimes mix camel milk with blood. They obtain the blood by shooting an arrow at close range into the jugular vein of a strong, reclining camel. When 1–2 liters have been collected, the wound is dressed with dung. Camels are not bled more than once a month.

The camel is a potentially important source of meat. At present, however, camel herds in the Sahara are often kept largely as symbols of wealth. Camels are sold only if their owners want to buy something, and they are slaughtered only for important feasts (pl. 53). Yet nomads eat camel meat whenever possible, sometimes even buying it at a butcher's shop. Fresh meat is dried in the open air, cut into small pieces, and saved for weeks or months (pl. 54). The dried meat, or tichtar, is either eaten alone or added in small bits to dishes of rice or pasta.

Since the nomads' needs for tea, sugar, and some luxury articles such as transistor radios have increased in recent times, camels are more often sold or bartered than they were formerly. The Tibbu of the Tibesti Mountains, for example, drive camels and sheep to the Fezzan and Kufra oases in Libya to exchange them for dates, tea, and sugar. The Kababish nomads in the Sudan until recently supplied most of the camels sold to buyers in Egypt (Schiffers 1972). However, the camel is still little exploited as a source of meat. Though camels are less productive than sheep and goats because of their slow growth rate and slow rate of reproduction, they are more valuable in that they are better adapted to withstand drought and do not degrade the habitat. The price of camel meat is also lower.

In their role as work animals, camels are used by the nomads chiefly for carrying water (100 liters at a time) and moving camp (pl. 55). The latter work involves two to four camels carrying the tent, saddles, some carpets, one or two wooden or metal chests, woolen or leather bags containing clothes and provisions, guerbas, water drums, and the cooking pot (pl. 56). Loading and unloading is always done quickly, before the camels become restless. Once the procession is under way, the camels settle into a slow walk. They walk only about 30 kilometers each day to allow adequate time for feeding and resting. Such a pace can be maintained for weeks. Each camel has a lead rope tied to its nose ring or around its lower jaw (pl. 57). The rope is held by a camel man or, where the camels are strung out in a line, tied to the tail of the camel ahead of it. The lines are long and slack enough—and the speed sufficiently leisurely—that there is no danger of the nose ring being torn off. Indeed, the camels can even snatch a mouthful of food now and then.

Camels play a role in social rituals and customs. Even today, no marriage in the desert is possible without camels. Not only does the camel carry the bride, but the bridegroom has to give as many as 50 female camels to his new father-in-law. He must also give him camels if he later wants a divorce. If a Reguibi has been injured or killed, reparation is made by a gift of camels—called a *taleb* for certain injuries and a *dya* for murder. A murderer is not executed, but instead must give a dya of 100 camels to the family of the man he killed. The dya is supposed to consist of 25 foals, 25 young, 25 3-year-old females, and 25 4-year-old females, but depending on the circumstances and the social positions of the victim and the murderer, the number, composition, and age of the camels can be altered, and guns may be added (Denis 1960). For a woman victim, half a dya is sufficient. The family, relatives, and friends of the murderer must all participate in the dya. The same levy is demanded of someone who frightens a camel and thereby causes its rider to be thrown fatally, or if a nomad does not help a person dying of thirst. An injury to a man's testicles is avenged by 100 camels, but to his eye by only 50 camels. Quarrels in which a man's incisor is broken require 5 camels in reparation; a broken molar, 8; a broken finger, 10; and a broken arm or leg, 25. These numbers of camels correspond to large sums of money.

The Tuareg do not have a fixed reparation scheme for murder or death by negligence. However, if a person is injured, the tribal chief determines how many camels he should receive in compensation, an exchange similar to the taleb of the Reguibat (Denis 1960). In northern Kenya, camel thieves are dealt with harshly by persecution and, after death, by emasculation.

The highest rank in the hierarchy of Mauritanian tribes is that of the warriors, or Hassan, who are for the most part descendants of a branch of the Arab Maquil, who invaded North Africa in the eleventh century (Farias 1967). Hassan status is sometimes conferred on those of less illustrious lineage; for example, our guide on a number of expeditions, Mokhtar Ould Bontemps, was considered a warrior because his father was a French officer stationed in Mauritania during the military occupation. The Hassan are thought of primarily as warrior-nomads who in former times provided the Marabouts and other tribes with essential protection. They still carry guns on all expeditions to emphasize their rank, even when they have no ammunition.

The Marabouts belong to a religious group of relatively high culture (even the women can read and write) descended from Berbers who lived in the Sahara before the arrival of the Arab invaders. They teach the children, but also breed camels and own shops. Since the independence of Mauritania in 1960, many Marabouts, including President Mokhtar Ould Dadda, have come to occupy important government posts. The Marabouts we encountered during our field trips were often friendly, discussing various matters with our guide or showing us the irrigation systems of their palm tree groves, but they never shook hands with us, as most Mauritanians did, because we were women.

A lower group in the Mauritanian hierarchy are the Zenagas, whose members formerly paid tributes of agricultural products, including animals, to the higher classes. The Zenagas also are descendants of the early Berbers, but from less noble families. They sometimes own large herds of camels or cattle.

An even lower group are the negroid descendants of slaves, who work in agriculture or as servants or herders for the nomads. Almost every nomad family we encountered had a black servant who received food and clothing for his or her work, but no wages. They are legally free, but they have either no opportunity or no incentive to become independent. In the few industries of Mauritania, blacks do most of the manual work.

At the bottom of the social scale are the musicians, who are generally black, and the blacksmiths, who are black or of Jewish extraction. Blacksmiths are half despised and half feared because they work with iron and are considered assistants to the devil. Besides their work with iron, blacksmiths brand camels, slaughter them, and put on their nose clips. Musicians and blacksmiths do not intermarry with other Mauritanian classes.

Main Saharan Tribes   The principal nomad tribes of the Sahara are the Reguibat in the west, the Tuareg in the central mountains, the Chaanba in the north, and the Tibbu in the east. All have different pastoral regimes, with the Reguibat to a large extent the only remaining pure nomads. Despite their immense territory, extending from 14° to 30° north latitude and from 5° to 10° east longitude, the Tuareg primarily graze goats in limited areas such as mountain valleys, with the milk animals generally kept near camp and the others farther away. They sometimes also tend gardens or palm trees in oases. Good pastures for camels exist only periodically, so the Tuareg tend to graze their camels, accompanied by men, 500 kilometers south in Niger, despite the grazing tax there. Some of the richer nomads keep their herds there permanently. The Tuareg comprise a number of subgroups arranged in a social hierarchy.

Chaanba sheep and camel herders occupy a large territory from eastern Morocco to the borders of Tunisia and Libya. They were at one time famous raiders but with the

French occupation became meharistes, providing most of the indigenous military troops to the French. Most Chaanba are the traditional occupants of rich grazing areas in erg, hamada, and wadi pastures, which enable them to be seminomads, undertaking only small, seasonal migrations with their camels. Most members of this tribe own palm trees in the many oases, and many have been sedentary for years, keeping shops instead of herding livestock.

The hardy Tibbu of the Tibesti region own mostly sheep and goats rather than camels, so they are not very mobile. In summer they leave their camels unattended in the mountains and, like the Chaanba, wait for them to come periodically to be watered at a well. It is quite common to encounter camels 60–80 kilometers away from a well if the summer pastures are green (Chapelle, in Monteil 1966). Many Tibbu have settled down; at first they continued to operate camel caravans but now they mostly farm.

The Reguibat   Unlike the other three tribes, the Reguibat have maintained their purely nomadic way of life. (It is impossible to predict whether this will continue, because of the recent drought and the present fighting in the desert.) Their lands are far from the main trans-Saharan vehicle routes, from tourism, and from towns and industrial centers, so that the nomads have been able, for the most part, to preserve their traditional way of life. The Reguibat tribe are the widest-ranging camel nomads of the Sahara (with the possible exception of some Somalis), migrating over a largely barren area comprising 600,000 square kilometers (slightly larger in area than France), from southern Morocco almost to the Senegal River and from the Atlantic to western Algeria. They have no attachment to cultivated lands.

The Reguibat are famous for their long migrations and their great resistance to hunger and thirst—adaptations they share with their camels. Even the young camels, which are weaned early to provide more milk for the nomads, must survive on the scant pastures of northern Mauritania and western Algeria. Before the recent drought, a Reguibat family and its herds used to travel up to 1,000 kilometers each year through the western Sahara. The Reguibat are called *ahel moussa*—people of the clouds—because they follow the rains, while other tribes confine themselves to traditional grazing areas.

In good years the Reguibat live almost entirely on milk, so each family must have many camels to convert the sparse vegetation of the arid land into milk. Sweet (1965) has calculated that in Arabia each lactating female camel gives 1–7 liters of milk per day (depending on the season and the pasturage) for a period of 11–15 months, with at most only half the females lactating at any one time. Thus one tent (i.e., family) needs about 20 camels (males plus females) to supply it with a continuous source of milk.

Because Reguibat herds tend to be large (as recently as 1971 Gauthier-Pilters met nomads who had herds of 1,000 or more animals), camels can be sold or bartered for staples during times of drought. Even if many camels in a herd starve in lean years, a nucleus will probably survive to enable a nomad to rebuild his herd. Indeed, since the size of a nomad's herd is a reflection of his wealth, he will have as many camels as possible; except for drawing water for the animals, it is almost as easy to herd 200 camels as 50.

Unfortunately, the increase in the number of animals in the Sahel has necessitated drilling many new wells, which has aggravated the consequences of the drought. Although the supply of water has increased, the amount of vegetation for grazing has not, and as a consequence the vegetation is being degraded. Such is not true in the desert, where pastures and wells remain far apart and men and camels continue their extensive migrations, so that overgrazing is unknown away from the wells.

The Reguibat, who are descendants of Berbers, are divided into two main groups, the Reguibat Sahel and the Reguibat Lgouacem, the latter living in the eastern part of their range. Originally the Reguibat were sedentary cultivators living south of Morocco between the lower Dra and lower Seguiet el Hamra wadis. Gradually they became seminomads herding sheep and goats, and then camel nomads. By the end of the nineteenth century they had fought and defeated several rival tribes of nomads and were herding in the Zemmour and near the Seguiet el Hamra. They continued to fight a long series of razzias and counterrazzias until 1910, when they conquered their fiercest rivals, the Oulad Bou Sbaa, and became the strongest tribe in the northwestern Sahara. Their power was curtailed only after 1934, when the French occupied Tindouf in western Algeria and thus completed their military occupation of this part of North Africa. The Reguibat returned to a peaceful way of life after the French occupation and increased their camel herds considerably, something they had been unable to do when they were fighting. This pacifism has only changed recently with fighting over the possession of the former Spanish Sahara.

Since the lack of vegetation and water in the desert makes dispersion necessary, most Reguibat move in small groups of three or four families, with one family to a tent, called *friq*. In the Sahel, however, where there is an abundance of fodder and many wells, big camps of 30–40 tents are feasible but are much less mobile, so these groups make smaller migrations with their herds. The Reguibat tent is very spacious (often 8 × 10 meters) and furnished with mats, carpets, and cushions (pls. 58 and 59). It seems extremely comfortable to someone who has journeyed through the inhospitable terrain surrounding it. In all camps the women are unveiled and relatively emancipated, unlike the women of sedentary Arab tribes. They take an active part in the conversation when a stranger is visiting, although if there is a cooked meal they only eat what is left after the men and visitors have eaten.

The best camel breeders are those who travel farthest to take advantage of the most rainfall, which usually begins earlier in the south than in the north and is frequently localized. During the recent extensive drought many nomads were forced to settle down after they had lost their herds (pl. 60). Despite the recent climatic and political misfortunes of Mauritania, the Reguibat continue to have the best chance of surviving in the desert. So far they have been little changed by their contacts with modern civilization. Whether they will continue to prefer the rigors of nomadism to the soft life of the towns, however, remains to be seen.

Negative Effects of Settling Down   The desert pastures of the Sahara, which can support more than a million people, can be exploited only because of the great mobility of the nomads and their animals. Nomadism, which requires little labor and capital, exploits regions that at the present time cannot be used for agriculture or for intensive livestock breeding. When camels comprise most of the livestock, ecological equilibrium prevails provided man submits to the needs of the herds. Any reduction in mobility, however, destroys the equilibrium, since it causes the degradation of the vegetation and subsequent impoverishment of the animals.

Overgrazing has always been common around wells and towns, but it was strictly localized. Nowadays construction sites, roads, railways, and settlements tempt the nomads to pursue an easier way of life where social life, food, and water can be obtained with less effort. The result is that nomads often stay with their herds far too long in one place and thereby degrade the vegetation to a much greater extent than in former times. This loss in mobility is often the first step toward settling down permanently, a transition reflected by the replacement of camel-transported goatskin water bags with metal oil drums, which can be carried only by vehicles. In the transition to the sedentary life, migrations are first reduced, then part of a family settles down, and then the whole family does so, leaving their camels to be guarded by herders. Eventually the family may move from a tent to a house, often using a tent or other portable dwelling only in summer. This dual dwelling arrangement is still used by tribes that abandoned their nomadic way of life scores or hundreds of years ago (Planhol and Rognon 1970). In Mauritania, even important politicians who live in comfortable houses often like to spend their weekends and holidays in the tents of relatives living in the desert. A Mercedes parked by a nomad's tent is a common sight in the region around the capital, Nouakchott.

The causes of declining nomadism in most countries are both political and economic. During the history of civilization many countries have tried to settle their nomadic peoples, but only since World War II has this process in many parts of the desert become irreversible. Nomadism was first affected by postwar industrial and political changes, particularly in the eastern and central Sahara, but recently in the western Sahara too. Ever since the French established peace in the desert, the nomads have lost a great deal of prestige; they are no longer needed as protectors of the sedentary population, which formerly paid high tributes for such protection. A further consequence of peace is that the big tribal groups that had been the source of strength for the nomads in wartime are breaking up. Now everyone can go where he wants, so the headmen have lost much of their influence. With this increased emphasis on the individual, social bonds and traditional tribal structure are weakened. With the widespread use of motor vehicles to transport goods, many nomads have settled down. With the establishment of industries, many workers of low caste have left their duties as herdsmen for the nomads to become paid workers.

Today, humanitarian reasons are sometimes given to justify settling the nomads, but this argument can only be applied to poor nomads who do not own enough camels to support themselves. For the successful nomad, whose health and quality of life are generally superior to those of the sedentary population, settlement means physical, moral, and, unless some lucrative activity replaces the traditional way of life, social decadence. The camel herd represents food, wealth, security, and social prestige to the nomad. Losing his herd means losing everything.

The nomad who travels with his camels rarely becomes sedentary by choice. He is reluctant to change his independent way of life unless the loss of his camels makes this inevitable. In former times nomads sometimes became sedentary for short periods when they lost their herds, but this was seldom permanent. As soon as they were able to build up new herds again, they returned to the desert. Nowadays, however, nomads in contact with Western civilization may learn to value material goods and become dissatisfied with the simple, migratory life. If they stay in one place too long, they soon lose the qualities of endurance, initiative, and self-reliance that are indispensable for life in the desert, and are unlikely to return to nomadism.

It is wrong to believe that nomadism can be transformed or modernized without at least partially destroying it. During the recent drought all working camps along the railroad leading to the mines in northern Mauritania grew into huge slums where only a few men could find work. All the towns, too, grew far beyond their capacity to generate employment. The iron ore mining company, which is the only important industry in Mauritania, was not able to provide substantially more than the few thousand jobs it had provided before the drought. Between 1974 and 1976, because of the drought, the population of Nouakchott doubled from 60,000 to 120,000. Only a few of the "refugees" can hope to find work in the near future.

The policy of encouraging nomads to settle down, which many people consider not only desirable but inevitable, may be a good thing for national integration, but it is bad for the nomads and for the utilization of the desert as a resource. Sufficient economic development to provide permanent employment in areas where nomads are most numerous is simply unfeasible. The settling of nomads increases the number of unemployed workers in the towns and oases, and increases the government money that must be spent to sustain them. Even if work were available, the nomads are less adapted than the native villagers to regular employment. In addition, with large-scale settlement, much more food will need to be grown, which will put an increased demand on water supplies at a time when water reserves in many places are decreasing. As well, most nomads despise agricultural work, which formerly was done by slaves and later by their descendants.

If the western Sahara is to be retained as a resource for Mauritania, all efforts must be made to rehabilitate nomadism before it is too late. Any nomad who wishes to return to the desert should be encouraged to do so. Certainly many of the nomads whose animals died during the drought would rather return to their migratory life than remain slum dwellers if they were given the chance to build up new herds.

Camel management relies heavily on nomadism, because the installation of paid herdsmen would probably not be economical. Although large camel herds can be guarded by a few men because of the docile and gregarious nature of camels and because they respond to the vocal sounds by which they are herded, one wonders whether nonnomad paid herdsmen would know where to find new pastures or lost camels, would be inclined to pick up and move with the camels, and would have the patience and skill needed to find the often obscure wells and water large numbers of camels in summer. Without experienced men willing to perform these tasks, camel breeding will die out and the immense areas of desert, which now support large herds of camels and consequently hundreds of thousands of people, will support no one. Where agriculture in arid lands is impossible, nomadism is not only the best way, but also the only way of using the land for man's benefit.

10 Water Supply

Desert Wells Efforts to encourage nomads of the western Sahara to continue their age-old way of life will be futile unless desert wells are improved. Such a project would be relatively inexpensive and of immediate benefit, much more so than many other more costly schemes of doubtful value. Governments have little money to spend on wells for nomads, so help from the nomads would be important in any well improvement scheme. The widespread improvement of existing desert wells, which would be less costly than drilling for new ones, would be of immense and immediate benefit to the nomads, since the welfare of men and animals in the desert depends first and foremost on the availability of fresh water. In arid lands the distribution of wells, and the equipment available at wells, in relation to feeding grounds must be taken into consideration in formulating a plan for the rational use of the pastures. At present in Mauritania there are large pastures that are inaccessible to camels in summer because there are no wells nearby; there are also wells in other areas that are not fully used because they have not been properly constructed.

An example of an area that could sustain many more camels, and therefore people, if it had a larger number of properly built and maintained wells is the Zemmour, a region rich in vegetation both in winter and in summer. However, the Zemmour has only a few wells with permanent water, although many an *oglat*, or man-made water hole a few meters deep. The oglats are an uncertain source of water, as we found in 1972 when we visited Oumat el-Ham, 80 kilometers north of Bir Moghrein. We had expected to fill our goatskin water bags there for our return trip to Bir Moghrein, but found instead that the oglats were producing hardly enough fresh water for the nearby military encampment of four tents. We were therefore forced to cut short our trip and to go without water for a day during our return journey. The oglats are not geared for the rapid watering of large herds, although they have played an important role in local history and legend; there are often rock-piled tombs nearby of men who died fighting for the scarce water of an oglat, or from accidents that occurred during construction of an oglat, or of thirst because an oglat was dry or the water inaccessible without a rope and water bag.

Because the oglats in the Zemmour are an insufficient and undependable source of water, many nomads leave the area before summer when the immense barren areas all around cannot be crossed because they have few or no wells. We encountered excellent pastures in August in the Zemmour that were almost unused because of the poor watering conditions. Many of the nomads had taken their herds south to Bir Moghrein, one of the few places where the wells are properly equipped. Every day in summer there were large camel herds there waiting to be watered. Camels had to walk a long way between pastures and well, passing caravans were sorely inconvenienced, and the sheep, goats, and donkeys owned by residents of Bir Moghrein had little food because every bit of vegetation in a wide circle around the well had been eaten by camels waiting to be watered.

Of the 40 oglats and wells we visited in Mauritania, most were poorly constructed; only nine of the wells had drinking troughs of sorts, and the walls of only a few were lined with stones or cement to prevent water pollution. However, most of the wells were a permanent source of water, in use even in the drought year 1973.

Types of Wells   Unlike the permanent deep wells, the water content of the oglats is dependent on rainfall. In the Zemmour, where oglats are particularly numerous, sometimes several dozen together in a dry river bed, a number of animals can be watered by hand at one time. However, the oglats are dug in soft soil, so sand can readily drift or fall into the water. The water in an oglat at any one time is usually limited, although water may continue to seep into an oglat for 3 or 4 years after a flood.

In Mauritania most permanent wells (called *bir* or *hassi*) are 10–20 meters deep, although in the south they may be as deep as 50 or even 100 meters. Most have been constructed by the nomads, sometimes long ago, so it is not surprising that, because of a lack of materials and the great distance of wells from villages, they are of primitive construction. Their water comes not only from rains but from fossil groundwater that has been stored for many thousands of years in underground pores and fissures in the rocks. These wells are usually lined with rocks or cement so that they will not cave in.

There are two systems for drawing water, one dependent on manpower and the other on animal power. The first type is common in the Algerian Sahara, where there are fewer camels than in Mauritania. The water is drawn with the help of a pulley fixed on a vertical frame above the well mouth (pl. 61). Two men pulling alternately can draw 20–30 liters of water in 20 seconds from a 30-meter-deep well. Deep well water can also be drawn by hand in Mauritania, as was done for our hired camels and for most stock in 1973, when the camels were too weak for this arduous work, but most of the wells are geared for the animal power of camels and, occasionally, donkeys.

In Mauritania a nomad at a well usually supplies his own pulley, which is made of hard wood and is highly valued (pl. 62), his own rope of leather or twine, and a floppy *dellou*, or water bag made from an old rubber tire, which holds about 50 liters of water. The pulley is attached to the forked trunk of a tree that slants over the well mouth and is embedded deep in the ground (pl. 63). The rope is swung over the pulley, with one end fastened to the dellou and the other to the harness of a strong camel. As the camel is led by a man or child to the well mouth, the dellou is lowered into the well and fills with water. As the camel is led away from the mouth, it pulls up the dellou to the hands of a waiting nomad, who calls to the camel to stop and then pours the water into a trough or basin. The well mouth is usually situated so that the camel pulling up the water moves downhill, the length of the path along which it walks corresponding to the depth of the well. Often two camels pulling water alternately can work with one dellou at one pulley. Although it takes a camel only 15 seconds to pull a full dellou to the surface from a 20-meter-deep well, by the time each camel is turned about, the water is poured from the dellou, and the dellou is dropped into the well again, only about 100 liters of water per minute can be brought up by two camels alternately pulling one dellou.

However, the best-yielding wells have two pulleys, one on either side, at which two teams of two camels each can work with two dellous at once, one camel at each side simultaneously drawing up one dellou each while the other two dellous are dropped into the well (p. 64). They bring up about 200 liters per minute, enough to water 100–120 camels in a few hours. Only a few wells yield this much water, although many other wells could be adapted, at very little expense, to yield as much water.

In arid zones a fair number of medium-yield wells a reasonable distance apart would be of far greater benefit than a few big-yield wells attracting herds from great distances. The number of animals that can be watered at a well is always limited by the quality of the surrounding pastures, and wells with big water yields by their popularity may cause overgrazing of the surrounding vegetation. In the Niger Sahel there are some very big wells capable of supplying enough water each day for about 6,000 cows (each drinking 10–30 liters) and 50,000 sheep (each drinking about 3 liters). But the actual number of animals watered at such wells is far lower because the vegetation cannot sustain such a large number of animals. In the Mauritanian Sahel, too, there is the potential for overgrazing because of the large number of wells, but this danger does not exist in the desert proper, where wells may be 100 or more kilometers apart. In central and northern Mauritania there are seldom more than 500 or 600 camels per day at a well.

Many wells in the Sahara are named for the man who drilled or improved them, and he has priority at his own well. Otherwise, watering is done in the order in which herds arrive. In the Sahel, where the population is essentially sedentary, the mouths of the wells are surrounded by many forked trunks on which to fasten pulleys, each one belonging to a family of the group that drilled the well.

Well Structure   *Lining of well.* Most permanent wells are lined with stones or cement to prevent cave-ins. Because oglats are not lined, a permanent conduit and trough cannot be constructed for them. The fresh-water well closest to Bir Moghrein is 150 kilometers away and is not lined, so water from it, which is trucked to Bir Moghrein for human drinking, is comparatively expensive; in 1972, 200 liters cost $1.00. The slightly salty water of the wells of Bir

Moghrein is used only for cooking by the few thousand local inhabitants and for watering animals.

Wall around mouth of well. Without a wall around the mouth of a well, enough sand can fall into the water that the well must be dredged frequently (pl. 65). To do this, a man is lowered into the well to send many dellous full of sand to the surface for disposal. This work represents a loss of human energy and a loss of watering time for the camels. If dredging is required during a visit to a well, the nomads may water their camels only once and, in cases of severe dehydration, the camels may not be able to drink enough water to regain their original weight. If they are not fully rehydrated at the well, they will not be able to feed normally. Also, the quality of the water in a permanent well lacking a wall around the mouth can be seriously impaired, which could be rectified with only a small amount of cement to construct such a wall. Ideally the stonework or cement lining of the well should be built up about 1 meter above the surrounding terrain. Such a wall helps keep dirt, sand, animals, and people from falling into the water, and facilitates the handling of the dellou.

Well lid. In Algeria, but not in Mauritania, wells often have lids to prevent sand from blowing into them when they are not being used. Indeed, in nonsandy soil a lid can serve in lieu of a wall to keep sand out of smaller wells. The lids should open so that they lean against a stone pillar at the side of the well. The pillar can also serve as a marker for the well. It sometimes happens that people, even nomads, miss a well without landmarks in an unknown region and die of thirst not far from it.

Optimal size of well mouth. Well mouths should measure about 1.5 meters across, because drawing water can be difficult if the opening is substantially smaller or larger than this. Many very old wells have mouths several meters across, which formerly allowed several slaves to pull water at once. Wells with very large mouths tend to be deep and unlined, and thus dangerous and subject to pollution. They are also very difficult to improve.

Conduit. A slanting stonework or cement conduit that leads down from the well opening to the basin where the animals drink makes the work of the man who empties the dellou far easier. He does not have to lift the heavy container to transfer water to the basin; he need merely tip it into the conduit. Conduits also keep the animals away from the men as they work, and prevent water from being wasted as it is poured from the dellou. They allow easily frightened foals to drink without approaching men too closely, and people can fill their water bags without interfering with the animals. Conduits may be open, as at Bir Moghrein, or enclosed as pipes under the soil. Despite their usefulness, very few wells in Mauritania have conduits.

Installation for pulley. Most Mauritanian wells deeper than 8 meters have slanting tree trunks alongside them that lean over the opening to which pulleys can be attached. Such installations would be invaluable on all wells, for without them a man must pull up vertically the full weight of water. Frames such as those used in Algeria could be installed to save the immense effort required to pull up water manually. We once watched a man draw over 4,000 liters of water from an 8-meter-deep well during 1½ hours, a feat that would exhaust just about any one.

Drinking trough or basin. Although for purposes of watering camels the most important part of a well installation is the drinking trough, this container is usually completely inadequate, with camels milling about wild with thirst, the man drawing water shouting at the animals to give him room, and other men yelling and whipping away most of the camels so that a few at a time can drink undisturbed. Most wells have only a low metal tin that holds 50 liters, a quantity of water two camels can consume in 1 minute (pl. 66). Since 10 or more camels are often trying to drink at once, such basins are the center of a great deal of shoving and pushing. Even the cement basins attached to the most important wells are generally inadequate, increasing rather than reducing the difficulties of watering. Types of basins include:

Deep basins embedded in the ground. These basins can be used only when they are completely full of water. To fill them, as many as five people may be needed to hold back the thirsty animals. Young camels, which have relatively shorter necks than adults, must lie down to drink, and thus get in the way of the other camels. Animals often trip on the cement edge of a basin and fall into the water. These basins must be cleaned fairly often.

Basins with walls that are too high. Basins are sometimes elevated so that sand will not get into them. Where a basin is higher than the wall surrounding the mouth of the well, men drawing water must lift the heavy dellou up to the basin. This work is particularly tiring if the basin is separated from the well, and often results in a great deal of water being spilled.

Basins that are too small. Camels push and shove to get at the water in small basins and in the process often jostle the man who is hoisting the dellou, causing water to be spilled. The camels sometimes fall right over, their soft feet slipping in the mud. Only about five camels can circle a small basin at one time, some of them probably not drinking as much as they would like.

Basins that are too large. Basins are sometimes built large to accelerate watering, but they are generally inadequate because men or animals cannot draw water as fast as the camels surrounding the basin can drink it (pl. 67). For example, the Bir Moghrein main well has a low basin 4 meters square around which 30 camels can gather. When four camels are drawing water, they can supply 200 liters per minute, less than half of what the camels could consume in a minute if enough water were available. They do not like to drink from the bottom of the basin, where sand accumulates, so if an owner has only a few camels to water he does so in the small traditional metal tins, wasting time, effort, and water. A further disadvantage of large basins is that animals that come alone to the well can easily step into the basin to drink and while there may pollute the basin with their urine or feces, which must then be cleaned before camels, which prefer clean to dirty water, can again be watered.

A Model Well Installation Since a big camel needs on the average 20–30 liters of water a day and may go for 10 days in summer without drinking, it may consume up to 200 liters on a single visit to a well. Ideally this water should be unpolluted and readily accessible so the camel need not waste time in waiting, in being beaten back by men, or in fighting with other camels. For major wells that have two pulleys at which four camels can draw water, the basin should be about 2 meters long and 0.7 meters wide, so that 15 or so animals can drink at one time. The working animals will be able to supply 200 liters of water per minute, enough to provide a continuous flow to satisfy all those drinking. Wells with only one pulley should have a smaller basin, which ideally would provide sufficient water for eight camels at a time. All basins should be 40 centimeters deep and set on a cement base 20 centimeters high, with a margin not larger than 20 centimeters so as not to hamper the drinking animals (fig. 15).

Before 1964, during the French occupation of Bir Moghrein, both windmills and motors were used to pump water from the town wells to the surface. In 1 hour a 1-horsepower pump could draw enough water for 100 camels. But motors use gas and must be kept in working order, which is unfeasible for people unused to mechanical engines and who do not have ready access to gasoline supplies. Windmills could conceivably be used, but they too would need to be maintained. (Those at Bir Moghrein, like the motors, broke down years ago and have never been repaired.) Moreover, because wind- or motor-powered pumps would have to be used more or less continuously, much water would evaporate and be wasted between visits by nomads; if they were only connected when a nomad arrived at a well, they would not draw water fast enough to water his camels quickly. In addition, many wells are incapable of supplying large quantities of water on a steady basis; their capacity depends on the rock or soil into which they have been drilled. In the Eastern Erg, for example, where wells are often less than 10 meters

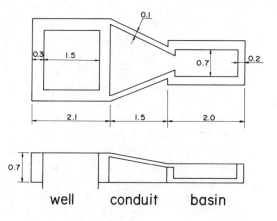

Fig. 15   Top and side view of an ideal desert well. Measurements in meters.

deep, a well may yield only 6–10 liters per minute, not enough to water many camels. In the Erg Iguidi, where water lies near the surface, it takes as long as 10 hours in April to water 100 camels.

It may be possible to drill Artesian wells in the now barren desert that would yield 5,000 or more liters of water per minute, but such a project could not be justified because of the limited vegetation and because of the expense of such a project. Besides, since most wells produce enough water to satisfy local needs, efforts should be directed to improving existing installations to facilitate and make safer the watering of herds. If the equipment were improved as suggested earlier, there would be a number of benefits: Camels could be watered more quickly, which would give them more time to graze. They would be more likely to rehydrate completely, which would allow them to graze to their maximum capacity—and only well-fed camels can compensate completely for water loss. If camels are totally rehydrated, they will need to drink less often and will be able to visit pastures farther from the well. By speeding up the process of watering, which can last as long as 3 days for a very large herd, the area around the well would be less subject to overgrazing. This is especially important where there are sheep and goats, which must be watered every day and consequently must obtain all their food near the well. Less water would be wasted from spillage, and there would be fewer accidents and injuries. A great deal of human effort could be spared— work that often must be carried out in full sunlight when temperatures in the shade may be as high as 45° C (pl. 68).

Any efforts to improve the desert wells of Mauritania should be directed first at the wells used most, although it may be difficult to ascertain which wells are indeed used most. Although nomads are aware of the movements of a few other migratory herds via the "Arab telephone," no one keeps track of the visits to wells of all the nomadic herds in the western Sahara. However, it is possible to gauge the relative use of a well by the extent of the camel pellet deposits. If pellets are deposited in a 100-meter or smaller radius from the well, the well is considered little used; if they are deposited in a 150-meter radius, the well is considered much used. We estimated that the most-used well at Char had 11.3 million pellets around it in 1973. If it is assumed (1) that each camel that visits a well is watered twice and stays 5 hours near the well, (2) that the average output of feces per camel is 38 pellets per hour, and (3) that the pellets last 5 years before disintegrating, then the number of visits that camels made to the well at Char per year was 9,300, mostly during the 5-month summer watering period. This value would be much lower now because of the many camel deaths during the drought.

Another, less direct way to estimate well use is to measure the extinction of plants around a well. The plants nearest a well are grazed almost completely by animals waiting for hours to be watered, so that only dried-out grasses, plants less than 10 centimeters high, trees with leaves 3.5 meters above the ground, and species not eaten by domestic stock (as *Cassia italica*) remain uneaten where a well is heavily used.

11 Recent Uses

Recent Military Use The French, who later made good use of camels throughout the Sahara, were first introduced to camels in Egypt at
the end of the eighteenth century during Napoleon
Bonaparte's campaign there. (The following information is
largely from a voluminous work of P. Denis [1966], a
former member of the French camel corps.) Camel units
were formed with riding camels from other countries, as
riding camels were unknown in Egypt, and saddles from
the Sudan (Gautier 1950). First 100, and soon thereafter
700, camels were mobilized and ridden by French soldiers
in full hussar dress. They were to assist the Orient Army
in their battles against the Mameluke cavalry, and they
adopted a technique similar to that used by the early Mus-
lims: in battle the camels were couched in a circle and the
men crouched behind them, firing over their bodies. If the
enemy fled, the French could quickly mount their camels
in pursuit. These units, however, only functioned for 2
years. When Napoleon returned to Paris, he brought his
camel with him and gave it to a zoo. It was stuffed when it
died and exhibited until 1933 in the Paris Museum of Natural History.

In 1835 French troops used camels to transport military
matériel during their early occupation of Algeria. Soon
three camel transport companies were formed, and in 1844,
the first large contingent of camels participated in a 110-
day expedition. In 1852, 1,500 camels and donkeys were
used to transport building materials for the construction of
a commanding officer's house in an Algerian oasis, a prec-
edent for the building later of many houses and mosques at
oases. At that time the capacity of the camel was over-
estimated; it was believed that a strong animal was able
to carry 300 kilograms plus a rider for 100 kilometers a day
for several consecutive days, had to drink only once a
week in summer, and needed to graze only 2 hours a day.

It is not surprising that many camels died. The French soldiers knew nothing about and cared little for their camels, so that until the end of the nineteenth century the French sought out indigenous camel men to care for their camels. Even so, the logistics of finding enough time, security, food, and water to care for as many as 2,000 animals in one place were almost insurmountable.

In 1883, the British created a camel corps in the Egyptian Sudan, which until 1921 took part in all military operations. The first official French camel corps were established shortly after this, but they were not successful because the French soldiers were still unable to handle their mounts properly and camels continued to die from overwork. In 1900, 20,000 of the 34,000 camels used by the French military died while in service. Other countries also suffered great camel losses because of their lack of knowledge of the camel. During the second Afghan war (1878–80) the British lost 70,000 camels. The Russians also lost most of their camels while fighting against Turkmenian tribes in the Kara Kum desert (Bulliet 1975). Much more recently, 20,000 Sudanese camels died in the cold mountains of Ethiopia during the British campaign against the Italians before World War II.

Only in this century did Europeans begin to use camels in a rational and efficient way, beginning with the creation in 1902 of the Saharan companies, based on the ideas of General Laperrinne, who played an important role in the ongoing pacification of the Sahara. Laperrinne visualized not large armies of mounted men as in the past, but small, mobile units that would be able to cope with dissident nomads, whose tribal quarreling was the main source of strife in the desert. The mounted camel men, called *méharistes* by the French, were at first nomads fully adapted to living and fighting in the desert who were utilized by the French with very little special training. By this time the Chaanba of the Algerian Sahara had been pacified, and they formed the bulk of the camel corps. They penetrated deeply into the desert, pursuing enemies and forming a reliable liaison service. They knew how to care for their camels and how to survive on natural resources, and were only too happy to raid their traditional enemies, the Tuareg, Tibbu, and Maures, who continued organizing razzias all over the desert. Each mehariste possessed two camels of his own, so that one was always available for work while the other pastured. The French had only to provide each man with arms and equipment.

Each unit of meharistes was led by a French officer. A unit acted independently when it became separated from another group or from base camp, often by several hundred kilometers. The meharistes became an elite corps for the conquest of the Sahara, and they increasingly preferred camels to horses. From 1927 on, camel men were the only mounted infantry in the Sahara. Through the meharistes, the Europeans and the desert nomads gradually began a period of socialization.

Typically, a group of meharistes moved slowly, with the men marching half the time to keep the camels in good condition. If they approached the enemy at night, the camels' mouths were tied shut to keep them quiet. Fighting took place on foot, even when the meharistes began their charge on camels. The Tuareg, for example, were armed not only with a gun but also with a spear, which they threw while still mounted on their camels before jumping to the ground to engage in hand-to-hand fighting. When possible, however, the French tried to subdue the enemy without fighting.

The meharistes often pursued rebellious nomads relentlessly. One of the most famous raids was led by Captain Le Cocq, who in March 1932 pursued the emir of Adrar, whose people had killed some of his men. The meharistes covered 770 kilometers in 8 days, averaging 100 kilometers per day during the first 5 days. In 1911, Captain Charlet, after tracking down Tuareg who had been illegally trading in slaves, set off on another raid, during which he and his men covered more than 7,000 kilometers (Peyré 1957). In general, military camels needed 6–8 months of rest each year; badly overworked camels might require a year's rest to recover fully.

The resistance of nomad tribes to the French conquerors was fiercest and longest lasting in the west. The Reguibat and Maures were excellent warriors who in times of trouble could escape from their pursuers into Spanish Sahara, which at that time was not under effective European control. They were subdued only in 1934, with the occupation of Tindouf. Even so, the Reguibat were again involved in razzias and fighting at the time Morocco became independent, in 1956, and again when Spain gave up control of Spanish Sahara, in 1975.

When rebellion in Algeria against France began in 1954, the Chaanba, who until then constituted most of the camel corps, could no longer be trusted and were largely replaced by Europeans. Despite the increasing use of motor vehicles—which were first used in the Sahara in 1916—the camel went unchallenged in the mountains and dune massifs, where travel by car was extremely difficult. During the rebellion, which spanned the years 1954–62, camel corps sometimes worked alongside motorized units in the more than 100 battles that were fought in the Sahara. By this time there were many centers to be defended, such as oil camps and convoys (since 1956), oil and gas pipelines, the rocket base near Béchar at the edge of the desert, and the atomic research center in the central Sahara. Vehicles were sometimes used to transport camels from one place to another, three in a truck. In 1960 two entire mehariste corps were moved in this way. The British have shipped military camels from one country to another, and camels have even been transported by plane where time is short. Camels are said to become seasick on ships and airsick when flying.

The meharistes not only had a thorough knowledge of the country and its inhabitants, a great resistance to deprivation, and a good sense of observation and orientation, but also had initiative and spontaneity and were vigilant. They were also adept at understanding and caring for their camels. On long trips into unknown parts of the desert, they became interested in the vegetation because the well-being of their mounts depended on it for food, and in other subjects as well—geology, zoology, prehistory. Meharistes like Cauvet and Cauneille contributed much to our knowledge of the desert at a time when it was inaccessible to most people.

After all of the Saharan tribes had been subdued, and before the French withdrew from Algeria, camel corps continued to patrol the desert, now becoming friendly with the nomads against whom they had fought. The French differed from other colonial troops in that they spoke Arabic and respected the nomads' customs and way of life. The last French corps was disbanded in 1962, but the Reguibat we met still spoke of their bravery and many regretted their departure. Camel corps also existed—and some still exist—in Iraq, Syria, Egypt, Arabia, Yemen, and Jordan, but their military use is now quite limited.

Razzias   Desert nomads in the past participated with relish in raids, or razzias, to steal camels, slaves, goods, and sometimes women, of rival tribes. This favored occupation gave Europeans the excuse to attack the nomads in efforts at "pacification." Raids, carried out mainly by the Tuareg, Reguibat, and Tibbu, sometimes took them 1,000 kilometers across the desert and netted them only a few camels. However, during a Tuareg razzia in 1844, 6,000 camels were captured from nomads west of Ouarane, in Mauritania (Monod 1958). The Reguibat and Tuareg often fought, raiding back and forth for months at a time. These journeys required great resistance to thirst, hunger, and fatigue, but nonetheless many nomads died. The Reguibat were impressed with how well the Tuareg camels were trained and with how quiet they were during razzias. To speed up mounting a camel in a razzia, the Tuareg trained their camels to crouch down only on their forelegs instead of lowering themselves completely to the ground (Monod 1958).

After the French subdued the Tuareg, in 1902, they concentrated on the Reguibat and the Beraber, another nomadic tribe of the western Sahara that constantly menaced oases in the Saoura and Tuat areas to capture slaves for sale in Morocco. After Tindouf was occupied in 1934 and the Rio de Oro was conquered by Spain, the era of widespread razzias in the Sahara ended.

In northern Kenya raiding is still practiced by young nomads to enlarge their herds of camels or cattle at the expense of their neighbors. Bands of such thieves, called *shifta*, formed after the Somali uprisings that followed Kenya's independence in 1963. Such raids, which are fiercely resisted, often lead to intertribal wars.

Scientific Exploration

Not only were large numbers of camels trained for warfare misused, but camels mobilized for peaceful purposes were also misused. In 1898, a scientific expedition led by Foureau, a French explorer, and Lamy, a military officer, both experienced in the Sahara, left from Ouargla, Algeria, to cross the Sahara. They had 1,000 camels loaded with a year's supply of food, and an abundance of munitions and soldiers; they did not want another disaster like that suffered by Colonel Flatters, who 20 years earlier had been sent to study the possibility of a trans-Saharan railway to stop the slave trade and who had been murdered along with his men by the Tuareg. During the first week of the Foureau-Lamy expedition, 150 camels died because they were overloaded and underfed, and the rest of them were dead by the time the party straggled halfway across the Sahara. It took the expedition a year to reach Chad, where it met up with two other expeditions from Niger and the Congo.

Until about 1950, scientists and explorers continued to traverse the Sahara with camels, but few do so today. Probably the greatest Saharan scientist—a man of broad interests, including geology, botany, zoology, and paleontology—is Théodore Monod. In his research he has covered on camel and on foot a distance greater than that between the earth and the moon, including trips of 1,000 kilometers without encountering a well. The camel for the scientist has the great advantage over the car of being able to go almost anywhere without a breakdown, of being able to fuel itself from local vegetation, and of allowing the scientist time to examine his surroundings closely as he travels. A plant, an insect, a lizard track, a prehistoric tool, or a special soil formation—things that would not even be seen from a moving vehicle—can be studied in passing, as it were. The scientist on a camel shares the hardships of the nomad and can understand the desert far better than his motorized colleague.

Salt Caravans   After the gold and slave caravans ceased operating in the Sahara, only the salt caravans remained. Salt has always been rare south of the Sahara yet vital to the physiology of men and animals, which need large amounts because of sweating. It comes mostly from the southern Sahara, mined from rock salt deposits, as in Idjil (Mauritania) or Taoudeni (Mali), extracted from saline water by evaporation, or leached from salt-containing earth, as in Bilma (Niger). In the ancient salt mine town of Teghazza (Mali), the houses and mosque were built of salt bars.

Today salt caravans (called *azalaï*) are less important than they were, and serve a smaller area (near the ocean people now obtain salt by saltwater evaporation techniques). The Saharan salt transport, still done exclusively by camels (which can carry a maximum load of four bars of salt totaling 140 kilograms), represents the most important commerce in the southern Sahara. In some years more than 20,000 camels carry salt for the 3-week journey from Taoudeni to Timbuktu, where it is exchanged mainly for millet. In 1900, 50,000 camels transported 6,000 metric tons of salt; in 1950, 31,250 carried 3,750 metric tons (Capot-Rey 1953); but in 1967, no more than 1,600 metric tons were transported by camels (Schiffers 1972). For some nomadic tribes, participation in an azalaï is still a traditional proof of virility. Many people from Timbuktu work at the salt mines of Taoudeni, 700 kilometers farther north, despite the extremely hard working and living conditions there (Planhol and Rognon 1970), and participate in azalaïs from the mines. The azalaï that transports salt southward from Bilma has to travel over a completely barren desert for 5 days and thus must carry food for the camels.

Small caravans sometimes still carry goods like tea, sugar, dates, and textiles a few hundred kilometers across the desert. Since time is of little value, long journeys can be undertaken for small profit. In 1962, a Tibbu caravan from Tibesti covered 2,000 kilometers in 3 months to exchange goods (Schiffers 1972). Today goods can be moved by camel from Bilma to Agadez for one-seventh the cost of truck transport (Vallet and Bordessoule 1978). Increasingly, travel agencies make arrangements for tourists to join working caravans, and sometimes arrange special caravans for tourists.

The Future of the Camel   An extensive literature has been compiled both on camel rearing in general (Griuner 1928–29) and on camel rearing in specific regions—in India (Krishnamurthi 1970; Malhotra et al. 1972), in Africa (Middaugh 1964), and in Turkmenistan (Donchennko 1956)—showing that camels are a vital resource in arid lands where other animals cannot survive. The vast stretches of arid land in many poor Saharan countries can be utilized only with the camel, via its meat, milk, wool, and even its droppings, which are used for fuel. If these countries settle their nomads in permanent settlements, the desert will be of little use. If the nomads are encouraged to continue their centuries-old way of life, the desert will continue to serve as an important resource, providing food and livelihood for millions of human beings.

In North Africa, the raising of camels for meat, even for export, could become a valuable industry. Sudan in 1956 exported 38,000 camels for meat to Egypt and also sent camels to Arabia. (Export figures are difficult to obtain because nomads are chary of being quizzed about the number of camels they own and the number they sell to butchers, in case they should be taxed.) Camels are shipped live to butchers because of the lack of refrigeration. If camel shipping could be expedited to cut down on death and weight loss during transit, many more could be profitably exported to meat-hungry nations.

With the increasing threat of world hunger, scientists have extended their research to include camel meat as a food source, either for man or for other animals. Al-Delaimy and Barakat (1971), for example, have found a way to use garlic to improve the shelf life of fresh camel meat; Barakat and Abdalla (1965) have calculated the ascorbic acid content of the edible liver (58.06 milligrams per 100 grams); and Afifi (1972) has analyzed the digestibility of camel fat as food for chicks (83.9 percent). Camel meat, like other meats, must be treated carefully so that it does not become infected by salmonella (Burmistrova et al. 1965). Its marketability has been studied by el-Gharbawi et al. (1974, 1975).

The possibility of producing camel meat commercially in Australia has also been studied. There is no doubt of the camel's potential as a meat animal. In 1962, after a 10-year period of drought, 600 slaughtered feral camels were found to be fat and nearly all the females were pregnant (McKnight 1969). Although camel meat is comparable to beef in fat and protein content (table 16), a camel carcass yields only one-third its weight in meat, which is less than the ratio in cattle, and people are reluctant to taste camel meat (Newman 1975). These drawbacks, together with the high mobility of camels and the problems of slaughtering them, make it unlikely that camel meat will ever compete with beef or mutton in Australia.

Camel milk is vital to the nomads. After a pregnancy, a

Table 16 Protein and Fat Content of Trimmed Meat from Camels and Cattle

Cut of Meat	% Protein	% Fat
Camel:		
Rump	23.4	15.7
Chuck	20.8	27.0
Rib	22.6	12.6
Cattle:		
Chuck	17.6	22.0
Loin	15.6	31.0
Round	18.7	17.0

Source: Newman (1975).

camel female may produce up to 3,000 kilograms of milk in 18 months (Frädrich-Leupold 1971) or nearly 1,800 liters in 6 months (Scheifler 1972). In Ethiopia seven well-fed females at various stages of lactation milked twice daily yielded an average of 6.6 kilograms of milk per day, or a ratio of daily yield to body weight of 0.0186 (Knoess 1977). Bulliet (1975) reports that in south Arabia most male calves are killed to maximize milk production.

Camel milk has a high vitamin C content, plus more fat, protein, and minerals than cow's or goat's milk (Knoess 1977). Frädrich-Leupold (1971) gives the following composition for milk from camels in Pakistan: 2.9 percent fat, 3.67 percent protein, 5.78 percent lactose, and 0.66 percent mineral salts. The following authors also give analyses of camel milk: Leese (1927), Kheraskov (1939), Balakaev (1958), Bestuzheva (1959), Grzimek (1959), Kon and Cowie (1961), Miller-Ben-Shaul (1962), Khan and Appanna (1967), Morrison (1968), and Rao, Gupta, and Dastur (1970).

In central Asia, camel milk (called *shubat*) has long been known for its curative powers. It is used in therapy for stomach infections and to cure tuberculosis (Akhundov, Amanov, and Dubrovskaya 1972; Akundov, Dyrdyev, and Serebryakov 1972; Monteil 1966). Efforts are being made to increase the production of camel milk so that eventually it may be the basis for a curative center in the Soviet Union similar to that founded in 1858 near Kuybyshev that utilizes *kumys*, or horse milk (Scheifler 1972). Camels in the Soviet Union are raised largely for milk production in cooperatives of 3,000–5,000 animals. One herdsman looks after 100–120 camels, which are unattended in summer but return to a familiar well at intervals to be watered by their herdsman (Prof. Nina Nichaeva, personal communication, 1975).

Camel wool and hides have great potential value. In Turkey and the southwestern Soviet Union, a camel supplies 2–3.5 kilograms of wool annually (Epstein 1969). In the Sahara, camels are shaved or the wool is gathered when the animals shed; in Tunisia, young camels yield about 3 kilograms of wool and adults yield about 2 kilograms (Burgemeister 1975). It is mixed with goat's wool and woven by the nomads into long bands, called *fleidj*. Twelve fleidj, sewn together, make a spacious tent 10 × 8 meters. The wool is also used for clothes, blankets, ropes, and bags. Camel wool is sometimes used for transmission belts and doormats. In 1938 over 500,000 kilograms of camel wool was imported into the United Kingdom (Leitch 1940). Nomads generally do not sell camel hides but, rather, use them to make saddles, rope, and leather vessels.

Appendixes

Appendix A Fieldwork on Camels in Algeria and Mauritania by Gauthier-Pilters*

Time of Study (funding agency in parentheses)	Principal Aims (publications in parentheses)	Number of Animals Studied	Study Area
March–August 1954 (Ministry of Foreign Affairs, France)	Behavior, herd structure (Pilters 1955a, 1955b, 1956)	100s of free-grazing animals	150 km around Sahara Research Center, Beni-Abbès, Algeria
April 1955–May 1956 (UNESCO)	Behavior, composition of pastures, food preferences, water content, quality and quantity of food intake, drinking rhythm, drinking, water intake, feces and urine output (1958, 1959a, 1959b, 1960, 1961)	f = 62† d = 195	Same
March–June 1961 (UNESCO)	Composition and productivity of pastures, food and water intake, drinking rhythm (1965, 1970a)	Numerous free-grazing animals	Algerian-Mauritanian area between Tindouf and Eglab, mainly Erg Iguidi
March–June 1964 (Institut Fondamental d'Afrique Noire, Dakar)	Composition and productivity of pastures, food and water intake (1969, 1971)	f = 33 d = 82	Central Mauritania (Adrar, Amsaga, Erg Akchar)
August–September 1969 (Centre National de la Recherche Scientifique, France, and Centre de la Recherche sur les Zone Arides)	Drinking rhythm and water intake for comparison with better-fed animals in the same region in 1955, state of pastures (1972b)	d = 106	Erg, hamada, and wadi near Beni-Abbès
August–September 1970 (Centre National de la Recherche Scientifique)	Drinking rhythm and speed, water intake, food intake (1977)	f = 3 d = 113	Central Mauritania, wells of Agui, Char, and Ben Amera

Date (Institution)	Study	f/d	Location
August–September 1971 (Deutsche Forschungsgemeinschaft, Godesberg) August 1972	Food and water intake of 4 working camels during 24-day 600-km trip, composition of pastures, state of wells (1975, 1977) Food and water intake of 4 working camels during 8-day 120-km trip, water intake of free-grazing camels, water input and output of Gauthier-Pilters and Dagg (1975, 1977)	f = 4 d = 4 f = 4 d = 9	Zemmour, northern Mauritania
July 1973 (Deutsche Forschungsgemeinschaft)	Food and water intake of 4 working camels during 12-day trip, water loss through urine and feces, drinking rhythm and water intake of free-grazing camels, water intake and output of Gauthier-Pilters and Dagg during 15 days (1977)	f = 4 d = 4 + 49	Central Mauritania, Adrar, wells of Char, Tenrharada, Ain Ouagf

*In August 1978 Gauthier-Pilters also studied guarded camel herds in northern Kenya.
†f = studies on feeding; d = studies on drinking.

Appendix B   Volume of Water Drunk and Urine Produced in Women
under Extreme Heat Stress

In the desert, the observation that human beings drink
a great deal of water but produce little urine led us to
measure these volumes in ourselves during field trips on
which we studied camels in the summers of 1972 and
1973. During our work we usually walked 10–15 kilometers a day, resting for 4 hours in what little shade
was available during the hottest part of the day. We ate
dry biscuits and coffee for breakfast; rice or spaghetti
for lunch; and spaghetti, rice, or soup for dinner. We
drank water whenever we were thirsty, which was most
of the time, measuring and recording the amount we consumed. Our input equaled this value plus the amount
of soup or any other liquid consumed, while our output
equaled the amount of urine we produced each day. We
never urinated more than three times a day, and sometimes only twice.

During 19 days of measurements we produced a daily
average of 340 milliliters of urine each (minimum 168,
maximum 571, $N = 38$). In 1972 the urine output was
13.2 percent of liquid input for Dagg and 12.9 percent
for Gauthier-Pilters, but in 1973 (which was hotter) it
was 8.3 percent and 5.2 percent, respectively. These volumes were considerably less than the volume of urine
excreted under normal conditions in temperate regions—
about 1–1.5 liters per day.

Unlike urine output, water input varied directly with
temperature. During our 1972 trip, when the maximum
daily temperature varied between 33° and 41° C, we each
drank at most 5.9 liters and at least 1.6 liters per day.
In 1973, when the maximum daily temperature varied
between 40° and 47° C and the minimum between 25°
and 31° C, Gauthier-Pilters drank significantly more than
Dagg (maximum 7.2 vs. 5.1 liters; minimum 4.2 vs. 3.5

liters) because she spent more time in the direct sun observing camels. Gauthier-Pilters also produced less urine each day during the 1973 trip, perhaps because she worked much longer in the desert and was better adapted to its hard conditions. Our minimum values of urine production per day were 168 and 192 milliliters, respectively (3.7 and 3.5 percent of the water consumed), well below the lowest volume of 230 milliliters per day obtained by Adolph et al. (1969) for men in North American deserts. This is perhaps because Adolph worked with men who were presumably heavier than we are (we weigh about 58 kg each). Most of the difference between our water input and urine output is accounted for by evaporation, although the Saharan winds were so omnipresent that we were seldom conscious of sweating.

During a 20-day camel trip through Mauritania in January and February, Monod (1964) noted that the least amount of water he drank in one day was 470 milliliters and the least amount urine he produced was 164 milliliters. As a percentage of the water taken in, the minimum amount of urine he produced was 11 percent, but averaged 30 percent per day. By contrast, Dagg, upon her return to Canada, produced 80 percent.

Bibliography

Abdalla, M. A., and O. Abdalla. 1979. Morphometric observations on the kidney of the camel, *Camelus dromedarius*. *J. Anat.* 129:45–50.

Abdalla, O., and I. Arnautovic. 1970. Morphological study of the lateral nasal gland of the one-humped camel. *Acta Anat.* 76:123–30.

Abdalla, O., I. Arnautovic, and M. F. A. Fahmy. 1971. Anatomical study of the liver of the camel (*Camelus dromedarius*). I. Topography and morphology. *Acta Morphol. Neerl. Scand.* 9:85–100.

*   Abdalla, O., M. F. A. Fahmy, and I. Arnautovic. 1970. Anatomical study of the lacrimal apparatus of the one-humped camel. *Acta Anat.* 75:638–50.

Abd-Ellatif, M., A. A. Kandil, and S. El-Kaschab. 1979. Study of body changes in Delta camel in Egypt. *Indian J. Anim. Sci.* 49:656–58.

*   Abdel Magid, A. M., and A. I. Abdel Razaq. 1975. Relationship and possible function of the nasal sacs and glands of the one-humped camel, *Camelus dromedarius*. *Acta Anat.* 91:423–28.

*   Abdel-Raouf, M., M. R. Fateh el-Bab, and M. M. Owaida. 1975. Studies on reproduction in the camel (*Camelus dromedarius*). V. Morphology of the testis in relation to age and season. *J. Reprod. Fertil.* 43:109–18.

Abdel-Wahab, M. F., M. S. Abdo, Y. M. Megahed, and S. A. Elmougy. 1974. Thyroxine content in the thyroid gland of domestic animals. VII. Iodinated tyrosines and thyronines in the serum of she camel at various reproductive stages. *Endokrinologie* 63:116–21.

Abdo, M. S., F. al-Chalabi, A. A. al-Kafaur, and A. S. al-Janabi. 1971. Studies on the ascorbic acid content of the ovaries of camel (*Camelus dromedarius*) during the various reproductive stages. *J. Fac. Med. Baghdad* 13:18–24.

Abdo, M. S., A. S. al-Janabi, and A. A. al-Kafaur. 1969. Studies on the ovaries of the female camel during the reproductive cycle and in conditions affected with cysts. *Cornell Vet.* 59:418–25.

Note. This bibliography includes all important references on *Camelus dromedarius*. References marked with an asterisk are cited in text.

Abdo, M. S., A. A. Farahat, and F. A. Fahmy. 1974. Further studies on prostaglandins. I. Effect of crude prostaglandins extracted from prostate glands of camels (*Camelus dromedarius*) on the endocrine glands of immature male and female rats. *Biol. Zentralbl.* 93:697–705.

Abdou, M. S. S., A. B. Elwishy, M. S. Abdo, and S. A. Elsawaf. 1971. Hormonal activities of the placenta of the one-humped camel, *Camelus dromedarius*. I. Gonadotrophic, adrenocortico-trophic and thyrotrophic hormones. *J. Anim. Morphol. Physiol.* 18:11–16.

Abu-Sinna, G. M. E., and S. M. Habaka. 1974. The cholesterol and phospholipid contents of the serum in the camel *Camelus dromedarius*. *Ann. Zool. Acad. Zool. (Agra, India)* 10:57–60.

Acland, P. D. E. 1932. *Notes on the camel in the eastern Sudan.* Sudan Notes and Records 15.

* Adam, J. G. 1962. Itinéraires botaniques en Afrique occidentale. *J. Agr. Trop. Bot. Appl.* 9:1–256.

Adamsons, K., S. L. Engel, H. B. van Dyke, B. Schmidt-Nielsen,and K. Schmidt-Nielsen. 1956. The distribution of oxytocin and vasopressin (antidiuretic hormone) in the neurohypophysis of the camel. *Endocrinology* 58:272–78.

* Adolph, E. F., et al. 1969. *Physiology of man in the desert.* New York: Hafner.

Afifi, A. K. 1964. The subcommissural organ of the camel. *J. Comp. Neurol.* 123:139–45.

————. 1964. The pineal body in the camel. *Anat. Record* 148:356.

* Afifi, M. A. 1972. Comparative studies of the digestibility of beef, buffalo, camel and mutton fats for chicks. *Brit. J. Nutr.* 27:97–100.

* Akhundov, A. A., G. N. Amanova, and V. V. Dubrovskaya. 1972. [Some results of treating pulmonary tuberculosis patients with antibacterial preparations together with "chal," a product of camel milk.] *Zdravookhr. Turkm.* 16:36–38.

* Akhundov, A. A., B. Dyrdyev, and E. P. Serebryakov. 1972. [Effect of combined treatment on water-electrolyte exchange in pulmonary tuberculosis patients.] *Zdravookhr. Turkm.* 16:40–44.

al-Bagdadi, F. A. K. 1966. The tongue of the camel (*Camelus dromedarius* and *Camelus bactrianus*). *Nord. Veterinaermed.* 18:337–46.

————. 1969. The adrenal gland of the camel (*Camelus drome-darius*): A study of the comparative anatomy and lipoids. *Zentralbl. Veterinaermed.*, ser. A, 16:354–64.

* Albright, W. F. 1942. *Archaeology and the religion of Israel.* Baltimore: Johns Hopkins Press.

* ————. 1961. *The archaeology of Palestine*, pp. 206–7. Baltimore: Penguin Books.

* Al-Delaimy, K. S., and M. M. F. Barakat. 1971. Antimicrobial and preservative activity of garlic on fresh ground camel meat. I. Effect of fresh ground garlic segments. *J. Sci. Food Agr.* 22:96–98.

Ali, H. A., K. A. Moniem, and M. D. Tingari. 1976. Some his-tochemical studies on the prostate, urethral and bulbourethral glands of the one-humped camel (*Camelus dromedarius*). *Histochem. J.* 8:565–78.

Ali, H. A., M. D. Tingari, and K. A. Moniem. 1978. On the morphology of the accessory male glands and histochemistry of the ampulla ductus deferentis of the camel (*Camelus dromedarius*). *J. Anat.* 125:277–92.

Alwan, A. S. 1968. Socioeconomic issues of nomads' settlement in the western desert of the UAR. *Land Reform* 1:28–35.

* Amoroso, E. C., O. G. Edholm, and R. E. Rewell. 1947. Venous valves in the giraffe, okapi, camel and ostrich. *Proc. Zool. Soc. London* 117:435–40.

* Antonius, O. 1922. *Grundzüge einer Stammesgeschichte der Haustiere*. Jena: Verlag Fischer.

Appanna, T. C., and C. R. Vyas. 1969. Effect of dietary camel milk protein on urinary creatinine excretion of rats. *J. Nutr. Diet* 6:106–10.

* Appleyard, H. M. 1967. Observations on cortical-cell size and arrangement in some animal fibres. *J. Roy. Microscop. Soc.* 87:1–6.

* Arnautovic, I., and O. Abdalla. 1969a. Unusual blind sac on the face of the one-humped camel. *Acta Anat.* 73:272–77.

* ———. 1969b. Elastic structures of the foot of the camel. Ibid. 72:411–28.

* Arnautovic, I., O. Abdalla, and M. F. A. Fahmy. 1970. Anatomical study of the vomeronasal organ and the nasopalatine duct of the one-humped camel. *Acta Anat.* 77:144–54.

* Arnautovic, I., and A. M. Abdel Magid. 1974. Anatomy and mechanism of distension of the dulaa of the one-humped camel. *Acta Anat.* 88:115–24.

Arnautovic, I., M. E. Abu Sineina, and M. Stanic. 1970. The course and branches of the facial nerve of the one-humped camel. *J. Anat.* 106:341–48.

Arnautovic, I., M. F. A. Fahmy, and O. Abdalla. 1972. Anatomical study of the liver of the camel (*Camelus dromedarius*). II. The course and distribution of the portal vein, hepatic artery and hepatic duct. *Acta Morphol. Neerl. Scand.* 9:211–20.

* Arnold, G. W. 1964. Factors within plant associations affecting the behaviour and performance of grazing animals. In *Grazing in terrestrial and marine environments*, ed. D. J. Crist. Oxford: Blackwell.

* Asdell, S. A. 1964. *Patterns of mammalian reproduction*. Ithaca, N.Y.: Comstock.

Awad, E. S., and L. Kotite. 1966. Camel myoglobin. *Biochem. J.* 98:909–14.

* Awkati, A., and F. al-Bagdadi. 1971. Lacrimal gland of the camel (*Camelus dromedarius*). *Amer. J. Vet. Res.* 32:505–10.

Badawi, H., M. el-Shaieb, and A. Kenawy. 1977. The arteria maxillaris of the camel (*Camelus dromedarius*). *Anat. Histol. Embryol.* 6:21–28.

* Balakaev, B. 1959. [*Vitamin content in milk of agricultural animals in the Turkmen SSSR.*] Referat. Zh. Biol., no. 67682.

Banerjee, S., and R. C. Bhattacharjee. 1963. Distribution of body

water in the camel (*Camelus dromedarius*). *Amer. J. Physiol.*
204:1045–47.

Banerjee, S., R. C. Bhattacharjee, and T. I. Singh. 1962.
Hematological studies in the normal and adult Indian camel
(*Camelus dromedarius*). *Amer. J. Physiol.* 203:1185–87.

Banerjee, S., and A. S. Bhown. 1964. Studies on camel hemoglobin. *Biochim. Biophys. Acta* 86:502–10.

———. 1965. Sequence of amino acids in the new peptides of
camel globin. *Ibid.* 100:503–8.

* Bannikov, A. G. 1958. Distribution géographique et biologie du
cheval sauvage et du chameau de Mongolie (*Equus przewalskii
et Camelus bactrianus*). *Mammalia* 22:152–60.

* ———. 1975. Wild camels in Mongolia. *Oryx* 13:12.

* ———. 1976. Wild camels of the Gobi. *Wildlife* 18:398–403.

* Baptidanova, Y. P., G. A. Schmidt, V. G. Shagaeva, and
V. E. Bondarenko. 1975. [Comparative morphology of intra-
uterine development in tylopods and ruminant artiodactyls.]
Zh. Obshch. Biol. 36:664–69.

* Barakat, M. Z., and A. Abdalla. 1965. The ascorbic acid content
of edible liver. *J. Food Sci.* 30:185–87.

Barakat, M. Z., and M. Abdel-Fattah. 1970. Biochemical analysis
of normal camel blood. *Zentralbl. Veterinaermed.*, ser. A,
17:550–57.

———. 1971. Seasonal and sexual variations of certain constituents of normal camel blood. *Ibid.*, ser. A, 18:174–78.

Barclay, N. E. 1966. Marginal bands in duck and camel erythrocytes. *Anat. Record* 154:313.

* Barker, H. M. 1972 [1964]. *Camels and the outback.* Rigby: Seal
Books.

Barmintsev, I. N. 1973. [Herd raising of horses and camels:
An important factor in producing animal industry products.]
Zhivotnovodstvo 4:24–30.

Barone, R. 1957. Observations sur l'arbre bronchique et les vais-
seaux pulmonaires d'un chameau (*Camelus dromedarius*).
Compt. Rend. Anat. 43:185–89.

Barone, R., and A. Belemlih. 1973. Le neopallium du dromadaire
(*Camelus dromedarius* L.). *Zentralbl. Veterinaermed.*, ser. C,
2:301–15.

* Bartels, H., P. Hilpert, K. Barbey, K. Betke, K. Riegel,
E. M. Lang, and J. Metcalfe. 1963. Respiratory functions of
blood of the yak, llama, camel, Dybowski deer, and African
elephant. *Amer. J. Physiol.* 205:331–36.

Bartha, R. Die physiologische Anpassung des Kamels an die
besonderen Umweltbedingungen der weitraumigen Trocken-
gebiete [Physiological adaptation to vast arid zones]. *Tropenlandwirt* 72:138–48.

* Baskin, L. M. 1974. Management of ungulate herds in relation to
domestication. *IUCN (International Union for Conservation of
Nature and Natural Resources) Publications*, n.s., 24:530–41.

* ———. 1976. [*Behavior of ungulates.*] Moscow: Academy of Sciences.

Bego, U. 1960. Die vergleichende Anatomie der Blutgefässe und
Nerven der vorderen Extremitäten bei Kamel, Lama, Giraffe
und Rind. *Acta Anat.* 42:261–62.

Berg, R., el-S. Taher, and M. S. eldin-M. Moustafa. 1967. Prenatal growth of some organs in the camel (*Camelus dromedarius*). I. Relations between body weight and body length,
heart and lung weight. *Zentralbl. Veterinaermed.*, ser. A.
14:774–76.
———. 1968. Comparison of prenatal growth of some organs in
the camel (*Camelus dromedarius*) and the Egyptian water buffalo
(*Bos/Bubalus/bubalis* L). Ibid., ser. A, 15:438–47.
———. 1969. Comparative studies on the prenatal growth of the
brain, thymus, stomach and oesophagus in the camel (*Camelus
dromedarius*) and Egyptian water buffalo (*Bos/Bubalus/bubalis*
L). Ibid., ser. A, 16:659–63.
Bernengo, M. G. 1970. [Observations on the morphology of
blood cells in Tylopoda and their relative serum values.] *1st
Lombardo Accad. Sci. Lett. Rend. Sci. Biol. Med.*, ser. B,
104:33–45.
* Bestuzheva, K. T. 1959. [*Chemical composition of colostrum and
milk of female-camels.*] Referat. Zh. Biol., no. 67681.
* Bhargava, K. K., V. D. Sharma, and M. Singh. 1963. A study of
mortality rate, sex-ratio and abortions in camel (*Camelus dromedarius*). *Indian J. Vet. Sci. Anim. Husb.* 33:187–88.
* ———. 1965. A study of the birth-weight and body measurements of camel (*Camelus dromedarius*). Ibid. 35:358–62.
Bhatt, P. L., and R. N. Kohli. 1959. A preliminary study on
camel's blood sedimentation rate. *Indian Vet. J.* 36:376–79.
———. 1962. Quantitative bio-chemical studies on camel's
blood. II. Inorganic phosphorus and sodium content. Ibid.
39:201–2.
Bhattacharjee, R. C., and S. Banerjee. 1962. Biochemical studies
on Indian camel (*Camelus dromedarius*). II. Inorganic constituents of serum. *J. Sci. Indus. Res.* 21C:106–7.
Bhown, A. S., and S. Banerjee. 1963. Biochemical studies on
Indian camel (*Camel dromedarius*). IV. Camel haemoglobin.
Indian J. Exp. Biol. 1:164–66.
———. 1972. Biochemical studies of Indian camels (*Camelus
dromedarius*) haemoglobin: Alkali resistance properties. *Indian
J. Biochem. Biophys.* 9:214–15.
Blaudin de Thé, B. 1960. *Essai de bibliographie du Sahara français et
des régions avoisinantes.* Paris: Arts et Métiers Graphiques.
* Bodenheimer, F. S. 1957. The ecology of mammals in arid zones.
In *Human and animal ecology: Reviews of research*, pp. 100–32.
Paris: UNESCO.
* Bohlken, H. 1960. The stomach and the systematic position of the
Tylopoda. *Proc. Zool. Soc. London* 134:207–15.
Bokori, J. 1974. Contribution to the haemograms of the buffalo
and of the camel. *Acta Vet. Acad. Sci. Hung.* 24:73–76.
Borricand, P. 1948. La nomadisation en Mauritanie. *Travaux Inst.
Recherches Sahariennes (Alger)* 5:81–93.
Boué, A. 1946. Le méhari Reguibi. *Revue Vet. Milit.* 2:141.
———. 1948. Les chameaux de l'ouest saharien. *Revue Elevage
Méd. Vét. Pays Trop.* 2:194–201.
———. 1951–52. L'originalité du chameaux. Ibid. 5:109–14.
Box, T. W. 1971. Nomadism and land use in Somalia. *Econ.
Devel. Cultural Change* 19:222–28.

* Brand, D. J. 1963. Records of mammals bred in the National
Zoological Gardens of South Africa during the period 1908 to
1960. *Proc. Zool. Soc. London* 140:617–59.

Braun, K., S. Z. Rosenberg, and L. Bellin. 1958. The electrocardiogram of a camel. *Amer. Heart J.* 55:754–57.

Bremaud, O. 1969. *Notes sur l'élevage camélin dans les districts du
nord de la république de Kenya.* Roneo. Maisons-Alfort, France:
Institut d'Elevage et de Médecine Vétérinaire des Pays Tropi-
caux.

* Bremaud, O., and J. Pagot. 1960. Pâturages, nomadisme et trans-
humance en zone sahélienne. In *Colloque général sur les prob-
lèmes de la zone aride,* Paris: UNESCO.

Bricteux-Grégoire, S., R. Schyns, and M. Florkin. 1971. N-
terminal amino acid sequence of dromedary trypsinogen.
Biochim. Biophys. Acta 251:79–82.

Brown, C. E. 1936. Rearing wild animals in captivity and gestation periods. *J. Mammal.* 17:10.

* Bulliet, R. W. 1975. *The camel and the wheel.* Cambridge, Mass.:
Harvard University Press.

Burgemeister, R. 1974. *Probleme der Dromedarhaltung und Zucht in
Süd-Tunesien.* Giessen: Institut für Tropische Veterinärmedi-
zin.

* ———. 1975. *Elevage de chameaux en Afrique du Nord.* Deutsche
Gesellschaft für technische Zusammenarbeit.

———. 1976. Die Verbreitung und Nutzung des Dromedars
[Distribution and use of dromedaries]. *Tropenlandwirt*
77:43–53.

* Burmistrova, O. G., V. M. Pylaeva, N. M. Furmanova, and M. A.
Ataev. 1965. [An outbreak of Salmonella-caused toxin infection
due to the consumption of camel meat.] *Vopr. Pitaniya* 24:89.

Cabannes, R., and C. Serain. 1955. Etude de l'hémoglobine du
dromadaire d'Afrique du Nord. *Compt. Rend. Soc. Biol. (Paris)*
149:1103–5.

* Capot-Rey, R. 1942. Le nomadisme pastoral dans le Sahara français. *Travaux Inst. Rech. Sahariennes (Alger)* 1:63–86.

* ———. 1953. *Le Sahara français.* Paris: Presses Universitaires
de France.

* Cartier, M., and M. Piette. 1968. Etude morphologique des
hematies des camélidés par microdensitométrie permettant
une reconstruction tridimensionelle. *Compt. Rend. Hebd.
Séances Acad. Sci. (Paris),* ser. D, *Sci. Natur.* 266:1665–67.

Cauneille, A., and J. Dubief. 1955. Les Reguibat Legouacem:
Chronologie et nomadisme. *Bull. Inst. Fondamental Afrique
Noire,* ser. B, 17:528–50.

* Cauvet, G. 1925–26. *Le chameau.* 2 vols. Paris: Baillière.

* ———. 1929. Dromadaires à 34 dents et dromadaires à 36 dents.
Bull. Soc. Hist. Natur. Afrique Nord 20:247–56.

Chandrasena, L. G., B. Emmanuel, and H. Gilanpour. 1979. A
comparative study of glucose metabolism between the camel
(*Camelus dromedarius*) and the sheep (*Ovis aries*). *Comp.
Biochem. Physiol.,* ser. A, *Comp. Physiol.* 62:837–40.

Chandrasena, L. G., B. Emmanuel, D. W. Hamar, and B. R.

Howard. 1979. A comparative study of ketone body metabolism between the camel (*Camelus dromedarius*) and the sheep (*Ovis aries*). *Comp. Biochem. Physiol.*, ser. B, *Comp. Biochem.* 64:109–12.

* Charnot, Y. 1953. De l'évolution des camélidés: Apparition du dromadaire au Maroc. *Bull. Soc. Sci. Maroc* 33:207–30.

* ———. 1958. Répercussion de la déshydratation sur la biochimie et l'endocrinologie du dromadaire. Thesis, Faculté des Sciences, Université de Paris.

———. 1959. A propos de l'écologie des camélidés. *Bull. Soc. Sci. Natur. Phys. Maroc* 39:29–39.

———. 1959. Mesure de la surface de la peau et détermination de la constante K du dromadaire dans la formule de Meeh. Ibid. 39:141–44.

* ———. 1960. Répercussion de la déshydratation sur la biochimie et l'endocrinologie du dromadiare. *Travaux Inst. Sci. Chérifien, Sér. Zool.* 20:1–167.

———. 1961. Histaminémie du dromadaire. *Compt. Rend. Séances Mens. Soc. Sci. Natur. Phys. Maroc* 27:131.

———. 1961. L'histaminoplexie du dromadaire. Ibid. 27:189–90.

———. 1961. Equilibre minéral tissulaire dans la déshydratation du dromadaire. *J. Physiol. (Paris)* 53:793–806.

———. 1963*a*. Cycle sexuel et déhydratation chez le dromadaire. *Compt. Rend. Séances Mens. Soc. Sci. Natur. Phys. Maroc* 29:138–41.

* ———. 1963*b*. Synchronisme de croissance de l'expansion palatale et du testicule au cours du cycle sexuel chez le dromadaire. *Bull. Soc. Sci. Natur. Phys. Maroc* 43:49–54.

———. 1964. Le cycle testiculaire du dromadaire. Ibid. 44:37–44.

———. 1965. Endocrinologie sexuelle et déshydratation chez le dromadaire male. *Compt. Rend. Séances Soc. Biol. (Paris).* 159:1103–5.

———. 1967. Régulation endocrinienne du métabolisme de l'eau chez le dromadaire. *Bull. Soc. Sci. Natur. Phys. Maroc* 47:217–26.

Charnot, Y., and J. Racadot. 1963. Mise en évidence de catégories cellulaires distinctes dans le lobe antérieur de l'hypophyse du dromadaire. *Bull. Microscop. Appl.* 13:144–48.

Chatty, D. 1972. *Structural forces of pastoral nomadism: With special reference to camel pastoral nomadism.* The Hague: Institute of Social Studies.

Chet Ram, N. D. Khanna, D. P. Sinha, and S. S. Prabhu. 1964. Studies on camel blood antigenic factors detected through cattle blood-group reagents. *Indian J. Vet. Sci. Anim. Husb.* 34:239–41.

Chiodi, H. 1970. Comparative study of the blood gas transport in high altitude and sea level Camelidae and goats. *Resp. Physiol.* 11:84–93.

Christian, E. 1926. Das Gebiss des Dromedars (*Camelus dromedarius*). D.V.M. dissertation, Tierarztlichen Hochschule, Berlin.

* Clair, M. 1962. *De la résistance du chameau à la soif.* Paris: R. Foulon.

∗ Cockrill, W. R. 1975. Impressions of veterinary education and the practice of veterinary medicine in China. *Brit. Vet. J.* 131:633–38.

Cohen, W. D., and N. B. Terwilliger. 1979. Marginal bands in camel erythrocytes. *J. Cell Sci.* 36:97–107.

Crandall, L. S. 1964. *The management of wild mammals in captivity.* Chicago: University of Chicago Press.

∗ Cross, H. E. 1917. *The camel and its diseases.* London: Baillière, Tindall & Cox.

∗ Curasson, G. 1939. *Sur quelques plantes toxiques ou reputées toxiques pour le bétail.* Bulletins de la Service Zootechnique et Epizootique de l'AOF.

∗ ———. 1947. *Le chameau et ses maladies.* Paris: Vigot Frères.

∗ Dagg, A. I. 1974. The locomotion of the camel (*Camelus dromedarius*). *J. Zool. (London)* 174:67–78.

∗ ———. 1979. The walk of large quadrupedal mammals. *Can. J. Zool.* 57:1157–63.

∗ Dagg, A. I., and A. de Vos. 1968. The walking gaits of some species of pecora. *J. Zool. (London)* 155:103–10.

∗ Dagg, A. I., and J. B. Foster. 1976. *The giraffe: Its biology, behavior, and ecology.* New York: Van Nostrand Reinhold.

∗ Dagg, A. I., and A. Taub. 1971. Flehmen. *Mammalia* 34:1–14.

Dakkuri, A., P. Naccache, and R. I. Sha'afi. 1972. Sodium and potassium transport in camel red cells. *Comp. Biochem. Physiol.*, ser. A, *Comp. Physiol.* 43:1019–23.

Danho, W. O. 1972. The isolation and characterization of insulin of camel (*Camelus dromedarius*). *J. Fac. Med. Baghdad* 14:16–28.

———. 1973. Pituitary lactogenic hormone from the camel (*Camelus dromedarius*): Purification and amino acid composition. Ibid. 15:57–62.

Danho, W. O., H. G. Gattner, D. Nissen, and H. Zahn. 1975. B-chain shortening of matrix-bound insulin with pepsin. II. Preparation and properties of camel despentapeptide (B26-30) and des-Phe[Bi]-des-Pentapeptide (B26–30) insulin. *Hoppe-Seylers Z. Physiol. Chem.* 356:1405–12.

∗ Davidson, A. 1974. Intensive care and re-introduction of neonatal ungulates. *Internat. Zoo Yearbook* 14:183–84.

De la Tour, G. D. 1971. Zur Vererbung der Höcker beim Kamel, Dromedar und Tulu. *Säugetierkdl. Mitt.* 19:193–94.

∗ Dementiev, G. P., and D. Zevegmid. 1962. Bemerkungen über das Wildkamel der Mongolei. *Zool. Gart.*, n.s., 26:298–305.

∗ Demon, L., P. de Felice, H. Gondet, L. Pontier, and Y. Kast. 1957. Recherches effectuées par la Section de Physique du Centre de Recherches Sahariennes en 1954, 1955 et 1956. *J. Rech. Centre Nat. Rech. Sahariennes* 38:30–63.

∗ Demougeot, E. 1960. Le chameau et l'Afrique du Nord romaine. *Ann. Econ. Soc. Civil.* 15:209–47.

∗ Denis, P. 1960. *La justice chez les nomades algériens.* Document of Centre de Hautes Etudes administratives sur l'Afrique et l'Asie modernes, Paris, no. 2353.

∗ ———. 1966. *L'évolution des troupes sahariennes françaises de Bonaparte à nos jours.* Roneo. Rennes: Published with the help of Centre National de la Recherche Scientifique.

* ———. 1970. Observations sur le comportement du dromadaire. Thesis, Faculté des Sciences de l'Université de Nancy.

* Dittrich, L. 1976. Food presentation in relation to behaviour in ungulates. Internat. Zoo Yearbook 16:48–54.

* Donchennko, V. V. 1956. [The one humped camel in Turkmenistan and the methods of the improvement of breed.] Referat. Zh. Biol., no. 72079.

Doolittle, R. F., D. Schubert, and S. A. Schwartz. 1967. Amino acid sequence studies on artiodactyl fibrinopeptides. I. Dromedary camel, mule deer, and cape buffalo. Arch. Biochem. Biophys. 118:456–67.

* Dowling, D. F., and T. Nay. 1962. Hair follicles and the sweat glands of the camel (Camelus dromedarius). Nature 195:578–80.

* Droandi, I. 1936. Il camello. Florence: Istituto Agricolo Coloniale Italiano.

* Dubief, J. 1959, 1963. Le climat du Sahara. Vols. 1 and 2. Mémoire., Institut de Recherches Sahariennes (Alger).

Durand, M., and M. Kchouk. 1959. Quelques constantes hématologiques chez le dromadaire tunisien. Arch. Inst. Pasteur (Tunis) 36:183–94.

Duran-Jorda, F. 1950. Secretion of red blood corpuscles as seen in the camel. Nature 165:280.

Durdyev, B. 1976. [Quantitative indices of the morphological composition of young camel blood in ontogeny.] Izv. Akad. Nauk Turkm. SSR, Ser. Biol. Nauk 6:84–85.

Durdyev, B., P. V. Kozlov, and A. Khangel'dyev. 1975. [Blood serum carotene content of young Arabian camels in ontogenesis.] Izv. Akad. Nauk Turkm. SSR, Ser. Biol. Nauk 2:81–83

Durr, I. F., and N. Cortas. 1964. The reduction of pantethine by an extract of camel intestine. Biochem. J. 91:460–63.

Dyusembin, Kh. 1972. [Milk ejection in the female camel.] Trudy Inst. Fiziol. Alma-Ata, Kazakh SSR 17:33–36.

Dzhu-Magulov, I. K. 1976. [Milk yield and milk fat content and their inheritance in interspecies hybridization of the Bactrian camel with the dromedary.] Izv. Akad. Nauk Kazakskoi SSR, Biol. 6:69–75, 86.

Eitan, A., B. Aloni, and A. Livne. 1976. Unique properties of the camel erythrocyte membrane. II. Organization of membrane proteins. Biochim. Biophys. Acta 426:647–58.

el-Azab, E. A., and B. Musa. 1976. Early detection of pregnancy in the camel using biological methods. Zuchthygiene (Berlin) 11:166–68.

el-Din M. Moustafa, M. S., R. Berg, and el-S. Taher. 1968. Prenatal growth of some organs in the camel (Camelus dromedarius). III. Relations of kidney and adrenal weights to body weight and between right and left kidney. Zentralbl. Veterinaermed., ser. A, 15:148–55.

el-Ghannam, F., E. A. el-Azaband, and S. el-Sawaf. 1974. Preliminary study on the application of Cuboni test for pregnancy diagnosis in the camel. Zuchthygiene (Berlin) 9:46.

* el-Gharbawi, M. I., M. A. Abdalla, and el-Moussana S. el-

Goundy. 1974. Studies on some market meats in Egypt. I. Changes in nitrogenous compounds during aging, freezing and storage. *Libyan J. Agr.* 3:125–30.

* el-Gharbawi, M. I., T. H. Foda, M. S. el-Dashlouty, and el-Moussana S. el-Goundy. 1975. Studies on some market meats in Egypt. II. Histological characteristics as influenced by aging, freezing and storage. *Libyan J. Agr.* 4:13–17.

el-Sheikh, A. S., A. A. Rasheed, and S. O. Amin. 1966. Histological changes in the foetal thyroid of the dromedary (*Camelus dromedarius*). *J. Anat.* 100:831–37.

Elwishy, A. B., and S. A. Elsawaf. 1971. Functional activity of the ovaries and uterine horns in fat-tailed sheep and camels (*Camelus dromedarius*). *Fortpflanzung Besamung Aufzucht Haustiere* 7:181–87.

Elwishy, A. B., A. M. Mobarak, and S. M. Fouad. 1972. The accessory genital organs of the one-humped male camel (*Camelus dromedarius*). *Anat. Anz.* 131:1–12.

Emmanuel, B., B. R. Howard, and M. Emady. 1976. Urea degradation in the camel. *Can. J. Anim. Sci.* 56:595–601.

* Emmett, C. 1932. *Texas camel tales.* San Antonio: Naylor.

* Epstein, H. 1969. *Domestic animals of China*, pp. 117–21. Farnham Royal, England: Commonwealth Agricultural Bureau.

* ———. 1971. *The origin of the domestic animals of Africa*, pp. 545–84. New York, London, Munich: Africana Publishing Co.

* Estes, R. 1972. The role of the vomeronasal organ in mammalian reproduction. *Mammalia* 36:315–51.

* Etemadi, A. A. 1966. Diaphragm and os diaphragmaticum in *Camelus dromedarius*. *Acta Anat.* 65:551–60.

Evans, J. V., J. Roberts, and N. S. Agar. 1970. Delta type Merino sheep: A rare blood type with some erythrocyte characteristics approaching those found in the camel. *Australian J. Exp. Biol. Med. Sci.* 48:25–32.

Fahmy, M. F. A., O. Abdalla, and I. Arnautovic. 1972. Anatomical study of the liver of the camel (*Camelus dromedarius*). III. The hepatic veins. *Acta Morphol. Neerl. Scand.* 9:221–28.

Fahmy, M. F. A., I. Arnautovic, and O. Abdalla. 1971. The morphology of the tarsal glands and the glands of the third eyelid in the one-humped camel. *Acta Anat.* 78:40–46.

* Farias, P. F. de Moraes. 1967. The Almoravids: Some questions concerning the character of the movement during its periods of closest contact with the western Sudan. *Bull. Inst. Fondamental Afrique Noire,* ser. B, 29:794–878.

Fazil, M. A. 1977. The camel. *Bull. Anim. Health Product. Africa* 25:435–42.

Finberg, J. P. M., R. Yagil, and G. M. Berlyne. 1978. Response of the renin-aldosterone system in the camel to acute dehydration. *J. Appl. Physiol. Resp. Environ. Exercise Physiol.* 44:926–30.

* Finbert, E. J. 1938. *La vie du chameau.* Paris: Librairie Fayard.

* Foley, H., and Lieutenant Musso. 1925. Les plantes du Sahara toxiques pour les animaux. *Arch. Inst. Pasteur (Alger)* 3:394–400.

183   **Bibliography**

Forbes, R. J. 1965. The coming of the camel. *Studies in Ancient Technology,* vol. 2, chap. 4. Leiden: Brill.

* Foster, J. B., and A. I. Dagg. 1972. Notes on the biology of the giraffe. *East African Wildlife J.* 10:1–16.

Fouad, S. M., A. M. Mobarak, and M. A. Aly. 1979. Micromorphology of the arteries of the penis of the one-humped camel (*Camelus dromedarius*). *Indian J. Anim. Sci.* 49:377–79.

* Fowler, H. D. 1950. *Camels to California.* Stanford, Calif.: Stanford University Press.

* Frädrich-Leupold, J. 1971. Kamele. In *Pflanzliche und tierische Produktion in den Tropen und Subtropen,* pp. 861–71. Handbuch der Landwirtschaft und Ernährung in den Entwicklungsländern, vol. 2. Stuttgart: Verlag Eugen Ulmer.

* Fraguier, G. de. 1955. Cheval et chameau. *Bull. Liaison Saharienne* 19:70–72.

* Free, J. P. 1944. Abraham's camels. *J. Near Eastern Stud.* 3:187–93.

* Frison, G. C., D. N. Walker, S. D. Webb, and G. M. Zeimens. 1978. Paleo-Indian procurement of *Camelops* on the northwestern plains. *Quaternary Res. (N.Y.)* 10:385–400.

* Gabriel, A. 1958. *Das Bild der Wüste.* Vienna: A. Holzhausens.

Gatt Rutter, T. E. 1967. Diseases of camels: Protozoal diseases. *Vet. Bull.* 37:611–18.

Gatt Rutter, T. E., and R. Mack. 1963. Diseases of camels: Bacterial and fungal diseases. *Vet. Bull.* 33:119–24.

* Gaudio, A. 1967. *Les civilisations du Sahara.* Paris: Verviers, Gérard.

* Gauthier-Pilters, H. 1958. Quelques observations sur l'écologie et l'éthologie du dromadaire dans le Sahara nord-occidental. *Mammalia* 22:140–51.

* ———. 1959a. Einige Beobachtungen zum Droh-, Angriffs- und Kampfverhalten des Dromedarhengstes und über Geburt und Verhaltensentwicklung des Jungtieres in der nordwestlichen Sahara. *Z. Tierpsychol.* 16:593–604.

* ———. 1959b. *Unter Nomaden und Kamelen.* Kempen-Niederrhein: Thomas-Verlag.

* ———. 1960. Ergänzende Beobachtungen zum aggressiven Verhalten und Kampfspiel bei Tylopoden. *Georg v. Opel Freigehege für Tierforschung, Jahrbuch 1959/60,* pp. 104–7. Frankfurt:
* Buchdruckerei Schäfer & Co.

———. 1961. Observations sur l'écologie du dromadaire dans le Sahara nord-occidental. *Mammalia* 25:195–280.

* ———. 1965. Observations sur l'écologie du dromadaire dans l'ouest du Sahara. *Bull. Inst. Fondamental Afrique Noire,* ser. A, 27:1532–1608.

* ———. 1969. Observations sur l'écologie du dromadaire en moyenne Mauritanie. Ibid., ser. A, 31:1259–1380.

* ———. 1970a. *Atschana—das heisst Durst.* Dusseldorf: Schwann-Verlag.

———. 1970b. Le dromadaire—fables et réalités. *MIFERMA—Informations* 19:47–52.

* ———. 1971. Que valent les pâturages sahariens? Ibid. 21:50–56.

————. 1972a. La consommation d'eau du dromadaire en été dans la région de Beni-Abbès. *Bull. Inst. Fondamental Afrique Noire,* ser. A, 34:219–59.

* ————. 1972b. Le puits pastoral dans le désert. *MIFERMA—Informations* 23:50–56.

————. 1973. Les nomades du désert. Ibid. 25:31–56.

————. 1974. The behaviour and ecology of camels in the Sahara with special reference to nomadism and water management. *IUCN Publications,* n.s., 24:542–51.

* ————. 1975. Observations sur la végétation d'été du Zemmour mauritanien. *Bull. Inst. Fondamental Afrique Noire,* ser. A, 37:555–604.

* ————. 1977. Contribution à l'étude de l'éco-physiologie du dromadaire en milieu naturel pendant l'été (1970–1973) en moyenne et haute Mauritanie. Ibid., ser. A, 39:385–459.

* Gautier, A. 1966. *Camelus thomasi* from the northern Sudan and its bearing on the relationship *C. thomasi–C. bactrianus. J. Paleontol.* 40:1368–72.

* Gautier, E. F. 1950. *Le Sahara.* Paris: Payot.

Geddes, L. A., W. A. Tacker, and J. P. Rosborough. 1974. Cardiac output in an anesthetized dromedary. *Amer. J. Vet. Res.* 35:131–33.

Geddes, L. A., W. A. Tacker, J. P. Rosborough, J. D. Bourland, P. A. Cabler, A. G. Moore, T. D. Pate, J. D. McCrady, and E. M. Bailey. 1973. Cardiovascular studies on an anesthetized dromedary camel. *Cardiovasc. Res. Center Bull. (Houston)* 11:53–71.

Geddes, L. A., W. A. Tacker, J. Rosborough, A. G. Moore, and P. Cabler. 1973. The electrocardiogram of a dromedary camel. *J. Electrocardiol. (San Diego)* 6:211–14.

George, N. 1951. The adrenals of the camel. *Brit. Vet. J.* 107:122–24.

————. 1957. Some observations on the foetal circulation in the camel. Ibid. 113:219–20.

* Ghobrial, L. I. 1970. A comparative study of the integument of the camel, Dorcas gazelle and jerboa in relation to desert life. *J. Zool. (London)* 160:509–21.

* ————. 1974. Water relation and requirement of the Dorcas gazelle in the Sudan. *Mammalia* 38:88–107.

Ghosal, A. K., T. C. Appanna, and P. K. Dwaraknath. 1973. Studies on the seasonal variations in the blood constituents of Indian camel (*Camelus dromedarius*). *Indian J. Anim. Sci.* 43:642–44.

————. 1975. A note on the effect of short-term water deprivation on certain blood characteristics in the camel (*Camelus dromedarius*). Ibid. 45:105–8.

Ghosal, A. K., P. K. Dwaraknath, and J. M. L. Patney. 1973. A note on plasma carotene and vitamin A levels in normal camels (*Camelus dromedarius*) of north-west Rajasthan. *Indian J. Anim. Sci.* 43:899–900.

Gillespie, I. A. 1962. Riding camels of the Sudan. *Sudan J. Vet. Sci.* 3:37–42.

* Gillet, H. 1961. Pâturages sahéliens: Le ranch de l'Ouadi Rimé (Zone Nord). *J. Agr. Trop. Bot. Appl.* 8:465–536, 557–692.

Gluhbegović, N. 1976. Uber die kollateralen Bänder des Kniege-
    lenkes des Kamels. *Verh. Anat. Ges.* 70:597–603.
Gode, P. K. 1958. Notes on the history of the camel in India
    between B.C. 500 and A.D. 800. *Janus* 47:133–38.
Gombe, S., and D. Oduor-Okelo. 1977. Effect of temperature and
    relative humidity on plasma and gonadal testosterone concen-
    trations in camels (*Camelus dromedarius*). *J. Reprod. Fertil.*
    50:107–8.
Grahame, T. 1944. The ureter and arterial blood supply to the
    kidney of the camel. *Vet. J.* 100:257–61.
*   Gray, A. P. 1972. *Mammalian hybrids*, pp. 161–62. Farnham Royal,
    England: Commonwealth Agricultural Bureaux.
*   Greenly, A. H. 1952. Camels in America. *Papers Bibliogr. Soc.
    Amer.* 46:359–72.
*   Griuner, S. A. 1928–29. [Bibliography on camel raising.] *Rept.
    Siberian Vet. Inst. Omsk* 10:329–37.
*   Grzimek, B. 1959. Zusammensetzung von Kamelmilch. *Zool.
    Gart.* 23:247.
*   ———. 1968. Heutige Kamele. *Grzimek's Tierleben* 13:143–57.
*   Gsell, S. 1914. *Histoire ancienne de l'Afrique du Nord.* 2d ed. Paris:
    Hachette.
Gulliver, P. P. 1971. Nomadism among the pastoral Tankana of
    Kenya: Its natural and social environment. In *Society and social
    change in Eastern Africa Nkanga.* Makerere: Institute of Social
    Research.
Gunstone, F. D., and R. P. Paton. 1953. Animal fats. I. The com-
    ponent acids of deer fat and of camel fat. *Biochem. J.* 54:617–21.
Gupta, A. K., K. K. Vyas, P. K. Dwaraknath, and P. K. Pareek.
    1979. Effect of breeding season, castration and exogenous tes-
    tosterone on blood-glucose level and eosinophil count of male
    camels (*Camelus dromedarius*). *Indian J. Anim. Sci.* 49:554–56.
*   Gutknecht, P. 1975. Elevage et pathologie néo-natale du chameau
    au Zoo de Mulhouse. Typescript. Paper read at 17th Sym-
    posium Internationale sur la Pathologie des Animaux Sau-
    vages,Tunis-Carthage.

Hafez, E. S. E. 1955. Foetal-maternal attachments in buffalo and
    camel. *Indian J. Vet. Sci. Anim. Husb.* 25:109–15.
Haltenorth, T. 1953. Zur Frage der Geniessbarkeit der Kamel-
    magenflüssigkeit. *Säugetierkdl. Mitt.* 1:79–80.
Hamed, M. Y., M. S. Abdo, M. G. Mohamed, and M. A. Aly.
    1974. Biological studies on the pineal body of the camel (*Cam-
    elus dromedarius*). *Bull. Fac. Sci. Assiut Univ.* 3:57–68.
*   Hansen, A., and K. Schmidt-Nielsen. 1957. On the stomach of
    the camel with special reference to the structure of its mucous
    membrane. *Acta Anat.* 31:353–75.
*   Hediger, H. 1952. Observations on reproduction in zoo animals.
    In *CIBA Foundation colloquia on endocrinology*, pp. 78–83. Lon-
    don: Churchill.
*   Hegazi, A. H. 1950. The stomach of the camel. *Brit. Vet. J.*
    106:209–13.
    ———. 1953. The spleen of the camel compared with other
    domesticated animals and its microscopic examination.
    J. Amer. Vet. Med. Assoc. 122:182–84.

186   Bibliography

————. 1954. The heart of the camel. *Brit. Vet. J.* 110:104–8.

Hifney, A., and N. A. Misk. 1977. The anatomy of the tendons of insertion of the extrinsic muscles of the eyeball in the buffalo, cow and camel. *Anat. Histol. Embryol.* 6:339–46.

Holler, H., and Y. M. Hassan. 1966. Bestimmung einiger Blutbestandteile bei Kamelen im Sudan. *Deutsch. Tierärztl. Wochenschau* 73:553–56.

* Home, E. 1806. Observations on the camel's stomach. *Phil. Trans. Roy. Soc. London,* pp. 357–84.

* Hutchison, B. 1950. *The Fraser.* Toronto: Clarke Irwin.

* Irwin-Williams, C. 1967. Associations of early man with horse, camel, and mastodon at Hueyatlaco, Valsequillo (Puebla, Mexico). In *Pleistocene extinctions,* ed. P. S. Martin and H. E. Wright, pp. 337–47. New Haven, Conn.: Yale University Press.

Ivanov, S. V. M. 1934. [M. biceps brachii and m. brachialis (internus) in camel.] *Arch. Russes Anat. Hist. Embryol.* 13:155–60, 300–4.

Jain, N. C., and K. S. Keeton. 1974. Morphology of camel and llama erythrocytes viewed with the scanning electron microscope. *Brit. Vet. J.* 130:288–91.

Jamdar, M. N. 1960. Comparative anatomy of the bony system of the camel (*Camelus dromedarius*): A preliminary communication. *Indian Vet. J.* 37:225–39.

————. 1960. Comparative anatomy of the bony system of the camel (*Camelus dromedarius*). II. Bones of the hind limb of camel. Ibid. 37:279–91.

Jatkar, P. R. 1968. Serum protein fractions of normal adult male camel. *Indian Vet. J.* 45:733–34.

Jatkar, P. R., R. N. Kohli, and P. L. Bhatt. 1962. Quantitative biochemical studies on camels' blood. III. Total serum-protein content. *Indian Vet. J.* 39:548–50.

Jayasinghe, J. B., D. A. Fernando, and L. A. P. Brito-Babapulle. 1963. The electrocardiogam of the camel. *Amer. J. Vet. Res.* 24:883–85.

* Jennison, G. 1928 [1971]. *Noah's cargo.* New York: Benjamin Blom.

* Johnson, D. L. 1969. *The nature of nomadism: A comparative study of pastoral migrations in southwestern Asia and northern Africa.* University of Chicago Department of Geography Research Papers, no. 118.

* Joly, F., A. Poueyto, P. Guinet, C. Sauvage, J.-B. Panouse, M. Vachon, L. Kocher, and A. Reymond. 1954. *Les hamadas sud-marocaines.* Travaux de l'Institut Scientifique Chérifien, ser. gén., no. 2. Tangier, Morocco: Editions Internationales.

Joshi, C. K., K. K. Vyas, and P. K. Pareek. 1978. Studies on the oestrous cycle in Bikaneri she-camel (*Camelus dromedarius*). *Indian J. Anim. Sci.* 48:141–45.

Kalra, D. B., and P. L. Arya. 1959. A preliminary study of the camel's urine. *Indian Vet. J.* 36:24–26.

Kanagasuntheram, R., C. V. Kanan, and A. Krishnamurti. 1970.

Nuclear configuration of the diencephalon of *Camelus drome-darius*. *Acta Anat.* 75:301–18.

Kanan, C. V. 1961. A study of the development of the auditory capsule of the chondrocranium in *Camelus dromedarius* at 5.4 cm C.R.L. stage. *Acta Morphol. Neerl. Scand.* 4:63–70.

———. 1961. Some observations on the ossification of the bones of the appendicular skeleton of *Camelus dromedarius*. Ibid. 4:254–60.

———. 1961. Some observations on the development of the nasal capsule of the chondrocranium in *Camelus dromedarius*. *Proc. Roy. Soc. Edinburgh*, ser. B., *Biol.* 68:91–102.

———. 1962. Observations on the development of the osteo-cranium in *Camelus dromedarius*. *Acta Zool.* 43:297–310.

*   ———. 1969. Spinal accessory nerve of the camel (*Camelus drome-darius*). *Acta Anat.* 74:615–23.

*   ———. 1970. The cerebral arteries of *Camelus dromedarius*. Ibid. 77:605–16.

———. 1971. Observations on the pattern and distribution of the coronary blood vessels of the camel (*Camelus dromedarius*). *Acta Morphol. Neerl. Scand.* 8:321–32.

———. 1971. The arterial blood supply to the diaphragm of the camel (*Camelus dromedarius*). Ibid. 8:333–41.

———. 1972. Observations on the distribution of external and internal ophthalmic arteries in the camel (*Camelus drome-darius*). *Acta Anat.* 81:74–82.

———. 1973. The external configuration of the cerebral hemi-spheres of the camel (*Camelus dromedarius*). Ibid. 85:145–52.

Khalifa, H., M. T. Fouad, Y. L. Awad, and M. E. Georgy. 1973. Applications of fast grey RA to the spectrophotometric de-termination of copper in liver of Egyptian camels. *Micro-chem. J.* 18:536–42.

———. 1973. Application of fast grey RA to the spectrophoto-metric determination of copper in soft tissues of Egyptian camels. Ibid. 18:617–21.

*   Khan, A. A., and I. S. Kohli. 1973*a*. A note on collection of semen from camel with the help of an artificial vagina. *Indian J. Anim. Sci.* 43:454–55.

*   ———. 1973*b*. A note on biometrics of the camel spermatozoa (*Camelus dromedarius*). Ibid. 43:792–93.

*   ———. 1973*c*. A note on the sexual behaviour of male camel (*Camelus dromedarius*). Ibid. 43:1092–94.

———. 1973*d*. A note on variations in blood serum cholesterol in camel (*Camelus dromedarius*) before and during rut. Ibid. 43:1094–95.

*   Khan, K. U., and T. C. Appanna. 1967. Carotene and vitamin A in camel milk. *J. Nutr. Diet* 4:17–20.

*   Kheraskov, S. 1939. [The manufacture of cheese from camel's milk.] *Molochno-Maslodel'naya Prom.* 6:14.

Kimura, S., R. V. Lewis, L. D. Gerber, L. Brink, M. Rubinstein, S. Stein, and S. Udenfriend. 1979. Purification to homo-geneity of camel pituitary pro-opiocortin, the common pre-cursor of opioid peptides and corticotropin. *Proc. Nat. Acad. Sci. (USA)* 76:1756–59.

Kivalo, E., and S. Talanti. 1962. On the hypothalamic-hypophyseal neurosecretory system of the camel and the seal. *Ann. Acad. Sci. Fennic.*, ser. A, *V. Med.* 89:4–8.

* Knoess, K. H. 1977. The camel as a meat and milk animal. *World Anim. Rev.* 22:39–44.

* Koford, C. B. 1957. The vicuña and the puna. *Ecol. Monogr.* 27:153–219.

Kohli, R. N. 1963. Cellular micrometry of the camel's blood. *Indian Vet. J.* 40:134–39.

Kohli, R. N., and P. L. Bhatt. 1959. A study on the normal specific gravity of blood, serum and plasma of the camel. *Indian Vet. J.* 36:494–97.

* Kon, S. K., and A. T. Cowie. 1961. *Milk: The mammary gland and its secretion.* Vol. 2. London: Academic Press.

Konuk, T. 1970. [The microscopic appearance of camel and llama erythrocytes.] *Ankara Ueniv. Vet. Fak. Dergisi* 17:518–22.

Kraft, H. 1957. Das Verhalten von Muttertier und Neugeborenen bei Cameliden. *Säugetierkdl. Mitt.* 5:174–75.

* Krishnamurthi, S. A. 1970. *The wealth of India.* New Delhi: Publications and Information Directorate.

Kulshrestha, R. C., R. G. Arora, and D. S. Kalra. 1977. Brucellosis in camels and horses. *Indian J. Anim. Sci.* 45:673–75.

Kumar, M., and S. Banerjee. 1962. Biochemical studies on Indian camel (*Camelus dromedarius*). III. Plasma insulin-like activity and glucose tolerance. *J. Sci. Indus. Res. (India)* 21:291–92.

Kurz. 1926. Die Furchung der Grosshirnrinde beim Kamel. *Z. Anat. Entwickl.* 78:1–25.

Kushner, H. F. 1938. [Composition of blood in camels in relation to the working ability of these animals.] *Compt. Rend. Acad. Sci. URSS*, n.s., 18:681–84.

Lal, J. B., P. L. Bhatt, and R. N. Kohli. 1962. Quantitative biochemical studies on camel's blood. I. Sugar and chloride content. *Indian Vet. J.* 39:64–66.

* Langman, V. A., G. M. O. Maloiy, K. Schmidt-Nielsen, and R. C. Schroter. 1978. Respiratory water and heat loss in camels subjected to dehydration. *J. Physiol. (London)* 278:35P.

* Leborgne, Cap. 1953. Vocabulaire technique du chameau en Mauritanie (dialecte Hassania). *Bull. Inst. Fondamental Afrique Noire* 15:292–380.

* Lee, D. G., and K. Schmidt-Nielsen. 1962. The skin, sweat glands and hair follicles of the camel (*Camelus dromedarius*). *Anat. Record* 143:71–77.

* Leese, A. S. 1927. *A treatise on the one humped camel in health and disease.* Stamford, England: Haynes.

Legge, C. M. 1935–36. The Arabian and the Bactrian camel. *J. Manchester Geog. Soc.* 46:21–48.

* Leitch, I. 1940. *The feeding of camels.* Imperial Bureau of Animal Nutrition, Rowett Institute (Aberdeen), Technical Communications, no. 13.

Lemaire, S., D. Yamashiro, and C. H. Li. 1976. Synthesis and biological activity of camel and bovine β-melanotropins. *J. Med. Chem.* 19:373–76.

* Leonard, A. G. 1894. *The camel: Its uses and management.* London:

Longmans, Green.

* Leroux, C. 1960. Aspects de la régulation thermique des animaux du désert: Observations personelles chez le dromadaire. Thesis, Ecole Nationale Vétérinaire de Lyon.

* Lesley, L. B. 1929. *Uncle Sam's camels.* Cambridge, Mass.: Harvard University Press.

Lewis, J. H. 1976. Comparative hematology: Studies on Camelidae. *Comp. Biochem. Physiol.*, ser. A, *Comp. Physiol.* 55:367–72.

* Lhote, H. 1958. *A la découverte des fresques du Tassili.* Paris: Arthaud.

Li, C. H., and D. Chung. 1976. Isolation and structure of an untriakontapeptide with opiate activity from camel pituitary glands. *Proc. Nat. Acad. Sci. (USA)* 73:1145–48.

Li, C. H., W. O. Danho, D. Chung, and A. J. Rao. 1975. Isolation, characterization, and amino acid sequence of melanotropins from camel pituitary glands. *Biochemistry* 14:947–52.

Li, C. H., D. Yamashiro, and S. Lemaire. 1975. Total synthesis of camel β-melanotropin by the solid-phase method. *Biochemistry* 14:953–56.

Lin, K. D., A. S. Bhown, and A. I. Chernoff. 1976. Studies on camel hemoglobin. I. Physico-chemical properties and some structural aspects of camel hemoglobin (*Camelus dromedarius*). *Biochim. Biophys. Acta* 434:110–17.

Little, A., A. J. McKenzie, R. J. H. Morris, J. Roberts, and J. V. Evans. 1970. Blood electrolytes in the Australian camel. *Australian J. Exp. Biol. Med. Sci.* 48:17–24.

Litvinova, A. A. 1956. [A case of finding "camel bread" in the fetal sac of the single humped camel.] *Trudy Turkm. S. Kh. Inst.* 8:235–36.

Livne, A., and P. J. C. Kuiper. 1973. Unique properties of the camel erythrocyte membrane. *Biochim. Biophys. Acta* 318:41–49.

* Lombardini, L. 1879. *Dei camelli.* Annali delle Università Toscana, Pisa, no. 2a.

* Lynch, J. J. 1977. Movement of some rangeland herbivores in relation to their feed and water supply. In *Proceedings of the 2d United States/Australia Rangeland Panel* (Adelaide 1972), pp. 163–72. Perth: Australian Rangeland Society.

* Lynch, J.J., and G. Alexander. 1973. Animal behaviour and the pastoral industries. In *The pastoral industries of Australia,* ed. A. Williams, pp. 371–400. Sydney: Sydney University Press.

* Lynch, J. J., and G. L. McClymont. 1975. Water as a nutrient for animals. Unpublished.

* McBride, G., G. W. Arnold, G. Alexander, and J. J. Lynch. 1967. Ecological aspects of the behaviour of domestic animals. *Proc. Ecol. Soc. Australia* 2:133–65.

Macfarlane, W. V. 1976. Ecophysiological hierarchies. *Israel J. Med. Sci.* 12:723–31.

* Macfarlane, W. V., and B. Howard. 1972. Comparative water and energy economy of wild and domestic mammals. *Symp. Zool. Soc. London* 31:261–96.

* Macfarlane, W. V., B. Howard, H. Haines, P. J. Kennedy, and

C. M. Sharpe. 1971. Hierarchy of water and energy turnover of desert mammals. *Nature* 234:483–84.

* Macfarlane, W. V., R. Kinne, C. M. Walmsley, B. D. Siebert, and D. Peter. 1967. Vasopressins and the increase of water and electrolyte excretion by sheep, cattle and camels. *Nature* 214:979–81.

Macfarlane, W. V., R. J. H. Morris, and B. Howard. 1962. Water metabolism of Merino sheep and camels. Abstract. *Australian J. Sci.* 25:112.

* ———. 1963. Turnover and distribution of water in desert camels, sheep, cattle and kangaroos. *Nature* 197:270–71.

* McKnight, T. L. 1969. *The camel in Australia.* Carlton: Melbourne University Press.

* Maire, R. 1933. *Études sur la flore et la végétation du Sahara central.* Mémoires de la Société Histoire Naturelle d'Afrique du Nord, vols. 1 and 2.

* Malhotra, S. P., J. S. Rao, D. Goyal, and F. C. Patwa. 1972. Population, land use and livestock composition in India and its arid zone. *Ann. Arid Zone* 11:116–27.

* Maloiy, G. M. O. 1970. Water economy of the Somali donkey. *Amer. J. Physiol.* 219:1522–27.

* ———. 1972a. Renal salt and water excretion in the camel *Camelus dromedarius*. *Symp. Zool. Soc. London* 31:243–59.

———. 1972b. Comparative studies on digestion and fermentation rate in the fore-stomach of the one-humped camel and the Zebu steer. *Res. Vet. Sci.* 13:476–81.

Malyshev, V. M. 1969. [*The morphology of the nerves of the pharynx and larynx in the Arabian camel.*] Referat. Zh. Biol., no. 31487.

Mares, R. C. 1974. The African nomad: East Africa. In *An introduction to animal husbandry in the tropics,* ed. G. Williamson and W. J. A. Payne, pp. 424–30. 2d ed. London: Longman.

* Marsh, G. P. 1856. *The camel: His organization, habits, and uses.* Boston: Gould & Lincoln.

Maskar, Ü. 1950. Über die biologische Verwandtschaft zwischen Lama und Kamel. *Experientia* 6:423–24.

* ———. 1957. Über den Zwerchfellknochen des Kamels. *Acta Anat.* 30:461–71.

———. 1961. Über eine Knorpelanlage im Oesophagus eines Dromedarfetus. Ibid. 44:206–9.

* Mathur, C. S. 1960. Nutrition in relation to satyriasis in camels. *Indian Vet. J.* 37:199–201.

* Mehta, V. S., A. H. A. Prakash, and M. Singh. 1962. Gestation period in camels. *Indian Vet. J.* 39:387–98.

* Meigs, P. 1952. La répartition mondiale des zones climatiques arides et semi-arides. *Zones Arides* 1:209–15.

Metcalfe, J., J. T. Parer, D. el-Yassin, J. Oufi, H. Bartels, K. Riegel, and E. Kleihauer. 1968. Cardiodynamics of the dromedary camel (*Camelus dromedarius*) during phencyclidine analgesia. *Amer. Vet. Res.* 29:2063–66.

Meyerstein, N., D. Mazor, Z. Etzion, and R. Yagil. 1978. Permeability of erythrocytes to glycerol and its acylated derivatives in the camel and dog. *Comp. Biochem. Physiol.,* ser.

A., *Comp. Physiol.* 61:261–66.

* Midant-Reynes, B., and F. Braunstein-Silvestre. 1977. Le chameau en Égypte. *Orientalia* 46:337–62.

* Middaugh, W. S. 1964. Livestock activities in Africa. *Cornell Vet.* 54:3–10.

* Mikesell, M. K. 1955. Notes on the dispersal of the dromedary. *Southwestern J. Anthrop.* 11:231–45.

Miller, J., E. Gudat, and H. Lindner. 1965. Vergleichende papier-elektrophoretische Untersuchungen an Seren von Kameliden und Rindern. *Arch. Exp. Veterinaermed.* 19:1027–36.

* Miller-Ben-Shaul, D. 1962. The composition of the milk of wild animals. *Internat. Zoo Yearbook* 4:333–42.

* Mimram, R. 1962. *Les glandes occipitales du dromadaire.* Cahiers de la Faculté des Sciences, Rabat, Série Biologie Animale, no. 1.

Mirgani, T. 1977. Fatty acid composition of hump triglycerides of the camel (*Camelus dromedarius*). *Comp. Biochem. Physiol.*, ser. B, *Comp. Biochem.* 58:211–14.

Mobarak, A. M., and A. B. Elwishy. 1971. Uterus of the one-humped camel (*Camelus dromedarius*) with reference to rectal palpation. *Indian J. Anim. Sci.* 41:846–55.

Mobarak, A. M., and S. M. Fouad. 1977. A study on ligamentum nuchae of the one-humped camel (*Camelus dromedarius*). *Anat. Histol. Embryol.* 6:188–90.

Monod, T. 1955. Longs trajets chameliers. *Bull. Liaison Saharienne* 6:38–42.

* ———. 1958. *Majâbat al-Koubrâ: Contribution à l'étude de l'"empty quarter" ouest-Saharien.* Mémoires de l'Institut Français d'Afrique Noire, no. 52.

* ———. 1963. *Ecosystèmes et productivité biologique: Déserts.* Morges, Switzerland: IUCN.

* ———. 1964. Majâbat al-Koubrâ. *Bull. Inst. Fondamental Afrique Noire*, ser. A, 26:1393–1402.

* ———. 1967. Notes sur le harnachement chamelier. Ibid., ser. B., 29:234–306.

* Montagu, I. 1957. Colour-film shots of the wild camel. *Proc. Zool. Soc. London* 129:592–95.

Monteil, V. 1952. *Essai sur le chameau au Sahara occidental.* Centre de l'Institut Français d'Afrique Noire, Etudes Mauritaniennes, no. 2.

* ———. 1953. *Contribution à l'étude de la flore du Sahara occidental.* Bulletins de l'Institut des Hautes Etudes de Maroc, Notes et Documents, no. 6.

* ———. 1966. *Les tribus du Fârs et la sédentarisation des nomades.* Paris: Mouton.

* Montgomery, P. O., C. T. Ashworth, and P. Fontaine. 1964. The camel capillary. *Nature* 201:624–25.

* Morrison, W. R. 1968. Fatty acid composition of milk phospho-lipids. III. Camel, ass, and pig milks. *Lipids* 3:107–10.

Morton, W. R. M. 1961. Observations on the full-term foetal membranes of three members of the Camelidae (*Camelus dromedarius* L., *Camelus bactrianus* L. and *Lama glama* L.). *J. Anat.* 95:200–209.

Moustafa, M. S. el-din M., R. Berg, and el-S. Taher. 1969. Prenatal growth of some organs in the camel (*Camelus dromedarius*): Relation between body weight and brain, thymus,
stomach and oesophagus weights. *Zentralbl. Veterinaermed.*,
ser. A, 16:536–42.
Musa, B. E. 1977. A new epidermal membrane associated with
the foetus of the camel (*Camelus dromedarius*). *Anat. Histol. Embryol.* 6:355—58.

Narain, D., and H. S. Sohal. 1968. The sex chromatin in the
pyramidal neurons of the camel *Camelus dromedarius*. *Indian
J. Med. Res.* 56:722–25.
Nawar, S. M. A., and G. E. M. el-Khaligi. 1975. Morphological,
micromorphological and histochemical studies on the parotid
salivary glands of the one-humped camel (*Camelus dromedarius*). *Gegenbaurs Morphol. Jahrb.* 121:430–49.
———. 1977. Morphological studies of the mandibular salivary
glands of the one-humped camel (*Camelus dromedarius*). *Anat.
Anz.* 142:346–62.
Nayak, R. K. 1977. Scanning electron microscopy of the camel
uterine tube (oviduct). *Amer. J. Vet. Res.* 38:1049–54.
Neuville, M. H. 1931. De certaines particularités dentaires des
camélidés. *Bull. Mus. Nat. Hist. Natur. Paris*, ser. 2, 3:77–81.
Newman, D. M. R. 1975. The camel—its potential as a provider
of protein in arid Australia. In *Proceedings of the 3d World Con-
ference on Animal Production*, ed. R. L. Reid, pp. 95–106. Sydney: Sydney University Press.
Nosier, M. B. 1973. Histological structure of the mammary glands
of the one humped camel (*Camelus dromedarius*). *Indian
J. Anim. Sci.* 43:639–41.
Novikov, I. I. 1940. [Chromosome behavior during spermatogenesis in camels *Camelus dromedarius* L. and *Camelus
bactrianus* L. and their F₁ hybrid.] *Trudy Inst. Genet.* 13:285–96.
* Novoa, C. 1970. Reproduction in Camelidae. *J. Reprod. Fertil.*
22:3–20.

Osman, A. M., and E. A. el-Azab. 1974. Gonadal and epididymal
sperm reserves in the camel, *Camelus dromedarius*. *J. Reprod.
Fertil.* 38:425–30.
Osman, D. I., K. A. Moniem, and M. D. Tingari. 1976. Studies on
the testis of the camel (*Camelus dromedarius*). III. Histochemical
observations. *Histochem. J.* 8:579–90.
———. 1979. Histological observations on the testis of the camel,
with special emphasis on spermatogenesis. *Acta Anat.*
104:164–71.
Osman, D. I., M. D. Tingari, and K. A. Moniem. 1979. Vascular
supply of the testis of the camel (*Camelus dromedarius*). *Acta
Anat.* 104:16–22.
Otterman, J. 1974. Baring high-albedo soils by overgrazing: A
hypothesized desertification mechanism. *Science* 186:531–33.
* Ozenda, P. 1958. *Flore du Sahara septentrional et central*. Paris:
Centre National de la Recherche Scientifique.

Patrushev, V. I. 1938. [Inheritance of biochemical characteristics in animals in connection with growth. III. On some indices of the blood composition of the hybrids between Bactrian camels and dromedaries in connection with heterosis.] *Compt. Rend. (Doklady) Acad. Sci. USSR* 19:285–90.

* Payne, W. J. A. 1966. Nutrition of ruminants in the tropics. *Nutr. Abstr. Rev.* 36:653–70.

* Pearson, L. C. 1965. Primary production in grazed and ungrazed desert communities of eastern Idaho. *Ecology* 46:278–86.

* Peck, E. F. 1939. Salt intake in relation to cutaneous necrosis and arthritis of one-humped camels (*Camelus dromedarius* L.) in British Somaliland. *Vet. Record* 51:1355–60.

———. 1942. Castor seed poisoning in a camel. Ibid. 54:184.

Perk, K. 1962. Seasonal changes in the glandular bulbo-urethralis of the camel. *Bull. Res. Council Israel,* sec. E, *Exp. Med.* 10E:37–44.

* ———. 1963. The camel's erythrocyte. *Nature* 200:272–73.

* ———. 1966. Osmotic hemolysis of the camel's erythrocytes. I. A microcinematographic study. *J. Exp. Zool.* 163:241–46.

Petri, J. 1927. Notiz über den Harnstoffgehalt des Kamelharns. *Hoppe-Seylers Z. Physiol. Chem.* 166:125–27.

* Peyré, J. 1957. *De sable et d'or.* Paris: Flammarion.

* Pierre, F. 1958. *Ecologie et peuplement entomologique des sables vifs du Sahara nord-occidental.* Publications du Centre de Recherches Sahariennes, Série Biologique, no. 1. Paris: Centre National de la Recherche Scientifique.

* Pilters, H. 1954. Untersuchungen über angeborene Verhaltensweisen bei Tylopoden, unter besonderer Berücksichtigung der neuweltlichen Formen. *Z. Tierpsychol.* 11:213–303.

* ———. 1955a. Observations éthologiques sur les tylopodes. *Mammalia* 19:399–415.

* ———. 1955b. Quelques observations sur le comportement des dromadaires, *Camelus dromedarius,* relevées dans le Sahara nord-occidental. *Bull. Soc. Vét. Zootech. Algérie* 3:9–13.

* ———. 1956. Das Verhalten der Tylopoden. *Handb. Zool.* 8:1–24.

Pkhakadze, G. M. 1932. [The histological structure of the testes in hybrids of the Bactrian camel and Arabian camel (dromedary).] *Trudy Inst. Genet.* 9:243–49.

* Planhol, X., and P. Rognon. 1970. *Les zones tropicales arides et subtropicales.* Paris: Colin.

* Pollard, G. C., and I. M. Drew. 1975. Llama herding and settlement in prehispanic northern Chile: Application of an analysis for determining domestication. *Amer. Antiquity* 40:296–305.

* Pond, A. W. 1957. The legend of the camel. *Natur. Hist. (New York)* 66:266–71.

Ponder, E., J. F. Yeager, and H. A. Charipper. 1928. Hematology of the Camelidae. *Zool. Sci. Contrib. New York Zool. Soc.* 11:1–7.

———. 1928. Studies in comparative haematology. I. Camelidae. *Q. J. Exp. Physiol.* 19:115–26.

Pottier, J. 1929. Etude sur les possibilités d'utilisation des plantes marines tunisiennes pour la nourriture du bétail. *Ann. Inst. Océanogr.* 6:321–62.

* Prakash, A., and V. Singh. 1962. Normal parturition in camels. *Indian Vet. J.* 39:551–53.

Pulling, J. A. 1973. Camels and camel hair. *Wool Record and Textile World,* June 29, pp. 6–7.

Purohit, M. S., and S. S. Rathor. 1962. Stomach of the camel in comparison to that of the ox. *Indian Vet. J.* 39:604–8.

* Purohit, M. S., and B. Singh. 1958. The poll glands in camel. *Indian Vet. J.* 35:296–98.

Rabagliati, D. S. 1924. *The dentition of the camel.* Cairo: Government Press.

Race, G. J., and H. M. Wu. 1964. Corticoids in the three zones of the camel (*Camelus dromedarius*) adrenal cortex. *Gen. Comp. Endocrinol.* 4:199–209.

Radmanesh, H. 1974. Choledochoduodenal junction in the dromedary. *Acta Anat.* 90:507–13.

Ralston, G. B. 1975. Proteins of the camel erythrocyte membrane. *Biochim. Biophys. Acta* 401:83–94.

* Rao, M. B., R. C. Gupta, and N. N. Dastur. 1970. Camel's milk and milk products. *Indian J. Dairy Sci.* 23:71–78.

Rasheed, A. A., and A. S. el-Sheikh. 1957. Developmental changes in the linear body and limb measurements of camel fetuses. *Ann. Agr. Sci.* 2:205–30.

Repérant, J. 1971. Les grandes lignes de l'histoire de la gyrencephalisation chez les camélidés. *Mammalia* 35:658–65.

———. 1971. Comparative morphology of the encephalon and the endocranial mold among the present-day Tylopoda (mammals, Artiodactyla). *Bull. Mus. Nat. Hist. Natur. Zool.* 4:185–322.

Retterer, E., and H. Neuville. 1916. De la rate des camélidés, des girafidés et des cervidés. *Compt. Rend. Soc. Biol. Paris* 79:128–31.

Rezakhani, A., and M. Szabuniewicz. 1977. The electrocardiogram of the camel (*Camelus dromedarius*). *Zentralbl. Veterinaermed.,* ser. A, 24:277–86.

Riegel, K., H. Bartels, D. el-Yassin, J. Oufi, E. Kleihauer, J. T. Parer, and G. Metcalfe. 1967. Comparative studies of the respiratory functions of mammalian blood. III. Fetal and adult dromedary camel blood. *Resp. Physiol.* 2:173–81.

* Ripinsky, M. M. 1975. The camel in ancient Arabia. *Antiquity* 49:295–98.

Rollinson, D. H. L. 1972. The distribution of nerves, monoamine oxidase and cholinesterase in the skin of the camel (*Camelus dromedarius*). *Res. Vet. Sci.* 13:304–5.

* Romer, A. S. 1966. *Vertebrate paleontology.* 3d ed. Chicago: University of Chicago Press.

* Rosenstiehl, D. F. 1959. Contribution à l'étude des pâturages camelins dans l'Azaouad. Thesis, Faculté de Médecine de Paris.

Roux, J.-P. 1959–60. Le chameau en Asie Centrale. *Central Asiatic J.* 5:35–76.

* Saint-Hilaire, I. G. 1861. *Acclimatation et domestication des animaux utiles.* Paris: Librairie Agricole de la Maison Rustique.

Saleh, M. S., A. M. Mobarak, and S. M. Fouad. 1971. Radiologi-
cal, anatomical and histological studies of the mammary gland
of the one-humped camel (*Camelus dromedarius*). I. The teat
(papilla mammae). *Zentralbl. Veterinaermed.*, ser. A, 18:347–52.

Schafer, E. H. 1950. The camel in China down to the Mongol
Dynasty. *Sinologica* 2:165–94, 263–90.

* Scheifler, H. 1972. Kamelmilch wird immer begehrter. *Tier*
12:10–11.

Schejter, A., Z. Grosman, and M. Sokolovsky. 1972. Isolation,
properties and partial sequence of the cytochrome c of the
camel, *Camelus dromedarius*. *Israel J. Chem.* 10:37–41.

* Schiffers, H. 1950. *Die Sahara*. Stuttgart: Frankh'sche Verlags-
buchhandlung.

* ———. 1971. *Die Sahara und ihre Randgebiete*. Vol. 1, *Physiogeo-
graphie*. Munich: Weltforum Verlag.

* ———. 1972. Ibid. Vol. 2, *Humangeographie*. Munich: Weltforum
Verlag.

* Schmidt, C. R. 1973. Breeding seasons and notes on some other
aspects of reproduction in captive camelids. *Internat. Zoo Yearbook* 13:387–90.

* Schmidt-Nielsen, B., K. Schmidt-Nielsen, T. R. Houpt, and S. A.
Jarnum. 1956. Water balance of the camel. *Amer. J. Physiol.*
185:185–94.

* ———. 1957. Urea excretion in the camel. Ibid. 188:477–84.

Schmidt-Nielsen, K. 1956. Animals and arid conditions: Physiological aspects of productivity and management. In *The future
of arid lands*, pp. 368–82. Washington, D.C.: American Association for the Advancement of Science.

* ———. 1959. The physiology of the camel. *Sci. Amer.*
201(6):140–51.

* ———. 1964. *Desert animals: Physiological problems of heat and
water*, pp. 33–70. Oxford: Clarendon Press.

* Schmidt-Nielsen, K., E. C. Crawford, A. E. Newsome, and K. S.
Rawson. 1963. The metabolic rate of camels. Abstract. *Fed. Proc.*
22:176.

* Schmidt-Nielsen, K., E. C. Crawford, A. E. Newsome, K. S.
Rawson, and H. T. Hammel. 1967. Metabolic rate of camels:
Effect of body temperature and dehydration. *Amer. J. Physiol.*
212:341–46.

Schmidt-Nielsen, K., and B. Schmidt-Nielsen. 1952. Water
metabolism of desert mammals. *Physiol. Rev.* 32:135–66.

* Schmidt-Nielsen, K., B. Schmidt-Nielsen, T. R. Houpt, and S. A.
Jarnum. 1956. The question of water storage in the stomach of
the camel. *Mammalia* 20:1–15.

Schmidt-Nielsen, K., B. Schmidt-Nielsen, S. A. Jarnum, and
T. R. Houpt. 1957. Body temperature of the camel and its relation to water economy. *Amer. J. Physiol.* 188:103–12.

Sergent, E., and A. Poncet. 1942. Etude morphologique du sang
des dromadaires sahariens. *Arch. Inst. Pasteur (Algérie)*
20:204–8.

Shakhov, S. D. 1972. [Amnion of the two-somite embryo of the
dromedary.] *Arkh. Anat. Gistol. Embriol.* 62:96–99.

———. 1974. [Embryometry of early intrauterine ontogenesis of
the dromedary.] Ibid. 67:64–69.

Shakhov, S. D., and E. G. Arustamyan. 1970. [Camel embryo in
the early embryonic stage.] *Izv. Akad. Nauk Turkm. SSR, Ser.
Biol. Nauk* 1:83–86.

————. 1971. [Amniogenesis heterochrony of *Camelus* genus.]
Ibid. 1:78–81.

* Shalash, M. R. 1965. Some reproductive aspects in the female
camel. *World Rev. Anim. Prod.* 1:103.

* Sharma, D. P., P. D. Malik, and K. L. Sapra. 1973. Age-wise and
species-wise haematological studies in farm animals. *Indian J.
Anim. Sci.* 43:289–95.

Sharma, S. S., and K. K. Vyas. 1971. Peculiar antepartum
characteristic behavior in single humped camel (*C.
dromedarius*). *Haryana Vet.* 10:59–62.

Sharma, V. D. 1964. Sutural bone in the pelvis of camel. *Indian
Vet. J.* 41:347–49.

* Sharma, V. D., K. K. Bhargava, and M. Singh. 1963. Secondary
sex ratio of normal births in Bikaneri camel. *Indian Vet. J.*
40:561–63.

Shatilov, M. I. 1972. Camel raising, a profitable branch of the
animal industry. *Zhivotnovodstvo,* Nov., pp. 23–24.

Shehata, R. 1961. A comparative study of Gartner's duct in the
camel. *Alexandria Med. J.* 7:489–96.

————. 1964. The mesonephric duct in female camel fetuses.
Anat. Record 149:443–47.

————. 1978. Comparative study of Gartner's duct in the camel.
Acta Anat. 100:532–37.

* Siebert, B. D., and W. V. Macfarlane. 1971. Water turnover and
renal function of dromedaries in the desert. *Physiol. Zool.*
44:225–40.

* ————. 1975. Dehydration in desert cattle and camels. Ibid.
48:36–48.

Simon, E. 1965. Endocranium, Endokranialausguss und Gehirn
beim einhöckerigen Kamel (*Camelus dromedarius*). *Acta Anat.*
60:122–51.

Simonetta, B. 1927. Sul sangue dei camelidi. *Pathologica* 19:116–19.

Singh, R., S. S. Rathor, and R. N. Kohli. 1962. A note on preliminary observations on the use of some general anaesthetics
in the camel. *Indian Vet. J.* 39:614–16.

Singh, U. B., and M. B. Bharadwaj. 1978. Morphological changes
in the testis and epididymis of camels (*Camelus dromedarius*).
Pt. I. *Acta Anat.* 101:275–79.

————. 1978. Histological and histochemical studies on the testis
of camel (*Camelus dromedarius*) during the various seasons and
ages. Pt. II. Ibid. 101:280–88.

————. 1978. Anatomical, histological and chemical observations
and changes in the poll galnds of the camel (*Camelus dromedarius*). Ibid. 102:74–83.

* Singh, V., and A. Prakash. 1964. Mating behavior in camels.
Indian Vet. J. 41:475–77.

Slimane-Taleb, S., A. Bererhi, and C. Zidane. 1968–69. Aspects
morphologiques des noyaux supraoptiques et paraventricu-
laires de l'hypothalamus du dromadaire (*Camelus dromedarius*).
Bull. Soc. Hist. Natur. Afrique Nord 59:165–70.

Sokolovsky, M., and M. Moldovan. 1972. Primary structure of cytochrome c from the camel, *Camelus dromedarius*. *Biochemistry* 11:145–49.

Soliman, M. K., S. el-Amrousi, and L. B. Youssef. 1966. Studies on the normal cerebrospinal fluid of healthy camels. *Indian J. Vet. Sci. Anim. Husb.* 36:40–44.

———. 1966. Physico-chemical properties of pericardial fluid of healthy camels. *Indian J. Exp. Biol.* 4:175–76.

* Spencer, P. 1973. *Nomads in alliance: Symbiosis and growth among the Rendille and Samburu of Kenya*. London: Oxford University Press.

Stepankina, M. K., and K. T. Tashenov. 1958. Water metabolism in the camel. *Fiziol. Zh. SSSR* 44:942–47.

Stevenson, P. H. 1921. The extrahepatic biliary tract of the camel. *Anat. Record* 22:85–95.

* Stocker, O. 1971. Der Wasser- und Photosynthese-Haushalt von Wüstenpflanzen der mauretanischen Sahara. II. Wechselgrüne, Rutenzweig- und stammsukkulente Bäume. *Flora* 160:445–94.

Sundby, F., J. Markussen, and W. Danho. 1974. Camel glucagon: Isolation, crystallization and amino acid composition. *Horm. Metab. Res.* 6:425.

* Sweet, L. E. 1965. Camel pastoralism in North Arabia and the minimal camping unit. In *Man, culture, and animals*, ed. A. Leeds and A. P. Vayda, pp. 129–52. Washington, D.C.: American Association for the Advancement of Science.

Sychev, N. A. 1930. [Zoological affinity and serologic type of camels.] *Zh. Exp. Biol.* 6:49–59.

Taher, el-S., A. K. al-Shaikhly, and S. Lawand. 1975. Morphological and micromorphological studies of the epiphysis cerebri of the dromedary *Camelus dromedarius* Linné, 1758. *Säugetierkdl. Mitt.* 23:223–30.

Taher, el-S., and R. Berg. 1969. Micromorphological studies on the coronary vessels of the camel (*Camelus dromedarius*). I. Micromorphology of the coronary arteries in camel fetuses. *Zentralbl. Veterinaermed.*, ser. A, 16:52–60.

Taher, el-S., M. S. el-Din M. Moustafa, and R. Berg. 1967. Prenatal growth of some organs in the camel (*Camelus dromedarius*). II. Relations of liver and spleen weight to body and heart weight and to one another. *Zentralbl. Veterinaermed.*, ser. A, 14:819–24.

Taher, el-S., M. A. el-Gaafary, and A. K. al-Shaikhly. 1975. Some studies of the centrum tendineum of the diaphragm of camel (*Camelus dromedarius*). *Anat. Anz.* 138:192–202.

* Talbot, L. M. 1968. The herbivore-vegetation-nomad complex: Recent research and its implications. Mimeographed. Read at IBP/CT Tech. Meeting, Tunisia.

Tartour, G. 1969. Studies on the metabolism of copper and iron in the camel. *J. Vet. Sci. Anim. Husb.* 10:14–20.

Tartour, G., and O. F. Idris. 1970. Studies on copper and iron metabolism in the camel foetus. *Acta Vet.* 39:397–403.

———. 1970. Serum iron and serum iron-binding capacity in the dromedary (*Camelus dromedarius*). *J. Zool. (London)* 161:351–54.

Tayeb, M. A. F. 1948. Studies on the anatomy of the ovary and corpus luteum of the camel. *Vet. J.* 104:179–86.

———. 1948. Urinary system of the camel. *J. Amer. Vet. Med. Assoc.* 113:568–72.

———. 1950. L'appareil glandulaire de la tête du chameau. *Rev. Elevage Méd. Vét. Pays Trop.* 4:151–55.

———. 1950. The pharyngeal cavity of the camel. *Brit. Vet. J.* 106:29–31.

———. 1951. A study on the blood supply of the camel's head. Ibid. 107:147–55.

* Taylor, C. R. 1968. Hygroscopic food: A source of water for desert antelope. *Nature* 219:181–82.

* ———. 1970. Dehydration and heat: Effects on temperature regulation of East African ungulates. *Amer. J. Physiol.* 219:1136–39.

* Taylor, K. M., D. A. Hungerford, R. L. Snyder, and F. A. Ulmer. 1968. Uniformity of karyotypes in the Camelidae. *Cytogenetics* 7:8–15.

* Temple, R. S., and M. E. R. Thomas. 1973. The Sahelian drought—a disaster for livestock populations. *World Anim. Rev.* 8:1–7.

Terent'ev, S. 1956. *Investigation of the working capacity of the Astrakhan camel.* Referat. Zh. Biol., no. 72082.

Tingari, M. D., and K. A. Moniem. 1979. On the regional histology and histochemistry of the epididymis of the camel (*Camelus dromedarius*). *J. Reprod. Fertil.* 57:11–20.

Tingari, M. D., K. A. Moniem, and E. Kuenzel. 1979. Observations on the fine structure of the testicular interstitial cells in the camel (*Camelus dromedarius*). *Q. J. Exp. Physiol. Cogn. Med. Sci.* 64:39–46.

Tomasch, J. 1969. Das Nierenbecken des Dromedars. *Z. Anat. Entwicklungsgeschichte* 128:235–42.

* Trabut, L. 1935. *Répertoire des nom indigènes des plantes spontanées, cultivées, et utilisées dans le nord de l'Afrique.* Alger: J. Carbonel.

Tret'yakov, V. N. 1973. The adaptation of Turkmen camels to desert conditions. *Izv. Akad. Nauk Turkm. SSR, Ser. Biol. Nauk* 4:52–56.

* Treus, V. D., and N. V. Lobanov. 1976. [Acclimatization of Tylopoda in Askaniya-Nova.] *Vestn. Zool.* 1:3–9.

* Trumble, H. C., and K. Woodroffe. 1954. The influence of climatic factors on the reaction of desert shrubs to grazing by sheep. In *Proceedings of a symposium on the biology of hot and cold deserts*, ed. J. L. Cloudsley-Thompson, pp. 129–47. London: Hafner.

Turner, J. C., H. M. Anderson, and C. P. Gandal. 1958. Comparative liberation of bound phosphatides from red cells of man, ox, and camel. *Proc. Soc. Exp. Biol. Med.* 99:547–50.

UNESCO. 1959. Nomades et nomadisme en zone aride. *Rev. Internat. Sci. Soc.* 11 (no. 4): 501–612.

———. 1963. *Nomades et nomadisme au Sahara.* Paris: UNESCO.

Vallet, M., and G. Bordessoule. 1978. Partir à dos de chameau. *Journal Partir* (Paris), Nov., pp. i–iv.

Van Lennep, E. W. 1961. The histology of the placenta of the one-humped camel (*Camelus dromedarius* L.) during the first half of pregnancy. *Acta Morphol. Neerl. Scand.* 4:180–93.

* Verma, B. C. 1975. Occurrence of Lower Paleolithic artefacts in the Pinjor member (Lower Pleistocene) of Himachal Pradesh. *J. Geol. Soc. India* 16:518–21.

Vignier, J. P. 1963. *Sur l'élevage du chameau au Tassili N'Ajjers.* Lyon: Bosc Frères.

* Villachon, M. A. 1962. Aliments et alimentation du dromadaire au Tassili N'Ajjer (Sahara central). Thesis, University of Toulouse.

* Vitale, M. A. 1928. *Il cammello ed i reporti cammellati.* Rome: Sindicato Italiano Arti Grafiche.

* Walls, G. L. 1963. *The vertebrate eye and its adaptive radiation.* New York: Hafner.

* Walter, H. 1970. *Vegetationszonen und Klima.* Stuttgart: Verlag Eugen Ulmer.

Walz, R. 1951. Zum Problem des Zeitpunkts der Domestikation der altweltlichen Cameliden. *Z. Deutsch. Morgenländ. Gesellschaft Wiesbaden,* n.s., 26:43.

* ———. 1954. Neue Untersuchungen zum Domestikationsproblem der altestenlichen Camelidae: Beiträge zur altesten Geschichte des zweihöckrigen Kamels. Ibid., n.s. 104:45–87.

* ———. 1956. Beiträge zur ältesten Geschichte der altweltlichen Cameliden, unter besonderer Berücksichtigung des Problems des Domestikationszeitpunktes. *Proceedings of the Fourth International Congress of Anthropological and Ethnological Sciences* (Vienna, 1952) 3:190–204.

* Webb, S. D. 1972. Locomotor evolution in camels. *Forma Functio* 5:99–112.

Welling, G. W., G. Groen, and J. J. Beintema. 1975. The amino acid sequence of dromedary pancreatic ribonuclease. *Biochem. J.* 147:505–11.

Welling, G. W., H. Mulder, and J. J. Beintema. 1976. Allelic polymorphism in Arabian camel ribonuclease and the amino acid sequence of Bactrian camel ribonuclease. *Biochem. Genet.* 14:309–17.

* Wendorf, F., R. Schild, R. Said, C. V. Haynes, A. Gautier, and M. Kobusiewicz. 1976. The prehistory of the Egyptian Sahara. *Science* 193:103–14.

* Wheeler Pires-Ferreira, J., E. Pires-Ferreira, and P. Kaulicke. 1976. Preceramic animal utilization in the central Peruvian Andes. *Science* 194:483–90.

Willemse, J. J. 1958. The innervation of the muscles of the trapezius-complex in giraffe, okapi, camel and llama. *Arch. Neerl. Zool.* 12:532–36.

* Williams, J. T., and R. M. Farias. 1972. Utilisation and taxonomy of the desert grass *Panicum turgidum. Econ. Bot.* 26:13–20.

* Williams, V. J. 1963. Rumen function in the camel. *Nature* 197:1221.

Woisard, Capt. 1958. Pour debuter chez les méharistes de l'erg oriental. Typescript. El Oued, Algeria.

Yagil, R., and G. M. Berlyne. 1976. Sodium and potassium metabolism in the dehydrated and rehydrated Bedouin camel. *J. Appl. Physiol.* 41:457–61.
————. 1977. Renal handling of creatinine in various stages of hydration in the camel. *Comp. Biochem. Physiol.*, ser. A, *Comp. Physiol.* 56:15–18.
————. 1977. Glucose loading and dehydration in the camel. *J. Appl. Physiol.* 42:690–93.
Yagil, R., and Z. Etzion. 1979. The role of antidiuretic hormone and aldosterone in the dehydrated and rehydrated camel. *Comp. Biochem. Physiol.*, ser. A, *Comp. Physiol.* 63:275–78.
Yagil, R., Z. Etzion, and G. M. Berlyne. 1975. Acid-base parameters in the dehydrated camel. *Tijdschr. Diergeneesk.* 100:1105–8.
Yagil, R., Z. Etzion, and J. Ganani. 1978. Camel thyroid metabolism: Effect of season and dehydration. *J. Appl. Physiol. Resp. Environ. Exercise Physiol.* 45:540–44.
Yakimoff, W. L., and E. F. Rastegaieff. 1926. Sur la question des leucocytes des chameaux. *Bull. Soc. Pathol. Exotique* 19:582–83.
* Yakovlev, L. A. 1945. [The eating of wool by camels as a result of salt deficiency.] *Veterinariia (Moscow)* 4/5:41.
Yasin, S. A., and A. Wahid. 1957. Pakistan camels: A preliminary survey. *Agr. Pakistan* 8:289.

Zannini, P. 1927. *L'osso del diaframma del cammello.* R. 1st Sup. Med. Vet. Pisa.
————. 1929. Sul "ossointerschiatico di Müller" studiato nel cammello e in diversi mammiferi: Note di anatomia comparata. *Ateneo Parmenso* 1:59–74.
* Zeuner, F. E. 1963. *A history of domesticated animals.* London: Hutchinson.

Index